A Collection of Oundle Families

– MARGARET BREWSTER –

An environmentally friendly book printed and bound in England by
www.printondemand-worldwide.com

http://www.fast-print.net/bookshop

A COLLECTION OF OUNDLE FAMILIES

A catalogue record for this book is available from the British Library

ISBN 978-178456-428-5

First Published 2016 by
Fast-Print Publishing of Peterborough, England.

INTRODUCTION

I grew up in Oundle and was lucky to have a wonderful childhood with my parents George and Nancy Slote and my sister Wendy. I married and moved away from Oundle in 1974.

In the year 2013 I was contacted by Susie Moore as she had some great ideas about arranging a reunion for past colleagues who attended the Oundle Secondary Modern School. After chatting about it we agreed I could help with the planning. The Reunion was to be held on 17th May 2014 at the Victoria Hall in Oundle. It was attended by over 200 people and was an incredible evening.

During the planning Susie collected various photographs and pieces of information passed on from ex-scholars via the Oundle Secondary Modern Facebook page. With my love of family history, I decided to research as many of the surnames of our guests and put together an insight of their ancestors lives in Oundle during the census years. These memorable collections were displayed for all guests to enjoy and they soon began to reminisce.

That was the start of 'A Collection of Oundle Families'.

Throughout the following pages there are many differences in individuals ages from one census to the next. The UK 1841 census website has the following information. Ages up to 15 are listed exactly as reported/recorded but ages over 15 were rounded to the nearest 5 years. (i.e. a person aged 53 would be listed on the census as age 50 years. The census pages are only transcriptions of the original household census forms the details were copied into the books by the enumerators.

Census read on following days.

1841 – 6 June. 1851 – 30 March. 1861 – 7 April. 1871 – 2 April.

1881 – 3 April. 1891 – 5 April. 1901 – 31 March. 1911 – 2 April.

ACKNOWLEDGMENTS

Thanks to the following for allowing me to use their photographs or for giving me information - Nigel Afford. Arthur Ball. The late Philip Brudenell. Stephen Brudenell. Jacqueline and Anne (nee Cotton). Virginia Francis (nee Burgess). Jackie Ganderton (nee Burgess). Joyce Hardick. Norman Hanna. Jean Donegani-Patt. Linda Rowton. Ray King from New Zealand.

Leoni from Staples in Peterborough for help with copying a collection of photographs.

Oundle School Archives

Peterborough Central Library

Peterborough Images.

Websites used:

www.findmypast.com
www.freebmd.org.uk
www.freereg.org.uk
www.familyhistorynorthants.co.uk - Northampton Strays

Thanks to the following newspapers for giving me permission to use announcements and articles from their publications.

Liam Reid from The British Newspaper Archive Support Team.

Bedfordshire Times and Independent. Bury and Norwich Post. Derby Telegraph. Grantham Journal. Hampshire Chronicle. Huntingdon, Bedford and Peterborough Gazette. Leicester Chronicle. Lincolnshire Chronicle. Lincoln, Stamford and Rutland Mercury. London Evening Standard. Northampton Mercury. Northants Evening Telegraph. Peterborough Advertiser. Reading Chronicle. Stamford Mercury. Sussex Agricultural Express. Yorkshire Gazette.

All newspaper articles reproduced up to 1909, out of copyright, by permission of – Newspaper Image ©The British Library Board. All rights reserved. With thanks to The British Newspaper Archive (www.BritishNewspaperArchive.co.uk).

All newspaper articles reproduced after 1909 but still in copyright, by permission of – 'Johnston Press plc'. Image created courtesy of THE

BRITISH LIBRARY BOARD. Image reproduced with kind permission of The British Newspaper Archive. (www.britishnewspaperarchive.co.uk).

I would also like to thank Simon Potter and the team at Fast-Print Publishing for helping me produce A Collection of Oundle Families.

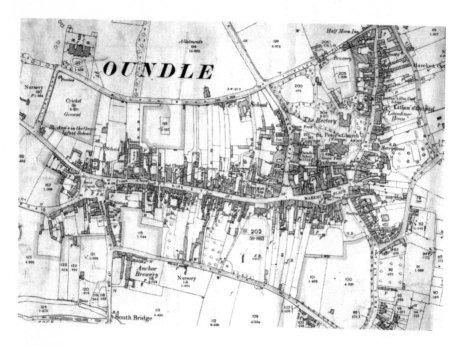

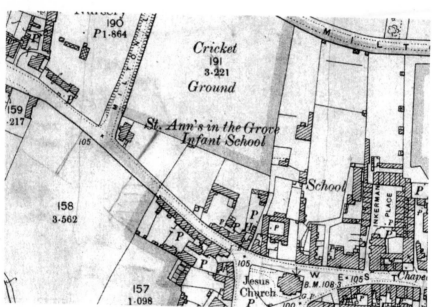

Maps courtesy of Oundle Archives

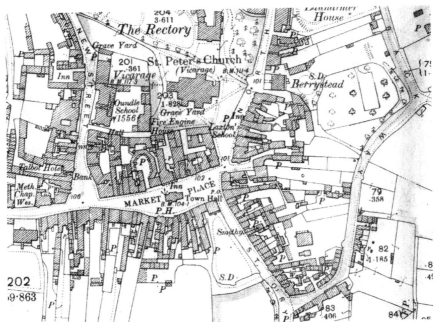

Maps courtesy of Oundle Archives

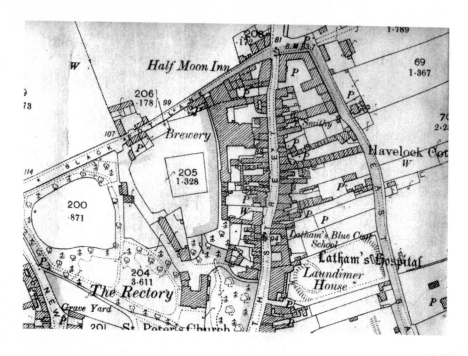

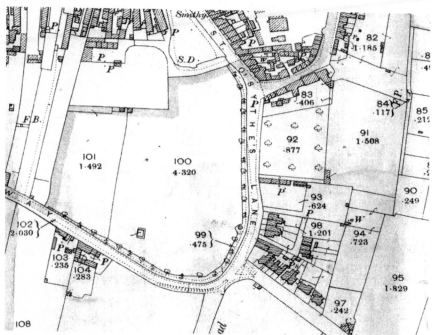

Maps courtesy of Oundle Archives

Contents

A COLLECTION OF OUNDLE FAMILIES

THE NEW OUNDLE IN 1827

We have at length to announce the completion of the improvements in the town of Oundle. This once old-fashioned town, with its sombre houses, narrow and dirty streets, and dangerous pavements, is now completely metamorphosed, that those who have not visited it since the alterations commenced will scarcely recognize it. It may not be uninteresting to some of our readers to state briefly the several alterations and improvements that have taken place: The range of buildings called the old butcher-row, which stood in the centre of the town, and which were so offensive to those in the immediate vicinity, have been wholly removed, and thus a very spacious and handsome street has been formed, in the centre of which a large market house in the gothic style of architecture, with a room over (called the town-hall) is erected. A number of shambles and fish-stalls, communicating with the market street have been erected, and in a peculiarly neat style. The cattle and sheep fairs have been removed from the streets of the town, and are now held in closes adjourning Glapthorn-road. Barroway pond, at the upper end of New-street, has been filled up, and the ground added to the church-yard. The whole of the pavement has been taken up, under drains have been made, the streets levelled, neat brick causeways farmed, and the carriage roads macadamized; and lastly, the town was lighted with oil lamps for the first time on Thursday 6th instant. The appearance of Oundle has also been much improved by the erection of several new and handsome houses, and by alterations and improvements in old ones particularly in those of tradesmen, who seem to have vied with each other in the neatness of their shop fronts. *Northampton Mercury 22 December 1827*

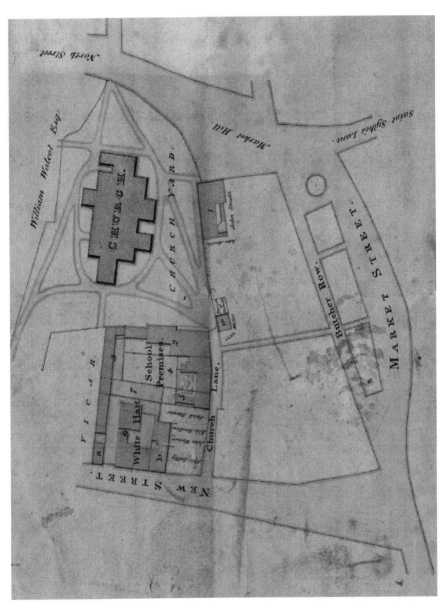

Map dated 1822 with courtesy of Oundle School Archive

The AFFORD families

The Afford families were living in Oundle from at least the 1600's as shown in the baptism transcriptions for St Peter's church Oundle. The occupation of Mason/Stone mason was carried down through most generations of the Afford family.

John Afford married Mary Glithero during 1786. Their children were Ann, Mary, Henry, George, John, Charles, Francis, William, although there may have been more who did not survive.

John and Mary's son John married Mary Sharman from Apethorpe in 1821. By 1841 John, a mason, and Mary lived along West Street with their six children Emma, Isabella, William a Stone mason, Mary, Walter and Lucy. In 1851 John and Mary were still living along West Street with Mary and Walter.

John and Mary's son Charles married Mary Ann Boughton during 1827. In 1841 they were living along Benefield Road with their son and daughter Harriet and Charles. An entry in the Death's column of the Northampton Mercury dated 5 August 1843 stated – At Oundle, on Friday week, Mrs Afford, wife of Mr C Afford, Stone mason, aged 55. By 1851 Charles, a widow, was visiting Henry and Ann Preston who lived along Victoria Terrace in Oundle.

John and Mary's son Henry married Elizabeth Broughton in 1814. Their children all baptised in Oundle were; John, George, Ann, Henry, Charlotte, Esther, Elizabeth, Mary, Francis, Jane and William. Henry and Elizabeth were living at the Lodge in Orton Longueville near Peterborough in 1841 with their family John, Esther, Elizabeth, Francis, Jane and William. Henry died in 1844 aged fifty-one. By 1851 Elizabeth, a mason's widow was living along West Street in Oundle with five of her children John and Francis were stonemasons, Esther was a stay maker, the younger children were Jane, William and Henry aged eight.

I, the undersigned, GEORGE MAILE, of Alconbury Weston, in the county of Huntingdon, cattle-dealer, *hereby give Notice*, that my Son, JOHNSON GEORGE MAILE, having left me, I will not in any way answerable or accountable for any Debts he may incur after this notice. Witness Jeffery Smith. GEORGE MAILE May 26, 1851. *Stamford Mercury 30 May 1851.*

Henry and Elizabeth's daughter Esther married George Johnson Maile during 1852.

OUNDLE POLICE, June 14. – Geo. Johnson Maile, of Oundle, drover, was charged by John Chapman, of Benefield, butcher, with cruelly beating a heifer, his property: adjourned for a fortnight. *Stamford Mercury 18 June 1852.* George Johnson Maile died during 1857 aged twenty-eight.

Elizabeth Afford, widow of Henry was a nurse in 1861 and had seven family members living with her at 36 West Street. Her daughter Easter (Esther) Maile, shown as a widow, continued to work as a stay maker, Francis and William were stonemasons, Jane was a stay maker, Edward Afford grandson to Elizabeth was a hostler and Easters children Harriet aged nine and Elizabeth Maile aged five attended school. By 1871 Elizabeth was shown as a Hospitaller at the Parson Latham's hospital along North Street she died in 1872 aged eighty-one.

Henry and Elizabeth's daughter Esther married John Burton in the district of Peterborough during 1869. By 1871 they were living along Gladstone Street in Peterborough with John's son and daughter George and Alice, also Esther's children Harriet Jane and Elizabeth who were both dress and stay maker's like their mother. By 1881 Hester (Esther) was a widow again she was a publican at the China Cup Inn along Eastgate in Peterborough where she stayed until she died in 1898. Her daughter Elizabeth lived with her.

Henry and Elizabeth's son John, a mason aged forty-four, married Mary Gilby, a widow, during 1859. They were living at the British School Yard No. 1 West Street Oundle in 1861 with Mary's daughters Mary, Leah and Fanny Gilby. Ten years later John and Mary continued to live along West Street with their son shown as A.E. Afford aged nine. John's wife Mary died in 1878 aged fifty-nine. In 1881 John, a widow, lived with William and Mary Jane Afford and their family. By 1891 John lodged with George and Susan Allen at the King's Arms along West Street. John was an inmate at the Workhouse along Glapthorne Road in 1901 and he died the following year aged eighty-seven.

Henry and Elizabeth's, son Francis married Sarah Allestree the daughter of Levi Allestree, in 1864. By 1871 Francis was an Innkeeper at the Victoria Inn along next to the Victoria Yard in West Street where they lived. Francis died in 1879 aged forty-seven. Sarah continued to run the Victoria Inn until she died in 1888 aged fifty-six.

Henry and Elizabeth's son William married Mary Jane Palmer, daughter of John Palmer from Oundle in 1868. At the time of the 1871 census William, a bricklayer, and Mary Jane had a one-year-old daughter Annie. By 1881 William and Mary Jane lived along Beals Yard near West Street. Their children were Annie Eliza, William Henry, Herbert, and Alfred Lewis. John Afford, a widower born in Oundle in 1816 also lived with them. William and Mary Jane continued living along West Street in 1891, their family were Annie, William an agricultural labourer, Herbert a mineral water labourer and Alfred and Flora attended school. Mary Jane worked as a nurse. Mary Jane died in 1893 aged forty-six, her death was recorded in the name of Jane. In 1901 William lived along North Street with his daughter Annie, son Alfred a general labourer and his niece Mary Lilley aged fifteen a domestic servant day girl. By 1911 William was described as an old age pensioner, he was a boarder with Arthur and Sarah Vessey who lived along West Street with their six children. Also in 1911 Herbert Afford son of William and Mary Jane, was an inmate at the workhouse and shown as being a mineral water manufacturer.

John and Mary's son George married Mary Freer during 1816. Their children were baptised in Oundle as follows – Catherine on 21 March 1817, Walter on 20 June 1819, Martha on 17 October 1821 she died in 1822 aged one, Martha on 25 December 1823 she died in 1825 aged two, Lucy on 24 February 1826, Isaac on 31 October 1828, Eliza on 25 March 1831, Edward on 25 December 1833, Elizabeth on 25 December 1836. – *Oundle baptism transcriptions.*

On Thursday, the 7th inst., George Afford, of Oundle, was convicted (before the Rev. Dr. Roberts) in the mitigated penalty of 10s for leaving carts and waggons standing in the public street, contrary to the provisions of the Oundle Improvement Act.) *Stamford Mercury 15 February 1828.*

A marriage announcement in the Northampton Mercury dated 6 February 1836 read – On Monday se'nnight, at Oundle, (by the Rev. Frederick Williamson, Mr Thomas Lovell, tailor and furrier, of Brigstock, to Miss Afford, eldest daughter of Mr George Afford, carrier. Catherine and Thomas Lovell were living at Wolverton near Pottersbury in 1851.

At Oundle on the 15th inst., (by the Rev J Nussey,) Wm. Sanders currier, of Higham Ferrers to Lucy Afford. *Lincolnshire Chronicle 26 March 1847*

In 1841 George Afford, a publican, lived along West Street with his wife Mary and their family. They were Louisa, Isaac, Eliza, Edward and Elizabeth. Georges' parents John, a mason, and Mary also lived with them. There were nine other people lodging at the premises. Mary senior died in 1842 aged eighty-three. Ten years later George and Mary continued to live along West Street with Eliza, Edward and Elizabeth. George's father John Afford, a widow, was living at the Latham's hospital. He died in 1854 aged eighty-eight. By 1861 George was the innkeeper at the Waggon and Horses along Mill Lane although Mary was not at home at the time of the census. Mary was visiting their daughter Catherine Lovell at Wolverton. Catherine's sister Lucy, a widow, and nineteen-year-old Lucy who was Mary's granddaughter were visiting Mary. At the time of the 1871 census George, a beer house keeper, and Mary had moved back to West Street. It was reported in the Northampton Mercury on 1 March 1873 that the license of the Old London Waggon, Oundle, was transferred from George Afford to George Allen.

Died - At Oundle on the 10th inst., Mr George Afford, in his 83d year. *Stamford Mercury 19 July 1878*

George and Mary's son George married Elizabeth Cook in 1839. At the time of the 1841 census they were living along West Street with their son Phillip. In 1851 George and Elizabeth had moved to Benefield Road where they lived with Martha, Matthew and their nephew George from Fletton. George, a builder, and Elizabeth continued to live along Benefield Road in 1861 where they made it the family home. Their family were Martha a dressmaker, Matthew, Grace, Selina and Cook George. Their two nephews George Afford from Fletton and William Hasseldine from London also lived with the family. George, Elizabeth and their children Matthew a mason, Grace who was a dressmaker, Selina and Cook were with them in 1871. Ten years later George and Elizabeth's son Cook George an Ag lab carter was their only son at home. Their grandsons William Bloxham Whittington aged eleven, George Herbert aged nine, John Richard aged six and Phillip James aged four all born in Oundle lived with George and Elizabeth. They were the sons of Martha and William Whittington who lived along North Street. George and

Elizabeth's daughter Martha married William Whittington during 1867. George's wife Elizabeth died in 1883 aged sixty-nine.

George and Elizabeth's son Matthew married Lucy Chester in 1876. They were living in Danford's yard during 1881. Matthew was a stonemason and bricklayer. They had two children Gertrude and James. They eventually moved to Winwick where Lucy was born.

George and Elizabeth's son Cook George married Ellen Sophia Clarke in 1882.

Oundle Divisional Petty Sessions – A charge against Cook George Afford, Oundle for wilful damage, was, by leave, withdrawn on the defendant paying the expenses of the action. *Northampton Mercury 19 December 1890*

By 1891 Cook George Afford lived along Benefield Road he was shown as being married although Ellen was not at home at the time of the census. Next door lived his father George Afford. They were both stonemasons. Ellen was living along West Street, where she was a seamstress; her children were Clara, Grace and Ernest. William Afford aged thirty-five worked as a groom and lived with the family, he was Cooks brother.

Cook George Afford, Oundle, was charged with deserting his wife and family at Oundle, - Mr Batten, of Oundle, of Batten and Whitsed, Peterborough and Oundle appeared for the defendant. – Mrs Afford said nine months ago he refused to allow her in the house, the Nag's Head, and turned her out. – The case was dismissed. *Northampton Mercury 24 April 1891*

In 1901 Cook and Ellen lived along Industrious Terrace, not far from Benefield Road in Oundle with their children Grace was a dressmaker, then there was George twelve and Albert eight years. Cook's grandfather George was an inmate at the Laxton's hospital along Church Lane. He died during 1902 aged eighty-six. Cook and Ellen had moved by 1911, they lived at 5 Burnham Terrace along East Road with two of their sons, George Ernest was a bricklayer and Albert Percy was a Stock Yardman. Cook's mother Elizabeth Afford was living in Inkermans Yard and was shown as having eight children three of whom had died.

Ernest Afford a soldier in the 1st Battalion of the Northamptonshire Regiment, was killed in action in Flanders during 1916. Ernest had only signed up six months prior. He was the son of Cook and Ellen. Albert Percy Afford son of Cook and Ellen joined the 27th Battalion of the Bedfordshire Regiment in 1917.

Mr Cook George Afford was the oldest inhabitant of Oundle when he died in his sleep at the home of his daughter at Roade near Northampton. He was ninety-four. The report in the Northampton Mercury dated 6 July 1951 stated Mr Afford worked for some years as a stonemason at Messrs Smith and Co.'s brewery. He was one of the founders of the old Oundle Pig Club, and was also fond of cricket. He was also a member of the Providence Lodge of Oddfellows.

George and Mary's son Edward married Amelia Allestree, daughter of Levi Allestree, in 1855. They lived with George and Mary at the time of the 1861 census with their children Albert four and eleven- month old Thomas. In 1871 they lived at the Ship Inn where Edward was a licensed victualler. Edward and Amelia had four children Albert, Thomas, Harriett and Edward. Ann Leimage from Elton was their domestic servant. Amelia died in 1876 aged forty-one. Edward remarried in 1878 to Mary Ann Shrive, a widow of the late Frederick Shrive, rope-maker and seedsman, who was also the publican of the Turks Head Inn. Mary Ann was the daughter of William Firmedows. By 1881 Edward was an innkeeper living along New Street with his wife, shown as Maria Ann, and their sons Albert and Edward both general labourers. Mary Jane Hall from Woodwalton was a domestic housemaid and Mary Brinsley from Oundle was a general servant for the family. There were also five lodgers at the Inn.

Photograph by courtesy of Peterborough Images showing area of Turk's Head

SPALTON – AFFORD – Sept. 9, at the parish church, Oundle (by Rev.J. Stewart). Frederick Pearson third son of the late J.N. Spalton, of Springwell House, Adwick-upon-Dearne, Yorkshire, to Harriet only daughter of Edward Afford, of Oundle. *Stamford Mercury 12 September 1884.*

An entry in the Oundle Petty Sessions on 8th March – 'Edward Afford, higgler, Oundle, and George Limage, labourer, Oundle, drunk while in charge of horses, on the 25th ult. – Afford was fined 10s.6d. and 9s.6d. costs, and Limage 5s and 9s 6d. costs. *Northampton Mercury 12 March 1887.*

Edward, son of Edward and Amelia, signed up for the 9th Lancers (Queens Royals) in 1886. He signed up for twelve years and was discharged in 1898 at the end of his twelve years of service.

In 1891 and through to 1901 Edward and Mary Ann still resided along New Street at the Turk's Head Inn where Edward was the publican and carter of corn. Mary Abercrombie, married daughter of Mary Ann (Shrive) was living with Edward and Mary Ann in 1901.

On Saturday Mr Edward Afford died aged 75. He had been in failing health for some time. Deceased was a native of the town, and when a young man crossed to America, and soon after his return became landlord of the Ship Inn. For the past thirty years, he has occupied the Turk's Head, also carrying on the business of a carter. He leaves a widow, his second wife, and several children by his former wife. The funeral took place on Wednesday in the Cemetery. *Northampton Mercury 25 December 1908*

At the time of the 1911 census Mary Ann Afford, aged seventy-nine, a widow lived along East Road. It was recorded on the census that Mary had three children two of whom had died from her first marriage. Jane Elizabeth Green was also a widow and lived with Mary Ann as her house-keeper. Jane was shown as having had two children both were still living at the time of the census.

Edward and Amelia's son Thomas was a Schoolmaster; in 1881 he was living at Star Road in Wells next the sea where he lodged with Eliza Straughter who was a shopkeeper of fancy goods. Ten years later Thomas was a police constable and lodged at the Police station along London Road in Kettering at the home of Levi Andrews an Inspector of Police and his wife Fanny. Thomas married Mary Margaret Kyle, daughter of James and Jane Kyle from Armston near Oundle, during 1891. By 1901 Thomas had changed his occupation to a poor law relieving officer; he and Mary lived 87 Newland in Northampton. They had a son Sidney A aged eight. Frederick Spalton aged nine was their nephew who also lived with them. Ten years later Thomas, Mary Margaret and their son Sidney who was a chemist apprentice continued to live at 87 Newland.

George and Mary's son Walter married Mary Ann Baldwin in 1837. In 1841 they were living along West Street with their daughter Margaret. At the time of the 1851 census Walter, a farmer and carter, and his wife Mary Anne living at 2 Odd Fellowes Place not far from West Street. Their children were Margaret, Lucy, Edward and Jane and Walter. Walter junior died in 1855 aged six. Ten years later Walter and Mary Anne had moved to Benefield Road where he had a farm of 30 acres. Their children were Lucy, Edward, Mary Jane, Sarah Eliza, George and Mary Anne. Walter and Mary's daughter Mary Jane married John Staniforth in 1872.

At Oundle, on the 1st inst, George Afford, aged 24; - and on the 3d, Mary Afford, aged 59. *Stamford Mercury 15 February 1878*

By 1881 Walter was at his home in Benefield Road, his daughter Mary Ann lived with her father.

Charge of wilful damage – Walter Afford, farmer, Oundle, and John Stainforth, his son-in-law, Oundle, were charged with wilfully damaging two scaffold cords, by cutting the same, to the amount of 4s in the second November, and by similar offence to the amount of 2s on the 3rd November respectively. – Mr Norris, of Peterborough, appeared for the plaintiff George Dew, builder, Oundle, and said the case was a somewhat complicated one. The plaintiff rented a paddock which had originally belonged to the defendant Afford, but had since been sold by him to Stainforth. Defendants retained the right of way to the stable which they still occupied. When plaintiff took the paddock Afford put up some hurdles to act as a gate, and when he sold the property took them away. His client had placed a small scaffold pole suspended on two ropes, so that he could keep a horse there, and defendants, who apparently wanted to get rid of plaintiff, had deliberately cut the ropes. The scaffold pole was placed in such a manner as to be in no way difficult to place on one side for any-one to enter. Not content with cutting the ropes, they had repeatedly driven the horse out of the paddock. – The complainant was then called and gave evidence to this effect, and said that he lay behind a wall and watched the defendant Stainforth cut the cords on Sunday; and Charles Dew, his uncle, said he saw Afford cut a rope on Saturday. – John Platt, a labourer, also gave corroborative evidence, and said he saw the defendants turn the horse out of the paddock several times. – The defendant Afford said he drove the horse out because it kept going to his clover stack, but Mr Norris stated that he had placed the stack in the paddock without any permission from the complainant, having absolutely no right to do so - Afford was ordered to pay £1 17s 6d fine and costs, and Stainforth £1 3s 6d fine and costs. *Northampton Mercury 9 November 1889*

Walter and Mary Ann's' son George married Roseanna Brown in 1875. George Afford died in 1878 aged twenty-three. In 1881 Rose Afford aged twenty-four was a widow with two children Walter aged four and Millicent aged one. They lived with Rose's brother John Martin and his family along Benefield Road. By 1891 Walter Afford senior lived with John and Mary Staniforth along Benefield Road. John was a silversmith born in Sheffield. Walter Afford junior, son of Rose also lived there. George and Roseanna's son Isaac Walter Afford married Caroline Shingles in the Fulham district in 1900. By the time of the 1901 census Walter and Caroline were lived at 1 Connaught Mansions along Sidbury Street in Fulham. Walter was a baker, his place of birth shown as not known but Caroline was born in Hammersmith. In 1911 Caroline was working as a house keeper for Arthur Court a stage coachman who lived in Chiswick. No sign of Walter in the census.

Walter and Mary Ann's son Edward married Elizabeth Saddington, daughter of Samuel Saddington, in Oundle during 1866. By 1871 Edward a farmer and carter lived at 1 Inkerman Square with his wife Eliza and their children Edward three and George eleven months. Ten years later Edward, a timber carter, and Eliza continued to live at 1 Inkerman Yard with Edward thirteen a Timber carter's assistant George ten, Henry eight, John six attended school and the youngest in the family was Frederick aged two. In 1891 Lizzie, (Elizabeth) was a house keeper for Charles Mckee. He was a brewer who lived at the Anchor Brewery along Mill Lane in Oundle. Lizzie's son Frederick was lodging with Robert and Elizabeth Coales who lived along St Osythes lane. Edward, a higgler, was lodging with George and Elizabeth Smith who lived along Benefield Road.

Edward and Elizabeth's son George married Emma Carrington during 1896 in the Wellingborough district. In 1901 George, a bricklayer's labourer, and Emma were living along the High Street in Rushden. By 1911 they had moved to 57 Grove Street in Higham Ferrers, they had a son George Henry aged eight.

Death of Mr G. Afford at Higham Ferrers – For many years a keen worker for Higham Ferrers Adult School, Mr George Afford of 53, Grove-street, Higham Ferrers, died at his home on Tuesday evening, aged 69. He had been ill for about two years, but had not been confined to his bed until recently. Born at Oundle, Mr Afford came to Higham Ferrers 35 years ago. There is a widow, Mrs Emma Afford, and one son. Mr Harry Afford of Watford. The funeral will take place on Friday afternoon, when the service will be conducted at Higham Ferrers parish church. *Northants Evening Telegraph 14 June 1939*

The ALLESTREE families

William Allestree married Elizabeth Bellamy during 1789 in Oundle. They were both born in Ashton. William and Elizabeth Allestree had the following children Matilda died aged three, Thomas Bellamy, Matilda, Levi and Esther.

On the 23d ult., at Oundle, Mrs W Allestree, aged 70. *Huntingdon, Bedford and Peterborough Gazette 8 April 1837.*

Married – On Tuesday, (by Rev. C. Hume) Mr Wm. Smith Woolley, butcher, to Miss Esther Allestree, daughter of Mr Wm. Allestree, butcher of Oundle. *Stamford Mercury 8 June 1838*

In 1841 William Alstree, butcher, was living along North Street with his son William. At Oundle, on 20th ult., Wm. Allestree, aged 79. *Stamford Mercury 3 July 1846*

Levi Allestree married Sarah Pitts in 1820 at Tansor where they both lived. The witnesses to their marriage were Thos' Bellamy Allestree and William Richards. Thomas Bellamy Allestree married Sarah Ladds from Oundle during 1819. He was a coach maker born at Ashton and lived in Thrapston. Thomas was a widow in 1851 and had moved to Higham Ferrers where he stayed until he died in 1861 aged sixty-eight.

Listed in the Oundle baptism transcriptions for Levi and Sarah Allestree were William 1823, Levi 1827, Harriett 1829, Sarah in 1831 and Milton born and died in 1834.

At Oundle, on Friday last, after a long illness, Mrs Sarah Allestree, wife of Levi Allestree, carpenter, aged forty-three. *Stamford Mercury 19 March 1841*

In 1841 Levi Allestree, a carpenter, was living along the Market Place in Oundle with his children. Ann was sixteen, Levi fourteen, Sarah nine and Amelia was five years old.

At Oundle on Tuesday last, (by the Rev. C. Hume) Mr. Thos. Haw of Cotterstock, to Miss Matilda Pitts Allestree, eldest daughter of Mr Levi Allestree, of Oundle. *Stamford Mercury 23 June 1843*

Levi senior died during 1843 aged forty-four.

Levi Allestree, aged sixteen, charged with stealing a gun, the property of J Smith Esq. of Oundle was delivered by proclamation - Northamptonshire Lent Assizes. *Northampton Mercury 10 February 1844.*

Commitments to the County Gaol – Levi Allestree, for 1 month for wilfully damaging certain filbert trees at Oundle, the property of William Pain. *Northampton Mercury 21 September 1844*

Committed to the County Gaol and House of Correction -Levi Allestree, charged with stealing a saw and a chisel from John Prentice of Oundle. *Northampton Mercury 23 November 1844.* He was sent for trial at Northampton on 8 April 1845. Levi was one of 300 convicts transported on the Equestrian 30 June 1845 arrived on 15 October 1845 to Van Diemen's Land Australia with 299 passengers. Sentence term - 14 years.

Levi and Sarah's daughter Amelia was a house maid for Edward Carr, a farmer, who lived at Mill End in Warmington in 1851. Amelia married Edward Afford during 1855. In 1861 they lived at the Wagon and Horses along Mill Lane in Oundle where Edward's father was the innkeeper. Amelia and Edward had two sons Albert four and Thomas was eleven months. By 1871 they had moved to the Ship Inn where Edward was a Licensed Victualler. Their children were Albert, Thomas, Harriett and Edward all attended school. Ann Limage aged seventeen from Elton was a domestic servant for them. Amelia died in 1876 aged forty-one. In 1878 Edward married Mary Ann Shrive. Mary was the daughter of Mary Ann and Frederick Shrive, a Rope maker and publican at the Turks Head in Oundle. The 1881 census shows Edward, an innkeeper, living along New Street with Maria Ann and his sons Albert and Edward. He employed Mary Jane Hall from Woodnewton and Mary Brinsley from Oundle as servants. There were five lodgers in residence. Edward was shown as being the innkeeper at the Turks Head in 1891, Mary J Hull from Woodnewton was a barmaid for him. In 1901 Edward was a publican and carter of corn still at the Turks Head; he died in 1908 aged seventy-five.

Levi and Sarah's daughter Ann married John Bunning, coal merchant son of William Bunning, in 1851.Details of their family can be found in the Bunning family section.

Levi and Sarah's daughter Harriet married John Cunnington a widower and innkeeper born in Lowick in 1857. In 1861 they were living at the Crown Inn along the Market Place with their son Tom aged one and John's mother Lucy, a widow. John employed Mary Binder from Oundle as a house servant and George Smith from Barnwell who was a groom and labourer.

Levi and Sarah's daughter Sarah married Francis Afford during 1864. Francis was the son of Henry and Elizabeth Afford who lived along West Street. By 1871 Francis and Sarah were living along West Street where Francis was a bricklayer and innkeeper. Francis died in 1879 aged forty-seven. Sarah continued to be the innkeeper until she passed away in 1888 aged fifty-six.

At the time of the 1861 census William Allestree, eldest son of the late Levi and Sarah Allestree, was living at 3 Henry Street in Wisbech St. Peters where he was a journeyman joiner. He employed Sarah Anker, a widow from Whittlesey, as his house keeper, she had two young daughters Sarah and Susan. They were all living along Henry Street in 1871, although Sarah was shown as 'Hanker' (Hawker). William died in 1879 at Henry Street aged fifty-six.

Grave of William and Elizabeth Allestree St Peters church-yard

The BARNES family

William and Catherine Barnes had the following children, Mary 1775 she died in 1778, Thomas 1778 he died not long after he was born, Mary c.1779, Sally and Elizabeth (twins) c.1783, Thomas c.1789 and William c.1794. Catherine died in 1832 aged eighty-three.

William and Sarah Barnes had a daughter Mary c.1821.

At the time of the 1841 census Thomas Barnes, a brewer, Mary Barnes and Henry Barnes, an Ag lab who were all shown as aged twenty lived along West Street, also living there were John Wilson aged twenty-five and Charlotte Broughton aged twenty. During the winter of 1841 Henry Barnes married Charlotte Broughton, the witnesses were Thomas and Mary Barnes. Charlotte was the daughter of William and Frances Broughton who lived along West Street.

Henry Barnes, widower, married Mary Brown, both from Oundle during 1815. The witnesses were shown as J. Freshwater and Mary Mills. They had a son Thomas in 1816. In 1841 Henry and Mary lived along Benefield Road with their sons, fourteen-year-old Jas (James Henry) and ten-year-old William. By 1851 Henry, an Ag lab, and Mary a laundress had their daughter Mary Ann, a laundress and their granddaughter Mary aged seven living with them. (In 1841 Mary Ann was a servant living and working for Miller Benskin a currier along Mill Lane.) Henry and Mary's son William was a livery servant living at the Grammer School House along Church Yard. Henry and Mary were living at 2 Alms House in 1861. Their daughter Mary Ann lived along Benefield Road where she was a laundress. Henry died during 1866 aged eighty-four. Mary continued living at the Alms House.

William and Catherine Barnes son Thomas, a baker, and his wife Ann lived along New Street in 1841 with their daughters' Sarah Ann twenty-five, Emma eleven and Agnes nine. Also, living with Thomas and Ann were John Dainty a baker, Edward Smith and Jane Ruff were servants. Thomas was employing his son Thomas, and William Williams in the baker and maltster business. In 1851 Thomas and Ann had a houseful with daughter Emma and son Thomas, Emma Bellamy and John Breadwell servants from Oundle, William Williams a baker from Dudley, also three visitors William Shelton aged three from Surrey, George Barnes, a baker and maltster from Oundle and husband of Mary, and Emma Barnes eleven from Harringworth. Agnes was living with James and Mary Dainty at Easton in 1851. Mary was her sister. Ann died during 1859.

Thomas and Ann's son Thomas married Sarah Jane Gray during 1857. By 1861 they were living with Thomas senior at 13 New Street with their children Herbert four and Georgina aged one. Thomas senior had retired; his son Thomas had taken over as the maltster and baker. They employed three servants, Joseph Tynch a maltster man from Nassington, Fanny Ruff a house maid from Hemington and Susan Martin a nurse maid from Oundle. Georgina died in 1864 aged three and Herbert died a few weeks later aged five. Thomas senior died during the winter of 1864 aged seventy-six. At the time of the 1871 census Thomas and Sarah had two more children Annie nine and Frederick seven. In 1881 Thomas and Sarah had two daughters at home Annie and Lucy Ethel aged nine. Ethel Lucy had reversed her name by the 1891 census she was living with her parents who had moved to West Street, Thomas was a retired brewer. Sarah Jane died during the latter months of 1891 aged fifty-three. Thomas had no family at home in 1901 although he did employ Agnes Bowman from Alwalton as a domestic servant. In 1911 Thomas was living at York House along West Street he employed Clara Clark from Spalding as his house keeper and Mable Smith from Oundle as his general servant. Thomas had recorded on the census that he and Sarah had been married for twenty-six years, had six children three of whom had died. Thomas died during 1919 aged eighty-five.

New Street c.1880 where Thomas Barnes was a maltster.
Photograph courtesy of Oundle Archives

Thomas and Ann's daughters' Emma and Agnes were living along St O'sythes Lane in 1861 where they were both Principles of a Ladies seminary Paulina Walker was their governess who came from Blatherwycke. The three pupils were Augusta Dainty, their niece, and Emily Coles both eleven then Jane Preston was nine. Ann Leigh from Holbeach was their servant.

Henry and Mary's son James married Ruth Clarke during 1849. Ruth was the daughter of David and Mary from North Street. In 1851 James, a shoemaker, and Ruth a dressmaker lived along New Street with their one-year-old son James. He died in 1852. By 1861 they had moved and lived along North Street James was a bootmaker employing two men and four boys. Ruth had a young family to look after with Mary Ann five, Elizabeth three and one-year-old James. Charlotte Strange from Northampton was their house servant. James employed three men in 1871 in his shoe maker business along North Street. Ruth was busy with the family with Mary Ann, Elizabeth, James Henry, eight-year-old Herbert Albert and four-year-old Emma all attended school. Charles Henry Clarke from Devon lodged with them he was 2nd assistant of the Excise branch of H.M. Inland Revenue. Ruth had begun her dressmaking again by 1881 their daughter Mary joined her, James continued being a boot maker their son Herbert was his assistant, Emma attended school. Thomas Bryan a bank clerk from Rutland lodged with the family.

MELANCHOLY DEATH – Mr James Barnes, of this town, has just received the sad news of the death of his eldest son, Mr James Henry Barnes, through an accident at West Lynn, Massachusetts, United States. Mr Barnes was a young man of promise, and had only recently left this country for America in search of employment, and was soon engaged on his arrival as agent of a large Industrial Life Office in West Lynn, under the superintendence of Mr I. France, who speaks very highly of the unfortunate young man's ability and industry. It appears from the report of the accident that on the afternoon of the 8th ult., Mr Barnes left the Lynn station, and was walking on the line as a near cut to his place of business. He was overtaken by an express train, and thrown with great violence on the side of the track. He was at once removed to the hospital at Boston, where upon examination it was found no bones were broken, but he had received injuries to the head of a very serious nature. The poor young fellow lingered in a state of unconsciousness until the 26th May, and then passed away. Deep sympathy is felt in Oundle with the parents. *Northampton Mercury 10 June 1882*

James and Ruth's daughter Mary Ann married Thomas Francis Kynaston during 1885. By 1901 they were living in Wales where Thomas was a sub postmaster.

James and Ruth only had Emma at home in 1891. Jane Kennedy a governess from Cannock lodged with them. In 1901 James was a bootmaker and shopkeeper at home, he and Ruth still had Emma at home, also their twelve-year-old granddaughter Mary Kynaston, daughter of Thomas and Mary Ann from Wales was with them.

OBITUARY – We regret to record the death of Mr James Barnes, an old and highly respected inhabitant. He was the oldest tradesman in the town having carried on the business of boot-maker for considerably over half a century. Deceased was an ardent Wesleyan, and was for many years Sunday School Superintendent. He was an Oddfellow, being one of the earliest initiated into the Loyal Providence Lodge, M.U., of which he was a P.P.C.M. For a long time, he was collector of the quit rents for the Lord of the Manor, and was in his day a noted quoit player. Mr and Mrs Barnes celebrated their golden wedding last year. Besides the widow, there are three daughters and one son. – FUNERAL – The interment of Mr James Barnes who passed away on Saturday at the age of 83, took place on Saturday. Full report can be found in the *Northampton Mercury 27 May 1910*

Ruth was living at Jericho in Oundle in 1911 with her daughter Emma and seventeen-year-old grandson Harold Barnes whose occupation was a printer. Ruth died a few months after the census was recorded in 1911.

James and Ruth's son Herbert Albert married Eleanor Lokier during 1889 in Shropshire. In 1891 they lived along West Street with their son John Henry aged one month. Eleanor died during 1899 aged thirty-two. Herbert married Sophia Webb from Northampton in 1900. By 1901 they were living along Rock Road with John Henry ten, Harold eight, Cynthia six, Cecil Colin five and Herbert Arthur two years old. Ten years later Herbert, a coal yard foreman, and Sophia had moved and were living along the Market Place with Cynthia a dressmaker's apprentice, Cecil an upholsterers apprentice and Herbert attended school.

OUNDLE – The swimming tests for life-saving, which consist in swimming 50 yards fully dressed and bringing a boy safe to land, have been executed by two Scouts of the Oundle 2nd Troop (M Fox and Cecil Barnes), thus entitling them to the medal. *Northampton Mercury 5 July 1912.*

The BEAL families

John Beal, clockmaker, married Harriet Underwood, during 1801. Their family included Harriet c.1803, Catherine c.1805, John c.1807, Elizabeth c.1809, Mary c.1811, Eleanor c.1813, Thomas c.1815 and Josiah c.1817. Their daughter Harriet died aged eleven and Catherine died aged thirty.

In 1841 John and Harriet lived along the Market Place with John, Elizabeth, Mary, Ellen (Eleanor) and Thomas. By 1851 John employed his two sons John aged forty-one and Thomas aged thirty-four in his watch and clock-making business. Ellen was their only daughter living at home. Harriet died during 1854 aged seventy-five. Their son John died during 1856 aged forty-nine.

At the time of the 1861 census John's daughters Elizabeth and Eleanor lived with him, as did his son Thomas who was a watchmaker managing the business. John died during 1863 aged ninety.

John and Harriet's daughter Eleanor married John Siddons, a farmer at Aldwinkle Lodge, during 1862. John was born in Kings Cliffe. (He was a widow in 1861 with a family of five children and a farm of 220 acres to run. John employed a house-keeper, governess, dairymaid and a carter). John died during 1866 aged forty-nine. In 1871 Eleanor was a widow living in Aldwinkle. She was a farmer of 230 acres employing 4 men and 3 boys. Also at home were her step-daughter's Lucy and Emily and her sister Mary Beal an annuitant. In 1875 Mary died aged sixty-four.

At the time of the 1881 census Elizabeth lived with her sister Eleanor Siddons in the Bradley cottage along South Backway near to the Church yard. Eleanor was a retired farmer living on Interest money. By 1891 they were living along St O'Sythes lane. Elizabeth died during 1895 aged eighty-five. Eleanor died during 1898 aged eighty-four.

John and Harriet's son Thomas married Dorothy Bodgener, from Suffolk, during 1869 in the district of Middlesex. By 1871 they lived along Market Place where Thomas was a watch and clock maker and jeweller, he employed one man. Thomas' sister Elizabeth also lived with them. In 1881 Thomas and Dorothy had no family at home.

Martha Wood from Gidding was their general servant. Thomas died during 1882 aged sixty-six.

John and Harriet's son Josiah married Mary Bryant from Suffolk during 1865 in the Marylebone district.

At the Oundle Flower and Poultry show the half-dozen silver cups, which were supplied by Mr T. Beal, silversmith, &c., Oundle, were exhibited in one of the marquees. In the Poultry section - class 19 – Bantams, any other variety of any age. For the best cock and two hens; 1st F. Worley, Northampton; 2nd Josiah Beal, Oundle. *Northampton Mercury 16 July 1870*

At the time of the 1871 census Josiah, a draper, and Mary were running their business in the Market Place. They employed three shopwomen, a shopman and two house servants. In 1881 Josiah, a linen draper master, and Mary lived along the Market Place. Josiah employed three linen draper assistants, an apprentice, a milliner, a dressmaker, a cashier's clerk, a cook and a housemaid. By 1891 Josiah employed three draper's assistants, two dressmakers, a milliner, a kitchen servant and a housemaid.

Josiah Beal died during 1892 aged seventy-four.

Another of Oundle's old inhabitants (Mrs Mary Beal) passed away on Monday last at a ripe old age of 89. Deceased was the relict of the late Mr Josiah Beal, who was for many years a leading draper of the town. The funeral takes place tomorrow (Saturday). *Northampton Mercury 4 April 1913*

Grave of John and Harriet Beal St Peters church-yard

Photograph with courtesy of Peterborough Images

The BEESLEY/BEASLEY families

William Beesley married Jane Garfield in 1829.they had a daughter Jane who only lived to be one year and ten months old. In 1841 William, a baker, and Jane lived in Polebrook with their family William aged nine and James seven. Also, living with them was Elizabeth Weston a housekeeper, Amos Bell a baker's assistant and Mary Ives a Servant. Jane died in December 1841 aged forty-five. William remarried during 1844 to Mary Keyston. The 1851 census shows William and Mary living in Polebrook. William's son William was a solicitor's clerk then there was Mary aged four and John aged one. Elizabeth Weston still lived with the family and was a widow and sister to William. Amos Bell also lived there where he continued working as a baker's assistant. Mary died in 1852.William, a widow carried on with his bakery in 1861 and employed Amos Bell and James Coles. By 1871 William lived with his sister Elizabeth Weston, John his son and Amos Bell. Elizabeth Chapman a widow from Benefield lodged with the family.

William and his late wife Jane's son William Beesley (junior) was a Solicitor's managing clerk in 1861. He lived with his cousin Martha Elizabeth Beeham and her son Henry a grocer's apprentice. He died 26 January 1862, aged thirty-one, in Oundle. *Peterborough Advertiser 1 February 1862.*

James Beasley, born 1834 in Glapthorne, married Elizabeth Ann Briggs in 1859. They lived in Prentices yard along North Street with their one-year-old son William Robert in 1861. James was a blacksmith. They moved to Deene by the time of the 1871 census where they stayed right through the census years. James and Elizabeth's other children were Elizabeth, Thomas, Lucy Ann, Amy, and Ida Maud,

Frederick Rowland Beesley, born in Titchmarsh in 1872, married Alice Maud Newell in 1897. Frederick was the son of James and Ann from Polebrook. By 1901 Albert Beesley aged three lived with his mother Alice at Danford's Yard.

Northampton Mercury 13 February 1903 – OUNDLE – Sad Fatality – A painful accident occurred in Oundle on Saturday morning to a little boy named Albert Beasley, only six years old, who was run over in the street and killed. The lad, who was a bright little fellow, went from his home in the St Osythe's lane about five minutes before the accident to the Market place, and Mr Beadsworth's threshing engine and tackle was proceeding through the town. The little fellow saw a boy named Clarke get on the shafts of the last vehicle but one, and he did the same. When he tried to dismount from his perch he stumbled, and the last vehicle passed over his body. At the time of the accident a young man named Holmes in the employ of Mr Sewell (grocer) was passing, and he picked the lad up and proceeded at once with him to Dr. Elliott's in the North-street, a train of blood from his burden leaving a trail along the street. Unfortunately, the doctor was away from home, and a second journey was made to Dr. Turner in West-street. Here again the doctor was away, and eventually the boy was taken to his home in St. Osythe's-lane, where he died about two hours after the accident. The case is of a most distressing character from the fact that the unfortunate victim was the cause of his younger sister's death two years ago in a scalding case. It will perhaps be remembered that the little girl was about to have a bath when the little boy accidently upset a large kettle of boiling water through clanking a whip. Terrible scalds were the result, and the death followed in a day or so. The family consisted of only these two bright little children, both of whom have been killed by accidents. The father is in the employ of Messrs. Smith and Co., brewers, and when the first accident took place was serving his country in South Africa. Great sympathy is felt by all the townspeople for the bereaved parents who were on most affectionate terms with their children. The inquest was held on Monday before Mr. J. C. Parker, jun. Deputy Coroner. -Dr Elliott said the little lad's skull was fractured. -The jury returned a verdict of "Accidental Death."

By 1911 Frederick was a night watchman at a brewery, living along St Osyth's Lane with Alice and their family. Charles Frederick was seven, Alice Maud six, Hilda four and Ivy May was one-year-old. They had been married for fourteen years had six children two of whom had died.

OUNDLE – ACCIDENT – A young man named Beesley, of St Osyth's-lane, received a broken leg on Friday night as the result of being run over by a grocery van after he had been knocked down by a motor cycle. He was also cut about the head. Dr. A. F. Elliott attended to his injuries. *Northampton Mercury 12 November 1926*

William John Beesley from Aldwinkle and his wife Annie Elizabeth moved to Oundle not long before the 1911 census was recorded. They had been living in London where three of their sons were born, John Earnest eight, George James five and Albert William was four, the youngest Henry Albert aged one was born in Oundle. William was a blacksmith working from home in West Street, Annie was a cook.

The BELL families

On Monday, last by the Rev. D. Brown of Barnwell, in this county, Mr Thomas Bell, printer and publisher of Oundle, to Miss Selby, only daughter of Michael Selby of Barnwell. *Northampton Mercury 8 July 1809*

A report in the Stamford Mercury dated 2 October 1829 states – On Tuesday evening last, about 10 o clock, as Thomas Bell, an apprentice to Mr Cumberland, of Oundle, was returning home from Stamford alone in a gig, he was stopped between Wansford and Yarwell by three highwaymen, who knocked off his hat and demanded his money; the young man protested that he only had a few halfpence, and the robbers, after searching his pockets and ascertaining the truth of that statement, left him, saying he was not the person they were waiting for. The night was so dark that the young man could not distinguish the features or dress of the robbers.

In 1841 Ann Bell c.1776 lived along the West End in Oundle. Ann Platt also born in the same year as Ann worked as a domestic servant for her.

Next to Mary lived Anthony Bell, a baker and his wife Elizabeth. Their son James aged twenty-two was a confectioner. He married Maria Budd during the summer of 1841. A report in the marriages section of the Northampton Mercury dated 25 September 1841 states 'On Tuesday last, at Oundle, Mr Wm Bell, baker, to Miss Budd.' (Confusion over Mr Bell's Christian name). In the 1847 Post Office Directory James Bell was listed as a bread and biscuit maker of West Street.

By 1851 James and Maria lived along West Street. James was a baker employing one man, his mother Elizabeth a widow also lived with them. James and Maria's children were Samuel eight, Anne four, Walter two and Herbert aged ten months. At the time of the 1861 census James had changed his occupation to a county court bailiff and continued to live along West Street at number 31 with his family. Annie was a dressmaker, Walter, Herbert, Emma eight, Mary six, Louisa four and Maria three all attended school. Charles was one month old.

On the 24th inst., at St Peter's Southwark, London, by the Rev. B.W. Raven, Samuel George, eldest son of Mr James Bell, of Oundle, to Eliza Maria, second daughter of the late Thomas King, of Bridge Street, Southwark. *Northampton Mercury 28 September 1867.*

James and his family were living in the yard behind Snowden Terrace in St Osyth's Lane in 1871. They had four children still at home, Mary Ann was a dressmaker, Maria and Charles Arthur attended school then Henry Edmund was one-year-old. James and Maria's daughter Emma was visiting Jane Reeves, the school mistress who lived along Stoke End. Their son Herbert was a Groom lodging with Francis Eady and his family at 4 the Queens Mews Paddington Kensington in London. Francis was a coachman also from Oundle.

Herbert Bell emigrated to USA during 1872, he married in 1879 to Elvira. They had a daughter Florence born in 1883 in Massachusetts. A report in the Northampton Mercury on 28 January 1916. The death has occurred at Leominster Mass., of Mr Herbert Bell, at the age of 65. He was a native of Oundle, being the son of Mr J Bell, a baker, of West Street, and at one-time County Court Bailiff.

In 1881 James and Maria continued living along St Osyth's Lane with their grandson Harry E Bell (Henry Edmund) aged eleven. James and Maria had moved by 1891 to Eastbourne Road in Birkdale Lancashire. Their granddaughter Ethel Bell aged fifteen also lived with them. Harry was boarding with Annie Powell at 72 Devonshire Lane in Sheffield at the time of the 1901 census. By 1911 Harry Edmund was a draper's van-man he boarded with Ann Ellison, a shop-keeper in Ecclesall, Yorkshire.

The Bell family from Benefield.

John Thomas Bell c.1858 was the son of Robert and Rebecca Bell and the grandson of Robert and Susannah Bell all from Benefield. Both Robert's were cordwainers. In 1871 John Thomas continued living with his parents in Benefield where he worked as a cordwainer.

John Thomas married Mahala Carter in 1875. They were living along Benefield Road during 1881 in one of the cottages named Snowdon's Terrace. He was a rural letter carrier and lived there with his wife Mahala and their one-year-old son William. They were still along Benefield Road in 1891 with their extended family. William twelve, Annie eight and Florence six attended school, then there was Reginald four, Mahala two and Lily aged four months. At the time of the 1901 census John and Mahala had moved to Carter's Row with their family. William was a rural post messenger as was his father. Reginald a telegraph messenger, Mahala aged twelve, Lily ten, John nine, Harriett seven, Isaac five and Shiloh aged two years. Mahala died in 1906 aged forty-seven. In 1909 John married Ellen Margaret Emms. By 1911 John Thomas, a town postman, and Ellen Margaret were living with their family along Carter's Road. Their family were Lois aged nine, Katie seven, Ethel and Kennard six, then fifteen-month-old Evelyn.

John and Mahala's daughter Mahala Ann married Frederick Smith in 1910 which was reported as follows. – MOTOR WEDDING – The first motor wedding in Oundle took place on Thursday week at the Parish church. The parties were Mr F Smith, Bedford, and Miss Mahala Ann, third daughter of Mr John Bell, of Benefield Road Oundle. The Rev. W.A. Hodgson performed the ceremony, and the wedding party was conveyed to church in a motor. The family party who met to celebrate the event included twelve brothers and sisters and five nieces and nephews, relatives of the bride. *Northampton Mercury 25 November 1910.*

John and Mahala's son William married Elizabeth Keziah Smith, from Thorpe Achurch, in 1906. By 1911 William, a postman, and Elizabeth lived along Benefield Road. Their children were Mahala Elizabeth aged three, John William aged two and Muriel Annie aged one. William's brother Isaac a grocer's assistant also lived with them. On 2nd December 1915 William Bell signed up for the Royal Fusilier's. He was discharged in 1919 after being wounded in Calais during 1917.

WOUNDED – BELL., QUARTERMASTER SERGEANT REGINALD, 1st/5th Battalion Bedfordshire Regiment. – Information has been received by his father, Mr J. Bell, a member of the Oundle Postal Staff that his son, Q.M.S. Bell has been wounded and is in hospital at Malta. *Northampton Mercury 26 November 1915.*

The section which covered the Local Casualties in the Northampton Mercury dated 10 May 1918 included – N.C. O's and Men – Died of wounds – Bell R. (22) son of Mr John Bell, postman, of Oundle, has died of wounds.

Mr John Bell, who has been a rural and town messenger at the Oundle Post Office, retires this week after 42 years' service. *Peterborough Advertiser 14 February 1920.*

Oundle Postmen c.1911. Photograph courtesy of Peterborough Images

The BINDER families

At the beginning of 1841 Henry Binder married Christian Coleman. An entry in the Northampton Mercury dated 12 June 1841 stated – June 3rd, at the Independent Meeting House, Oundle, by the Rev. Dr Simpson, Mr Henry Binder, of Barnwell Mills, to Christiana Coleman, third daughter of the late Mr Wm. Coleman, farmer, of Ringstead, in this county. Henry was born in Stanion and Christian in Ringstead both in Northamptonshire. At the time of the 1841 census Henry Binder, a miller and his wife Christiana were living along Mill Lane with Elizabeth Drage a schoolmistress aged forty-five. Throughout the census years Christian was shown as Christiana. By 1851 Henry, a corn factor, and Christiana living along West Street with Mary aged eight, Carolina two and Anne aged four months. In 1861 census Henry, a corn dealer, grocer and baker, lived at 52 West Street with Christiana and their family. Mary sixteen, Caroline twelve, Anne ten, Henry eight, Clara six, Frederick four, Charles two and one month old Beatrice. All their children were born in Oundle.

On the 16th inst, at Oundle, deeply regretted, Mr Henry Binder, corn dealer, aged 59. *Northampton Mercury 23 April 1870*

By 1871 Christiana, a widow, continued to live along West Street with her family, she was described as a grocer, baker and corn factor. Her children were listed on census as sons first, Frederick aged fourteen was an assistant in the family business, Charles twelve and John Coleman Binder eight were scholars, Mary twenty-six, Annie twenty, Clara sixteen and ten-year-old Beatrice who also attended school. Frederick died in 1872 aged fifteen. Christiana had moved to Benefield Road in Oundle by the time of the 1881 census where she continued to be a corn dealer, grocer and baker. Four of her children were living at home, Annie, Clara Fanny, Charles Ernest a corn-dealer's assistant and Beatrice Alice. Christiana's son John was a Boarder with William Hoddle, a leather cutter (Currier) and his wife Anne. They lived at 57 Lawrence Street in Northampton. John was a shop-man in the cabinet trade. Ten years later Christiana was living along Binders Row with her son Charles, a corn-dealer's assistant, and her granddaughter Annie Holt aged eighteen born in Rochdale.

Christiana Binder died on December 8th in Oundle aged seventy-three. *Northampton Mercury 14 December 1894.*

Henry and Christiana's daughter Caroline married James Holt during 1870. At the Independent Church, Oundle, on the 15th inst, by the Rev W M Jones, James younger son of the late Benjamin Holt, grocer, Rochdale, to Caroline, second daughter of Henry Binder, corn factor, &c., Oundle. *Northampton Mercury 19 February 1870.* By the time of the 1871 census they were living in Birkenhead where James worked as a hatter employing one man and one boy. They had a son Benjamin aged one month.

Henry and Christiana's daughter Mary Elizabeth married William John Coaten in 1873. December 31st at the Providence Chapel, by the Rev T Shelton, Mr W J Coaten of Oundle, to M E J Binder, eldest daughter of the late Mr H Binder, of Oundle. *Northampton Mercury 11 January 1873.*

At the time of the 1881 census William and Mary Elizabeth Coaten were living along the Market Place in Oundle, William was a plumber and painter. In 1891 they had Minnie Coaten aged seventeen, niece to William, living with them she worked as a dressmaker. John Coleman Binder, a grocer and brother to Mary's also lived with them. Ten years later William and Mary were living in the Market Place. William died in 1906 aged sixty-three. Mary was living along West Street in 1911 and showed her full name as Mary Elizabeth Isabella. She died during 1914 aged sixty-nine. They had no children.

Henry and Christiana's son Henry married Catherine Jane Brown from Chelmsford during 1878. In 1881 they were living along Grove Road in Ealing where Henry was a draper. Catherine was a dressmaker employing one person. They had a baby boy, unnamed, age shown as aged under one month. They employed a domestic servant and a nurse.

Henry and Christiana's daughter Annie married Robert Knight from Ringstead during 1883. In 1891 Robert was a solicitor's clerk and they were living in the Nene Cottage along Station Road in Oundle. Their children were Ida Nellie twelve, Percy Robert eleven and Ada Emily Sarah was nine years old. Robert's mother Elizabeth also lived with them in Oundle, she was a widow. By 1901 Robert was a superintendent registrar and they had moved to North Street. Percy lived at home with his parents and worked from home as a watch maker. Sarah Glover from Alconbury was their domestic servant. In 1911 Robert and Annie were still living along North Street their house was called 'Rookholme'. Percy continued his business at home as a jeweller.

Henry and Christiana's daughter Beatrice Alice married Charles Wright on the 21st August 1888 at the Independent Church in Oundle. This was reported in the Northampton Mercury dated 25th August 1888. At the time of the 1891 census Charles and Beatrice lived along New Street where Charles was a tailor and woollen draper. They had a son Charles aged one. Gertrude Dicks from Oundle was a servant for the family. Charles and Beatrice had moved by 1901, they lived at 18 Market Square in the town of Aylesbury where Charles was a tailor and outfitter. Their son Charles had a brother Frederick Coleman Wright both were born in Oundle. By 1911 they had moved to 49 Market Square, their son Charles was still living at home, his occupation was an assistant architect.

Henry and Christiana's son Charles Ernest married Sarah Elizabeth Dolby during 1896 in Axbridge. In 1901 they were living along West Street where Charles was a grocer, baker and corn dealer shopkeeper. Charles brother John Coleman Binder aged thirty-nine lived with them, he had the same occupation as Charles. Ten years later Charles and Sarah lived at Albion House in Oundle. They had been married for fifteen years and had no children. Rose Leah Earle aged sixteen was the family servant. Charles died on 1 August 1932 aged seventy-three.

Henry and Christiana's son John Coleman Binder married Louisa Clara Middleton during 1901 in the West Ham district of London. John Coleman Binder, a grocer, and Louisa Clara lived along West Street where they had a shop in 1911. They had been married for ten years.

Graves of Binder family in the town cemetery Stoke Road

The Binder family from Weldon

Caution to wheelwrights. – Whereas MILLIN BINDER, an Apprentice to William Ladds, of Oundle, in the county of Northampton, wheelwright, did on the 2d inst. abscond from the service of his Master, before the expiration of the term of his apprenticeship. Notice is hereby given, that a reward of Two Pounds will be paid by the said William Ladds to any person who shall give such information as will lead to his apprehension; and all persons are hereby cautioned not to employ him after this notice. – The said Millin Binder stands about 5 feet 7 inches high, has brown hair, is rather fresh-coloured, and has a scar on the back of his left hand. He had on when he left Oundle a light fustian frock coat. Oundle 12th December 1838. *Stamford Mercury 14 December 1838*

In 1841 Milton Selby Binder married Harriet Clipston. By 1851 Millin Binder, a journeyman wheelwright born in Weldon c.1819 lived along North Street with his wife Harriet from Oundle and their family John twelve, Mary nine, William six and Alice eleven months old. In 1861 Millin, a wheelwright and master who employed two men and three boys lived along Binders Hill not far from Stoke End, with his wife Harriet and their family. John and William were both wheelwrights, and Alice, the new additions to the family since 1851 were Elizabeth seven, Millin five, Lucy two and Henry five months.

Millin and Harriet's daughter Alice married Daniel Beeby during 1868 in Oundle. By 1871 Millin had four men and one boy working for him. He continued living along West Street with Harriet, William, Millin, Lucy and Harriet aged seven. Alfred Bradshaw aged seventeen from Tansor was an apprentice wheelwright living with the Binder family. Millin and Harriet's daughter Elizabeth was living at the East side of the Market Place where she worked as an assistant dressmaker for Susannah Stafford a milliner and dressmaker from Nassington. In 1881 Millin, a wheelwright master, and Harriet were living along West Street at the Ship Inn. Living with them were Millin a carpenter journeyman, Lucy a dressmaker, Henry a blacksmith journeyman, Harriet seventeen, Percy their grandson aged three months and Thomas Ruff a widow was boarding with the family, he was a butcher journeyman. Millin's wife Harriet died in 1882 aged sixty-one. Moving to 1891 Millin Binder (junior), a builder, was living along Benefield Road with his wife Emily. His father Millin a widower lived with his son. Millin Selby Binder died during 1894 aged seventy-six.

Millin and Harriet's son John married Sarah Jane Bishop during 1861. John died in 1867 aged twenty-eight. In 1871 Sarah Binder aged thirty-one a wheelwright's widow was living along West Street at the British Schoolyard. Her three children were Annie nine, Sarah five and John three all attended school. Also, living with Sarah was her sister Hannah Bishop aged twenty-nine and Sarah's nephew Arthur Bishop who was one month old. Sarah Jane married Luke Richards during 1878. By 1881 they were living along West Street at the British School Yard, Luke was a general labourer. Sarah Binder, their daughter, also lived with them, she was aged fifteen a domestic servant and John Binder, their son, aged thirteen who attended school.

Millin and Harriet's son William married Mary Ann Kirby during 1873 in the district of St Olave in London. In 1881, living along West Street at the Green Man Inn was Elizabeth Kirby, the publican, she was seventy-three and born in Glapthorne. Also, living with Elizabeth was William Binder, a wheelwright, her daughter Mary Ann and her grandsons Millin Jude aged six and William Bertie aged one. By the time of the 1901 census William Binder, a wheelwright and innkeeper was living at the Ship Inn with his wife Mary Ann. Their children at home were Millin Jude aged twenty-six and William Bertie aged twenty both wheelwrights, Arthur Henry aged sixteen and William's brother Henry aged forty a blacksmith.

OUNDLE – On Tuesday Mr Millin Binder, eldest son of Mr W. Binder, wheelwright, after partaking of his tea, died suddenly, it is supposes from a fit. As no doctor had attended the deceased, an inquest was held on Thursday morning, when a verdict of "Death from natural causes" was returned. *Stamford Mercury 10 February 1905*

SUDDEN DEATH – An inquest was held on Thursday at the Old hind Inn by Mr J.C. Parker, deputy coroner, on the body of Millin Jude Binder, aged 31 years, the eldest son of Mr William Binder a wheelwright and coach builder of Oundle. From the evidence, it appears the deceased went to Thurning to assist in felling trees with his uncle and other workmen. On returning home deceased had his tea and went into the yard and fell down dead. The father said his son had a fainting fit just before Christmas, and some weeks previous to that, otherwise he had enjoyed good health, and on Tuesday he was as well as usual. Dr Turner said the cause of death was most probably heart failure. A verdict of 'natural causes' was returned, and the jury expressed their sympathy with Mr and Mrs Binder in the sad bereavement. *Peterborough Advertiser 11 February 1905*

William Binder was working as a coachbuilder; he lived with Mary Ann along West Street in 1911. Their son Arthur had married, he and his wife Florence were living with William and Mary Ann. Arthur was a jeweller. He lived along at Coombe Brae along Glapthorn Road. Arthur died on 5 April 1936.

Millin and Harriet's son Henry married Elizabeth Ann Chappell during 1910. By the time of the 1911 census they were living at 5 Rock Road in Oundle. The census showed they had been married under one year. Gertrude Elizabeth Chappell aged fifteen was Henry's Step daughter. Henry died in 1936 aged seventy-six and Elizabeth Ann died in 1937 aged seventy-four.

Millin and Harriet's grandson Percy Binder was a timber sawyer in Wood Yard lodging with William and Annie Steele at North Luffenham in Rutland during 1911.

William and Mary Ann's son William Bertie married Mary Ethel Brudenell during 1907. In 1911 Bertie, a coach builder, and his wife Ethel lived at Woodbine Cottage along Glapthorne Road.

The BRINSLEY families

In 1841 George and Mary Brinsley living along Fen Street in Stilton with their children, George aged two and Sarah one-year-old, she died in 1842. The family had moved to Benefield Road in Oundle by 1851, George was a general labourer. They had three sons George, Matthew aged four and James aged two. Ten years later George Brinsley was a shepherd and lived with his wife Mary and their sons George, Matthew and James all agricultural labourers. They had extended their family since the last census and continued to live along Benefield Road with Rebecca aged nine, William seven, Mary four and Harriet was one-year-old.

Oundle Petty Sessions February 5th - Barnwell snaring – George Brinsley, of Oundle, was charged with the above offence, on the estate of the Duke of Buccleuch, at Barnwell, on the 25th ult. Six snares were discovered by the keepers, and a watch was set upon them, when defendant (who was engaged at Work on the turnpike immediately adjoining) was observed to go to the first trap, which was empty; from thence to the second, in which was a hare, which he took. – Defendant said he saw a hare dead in a snare, and thought he might take it, but denied setting the snares. - Previous convictions being proved, he was ordered to pay £2. 15s. 0d penalty and costs, in default of which he was committed for two months. *Northampton Mercury 10 February 1866*

In 1871 George senior, who was back working as a labourer and Mary only had James, Rebecca and William living at home. By 1881 George, a farm labourer, and Mary were shown on census as Brindsley had moved to Mill Lane, all their children had moved out of the family home. George and Mary were living at the Workhouse in Oundle when the 1891 census was recorded. George died in 1892 aged seventy-seven.

George and Mary's son James married Margaret Brown in 1872. By the time of the 1881 census they were living in the Hamlet of Kingsthorpe near Polebrook with their children Charles eight, Fred five and Margaret was three.

George and Mary's daughter Emma married Harry Saunders during 1900; Harry was born in Mildenhall Suffolk. By 1901 they lived along Back Row in Benefield Road with their son Reginald

Brinsley aged one. Harry and Emma Saunders had moved to Tilley Hill Close along Glapthorne Road by the time of the 1911 census with their family Reginald Brinsley aged eleven and Kathleen Doris Saunders aged one.

George and Mary's son George married Emma Sophia Bluff in 1864. Emma was the widow of James Bluff who she married in 1860, and was the daughter of John and Ann Ives from Benefield Road in Oundle. By 1871 George and Emma were living along Benefield Road with James aged eight and George aged one year and six months. Ten years later, surname shown as 'Brindsly' they were living at Bings Corner Cottage along Benefield Road towards Stoke Road with George a farm labourer, Elizabeth aged six, Caroline aged four and Emma aged one.

George and Emma's daughter Elizabeth married Stephen Coales in 1889. (See 'Coles' family details) In 1891 George and Emma lived along Benefield Road with their daughter Emma twenty and son John aged eight. Their daughter Caroline was a domestic servant for Henry Garner an innkeeper living along North Street.

OUNDLE FATAL ACCIDENT AT STOKE DOYLE – On Friday Mr. J. C. Parker (the deputy Coroner for the district) held an inquest at the Shuckburgh Arms Inn, Stoke Doyle, touching the death of George Brinsley, who was killed by a loaded cart running over him on the previous day. – Dr Somerset said he was called to deceased on Thursday afternoon. He was then lying in the roadway leading to Mr Everard's house. He examined him, and found him to be quite dead, and he should say that death took place through fracture of the skull. It was his opinion that nothing could have saved the boy's life. The father of the deceased, who lives at Mill-lane, Oundle, was then called, and said deceased was his son, and 13 years old last October. Witness last saw him alive on Thursday morning. - Jeremiah Hankins said he lived at Stoke Doyle, and worked for Mr Freeman. On Thursday, he saw deceased going into the yard leading to Everard's. He was leading a horse attached to a loaded cart. There were four or five sheaves lying on the ground against the gate inside, and as he was looking behind to see the cart did not catch the gate post he fell over the sheaves and under the cart wheel. Witness called out to the horse to stop, but failed to attract its attention. He was five or six yards off deceased when the accident happened. Witness then called to the other men in the stackyard. – Verdict, "Accidental death." *Northampton Mercury 25 August 1899*

George and Emma's son John James was a blacksmith's apprentice for John Smith at The Poplars along Benefield Road in 1901. John James married Amelia Ann Carter in 1904. By 1911 John James, a blacksmith, and Amelia lived along Rock Road with their daughters Florence May aged two and Millicent Rebecca aged six months.

George and Mary's son William married Elizabeth Hollis during 1873. In 1881 they were living along Mill Lane with their children Arthur six, Emily four, John two and Albert was new born. By 1891 William and Elizabeth continued to live along Mill Lane with their family. Arthur was a farm labourer, Emily a domestic servant, John a farm labourer, then Albert was ten, Alfred aged eight, George aged five and William aged two. At the time of the 1901 census William and Elizabeth lived at 9 Mill Lane with their son Albert a grocer's assistant, Alfred an Ag lab, William twelve and Margaret eight.

Annual Fete and Flower Show at Ashton – a section of the report – A fine show of assorted plants, ferns, palms, etc., were exhibited on the centre table, belonging to Messrs. W. and J Brown, of Oundle, Stamford and Peterborough. A case that attracted much attention contained a hornet's nest. It was the property of Mr Brinsley, of Mill-lane, Oundle, and is really a remarkable piece of insect work. It was taken from a root in the woods of Biggin Grange, and is said to be over 100 years old. *Northampton Mercury 29 July 1904*

William and Elizabeth's son Arthur William married Kate Andrews during 1896. In 1901 Arthur, a railway platelayer, and his wife Kate lived in North Street Stanground with Kate M four and Naomia one-year-old. Elizabeth Naomi died during 1909 aged nine. By 1911 Arthur and Kate were living along Church Street in Stanground with their daughter Kate a dressmaker.

William and Elizabeth's daughter Emily Mary married Thomas Alfred Moore during 1899. In 1901 Thomas and Emily Moore lived at Arthington Road in Braybrook Northants with their son George Thomas six months. They were still in Braybrook by 1911 with their children George ten and Edwin eight.

William and Elizabeth's son John was a boarder with Thomas and Elizabeth Gadsden who lived at Wootton in Bedfordshire during 1901. John married Kate Whitbread, daughter of Charles and

Susannah at Marston Moretaine in Bedfordshire during 1902. Kate died in 1909 aged twenty-eight. By 1911 John, and his son Albert aged seven, were living with Charles and Susannah Whitbread at Marston Moretaine.

William and Elizabeth's son Alfred married May Turner during 1904. In 1911 Alfred, a garden labourer, and May lived at 7 Mill Lane with their family Gladys six and Alfred three.

William and Elizabeth's son Albert Edward married Nellie Dorrington during 1906. In 1911 they lived not far from Albert's parents along Benefield Road. Albert Edward, a bread baker, and Nellie had a three-year-old son Ernest.

In 1911 William and Elizabeth continued to live at 9 Mill Lane with William a farm labourer and Margaret a general servant.

A £ - CLOTHES LINE POST – OUNDLE MEN'S COSTLY ENTERPRISE – A man who cut down a sapling because his friend wanted a clothes-line post, accompanied that friend to Oundle Police Court on Thursday when William Brinsley, labourer, 13 Mill-road and Ronald Lewis Coles, labourer, 39 Benefield Road, were charged with cutting down an ash tree on land the property of Sylvia Watts Russell, and doing damage to the amount of 15s. at Oundle on November 30. Brinsley pleaded guilty and Coles not guilty. Ernest Baxter, Benefield Road Oundle, said he saw a man whom he recognised as Brinsley cutting down an ash in Mrs Russell's spinney. Coles was watching from the road and each time a car came by, he spoke to Brinsley, who went into the spinney until it had passed. Frederick Carman, a gamekeeper, said on going into the spinney he saw the freshly cut stump of the ash tree. P.C. Johnson said Brinsley denied having cut down the tree, but Coles told him, "Bill did cut it down." Later Brinsley admitted doing the damage. Brinsley said Coles had helped him with the load of wood he had purchased. Coles asked him to cut down the ash tree as he wanted a clothes-line post, and he was silly enough to do it." Each defendant was fined £1. *Northampton Mercury 13 December 1929*

Tools in two allotment huts on the Benefield-road allotments have been destroyed by fire. They belong to Mr. W Brinsley and Mr. Coles. *Northampton Mercury 3 August 1934.*

The BRUDENELL families

The 'Brudenell' families lived in Oundle from at least the early 1700's. George Brudenell from Ashton married Arabella Sugars from Oundle at St Peter's church in 1743. Their son George was baptised in July 1745.

Thomas and Lucy Brudenell's children were John c.1793, he died in 1794, Lucy c.1795 and Barbara c.1797. Thomas died during 1817 aged forty-nine. Barbara died during 1830 aged thirty-three.

In 1841 Lucy Brudenell senior was a Parish Relief, her daughter Lucy a dressmaker lived with her along West Street and was still there in 1851. Her mother died during 1850 aged eighty-seven. Lucy was an inmate at the Latham Hospital for eighteen women in 1861.

There were 'Brudenell' families who lived in Warmington from around the same era. Their descendants eventually moved to Oundle.

Job Brudenell married Elizabeth Starsby/Sharsby in 1724. Their children included Job, William and Elizabeth.

Job and Elizabeth's son William married Jane Richardson during 1760. Their children were John, Daniel, William, Mary and Elizabeth.

William and Jane's son John married Mary Elderkin during 1790; their children were Elizabeth, John, Daniel, Mary Crooks Brudenell, Valentine, Mary, William, Isaac and Jane who were baptised at St Mary the Virgin church in Warmington.

John and Mary's son Daniel married Frances Cawthorne on 20 December 1814 at Warmington. Some of their children were Joseph Cawthorne, Jane, William, Charles, Frances, Ann, Phebe, John. In 1841 Daniel and Frances lived along Long Lane in Warmington with Charles, John and Ann. Frances died during 1848. In 1851 Daniel was a road labourer living in Warmington.

Daniel and Frances son William married Jane Duery during 1838. At the time of the 1841 census they were living along Long Lane in Warmington where William was born. By 1851 William and Jane had moved to North Street in Oundle with their family, Herbert nine, Caroline seven, John five, Louis two and Mary one-year-old. William, a Carpenter, and his wife Jane lived at 16 East Court, along North Street in 1861. Their children at home were Herbert Dury a groom,

Caroline Eliza a house servant, John Thomas an errand boy, Louis/Lewis William a farmer's boy, Mary Jane, Enzor Aaron, Edwin Alfred, Leonard Moses and Sara Agnes. By 1871 Jane was a widow and worked as a seamstress, her children at home were Mary Jane who was recorded as very Deaf and assistant to her mother, Enzor Aaron a day servant and Leonard Moses was a rope maker's assistant. In 1881 Jane was working as a laundress, her son Leonard Moses, a general labourer they were living in one of the Havelock Cottages along North Street.

William and Janes' son Leonard married Sophia Williamson in 1882. Sophia was the daughter of William and Mary Ann from Warmington. Leonard died in 1888 aged thirty-one. In 1891 Sophia was living along North Street in Oundle with her children Ethel Jane aged six, Leonard five, Edwin Alfred three and Sydney Moses was two years old. Sophia married Charles William Catton during 1897. Charles was a carpenter/joiner they lived in Old Fletton in 1901 with Sophia's children Ethel, Leonard a mechanical engineer, Edwin and Sidney. Sydney joined the 3rd Northamptonshire Regiment in 1907 aged seventeen years and eleven months. Sydney's trade was shown as a baker.

By 1911 William and Sophia Catton had moved to 1 Illinois Houses along Burton Street in Peterborough with Sophia's grown up family Ethel Jane, Leonard a cycle maker and Sidney Moses a boot maker.

Daniel and Frances son Joseph Cawthorne married Elizabeth Prentice during the summer of 1844. Elizabeth died in May 1845 (see the Prentice family details).

At Uppingham, on the 21st ult., (by the Rev. J. G. Dimock) Mr Jos. Cawthen Brudenell, of Oundle, to Matilda second daughter of Mr. J. Penny, schoolmaster, of the former place. *Stamford Mercury 2 February 1849*

At the time of the 1851 census Joseph Cawthorne Brudenell a master tailor lived along North Street with his wife Matilda and their children Harry aged one and William seven months old. In 1852 they had a daughter Matilda Penny she was given a private baptism and only lived for six weeks. By 1861 Matilda was a dressmaker, their sons William aged ten and John aged eight attended school. Ten years later Matilda was a milliner and dressmaker who employed two apprentices, Elizabeth Luffley and Emily Cooper Andrews. Joseph and Matilda's son John Thomas was a grocer and tallow chandler's apprentice he lived at home with his parents. Matilda died in 1875 aged fifty-three. In 1881 Joseph was living on his own in North Street where he continued with his work as a tailor. He died during 1889 aged seventy-seven.

John and Mary's son Valentine married Elizabeth (surname not known) during 1825.

The stable of Mr V. Brudenell, baker of Warmington near Oundle, was broken into on Sunday night last, and a mare was stolen. Her feeting could be traced over three fences, but she has not since been heard of. Stamford Mercury 8 December 1837

Valentine and Elizabeth lived in Warmington in 1841 with their four children, Daniel and Valentine fifteen-year-old twins, Mary Ann eleven and Eliza was one-year-old.

Valentine and Elizabeth's son Valentine junior, a cattle dealer, married Elizabeth Shelton during 1850. They lived with Valentine's parents in 1851 and had a five-month old son Charles Parker Brudenell.

In 1851 Valentine (senior) a baker and farmer of 30 acres who employed one labourer, Elizabeth was kept busy in the home. Their son John was a baker their daughter Eliza was a domestic and Martha Elizabeth stayed at home as she was only six.

WARMINGTON near Oundle. 19 COWS and 150 EWES and THEAVES with Lambs. To be sold by Auction, without Reserve, By Deacon and Son. On Wednesday, the 28th March 1855, on the premises of Mr Valentine Brudenell, junior, at Warmington, (who is leaving his farm) – 17 Excellent Barren Cows, 2 superior Milch Cows in Calf, 95 two-shear Ewes and 55 Theaves with Lambs. The above stock will be found well worthy the attention of Graziers and Breeders, as the cows are young and in good condition, the Sheep sound and healthy, and descended from the celebrated Lincolnshire flocks of Messrs. Winn, Hoyles and Bailey. The company are requested to meet the auctioneers at Twelve o'clock, when Refreshment will be provided, and then proceed to Sale. *Stamford Mercury 23 March 1855*

Valentine and Elizabeth's son John a cattle dealer, married Elizabeth Davey during 1858. By 1861 they were living along Church

Street in Warmington with their one-year-old son Leonard. Valentine and Elizabeth senior lived not far from them and only had their daughter Martha at home.

At the Oundle Petty Sessions on May 24th Mr Lettice, of Warmington was charged by Mr. V. Brudenell, jnr., with allowing two cows to stray on the highway. – From the evidence of complainant, the cows were "lying" on the road, necessitating complainant getting out of his gig, which was as positively denied by the keeper of the cattle. The Bench considered the fact of the cattle lying on the road was straying within the meaning of the Act, and convicted in the nominal penalty of 6d. – Mr Deacon applied for and obtained a case for the superior court as to the point of law raised. The parishioners of Warmington, under the parish award, are entitled to the herbage on the highways in the parish, subject to certain restrictions, and the above proceedings appear to point to the sweeping away of such privileges. *Northampton Mercury 29 May 1869.*

At the time of the 1871 census Valentine senior, a cottager, and his wife Eliza were living in Warmington. Next to them was their son John a pig jobber and Elizabeth with their children Leonard, Herbert, Harry and Walter.

Petty Sessions – Magistrate's room May 4th before the Rev. G. H. Capron and Lieut Col. Tyron – V. Brudenell, snr. of Warmington, was convicted of using a gun without a license, and ordered to pay £2.10s. penalty and costs. *Northampton Mercury 9 May 1874.*

The two families continued to live side by side in 1881, John and Elizabeth had another son John Arthur also at home were Harry and Walter. By 1891 John, a cattle dealer, and Elizabeth lived along Church Street with Walter and John who were both butchers. John's father Valentine was a widow and lived with his son. Ann Titman from Polebrook was a live-in nurse.

Valentine's twin brother Daniel married Mary Lettice during 1848, possibly a childhood sweetheart as they grew up a few doors away from one another in Warmington. At the time of the 1851 census they were living with Mary's parents Robert and Ann Lettice in Warmington with their one-year-old son Joseph. Daniel died very young as ten years later the census shows Mary was a dealer's widow. Mary and her sons Joseph eleven and Horace aged eight lived with her mother Ann Lettice, also a widow.

Daniel and Mary's son Horace married Sarah Jane Ireson during 1876; she was the daughter of Francis and Elizabeth Ireson from Warmington. Francis was a stonemason and publican at the Masons Arms. By the time of the 1881 census Horace was a grocer, he and Sarah had two children Lewis and Mary E, they lived in Warmington. By 1891 Horace and Sarah Jane 's family had grown with the addition of Harry Lettice Brudenell, Joseph Horace and Victoria Maud brothers and sister for Lewis Dan and Mary Ethel. Horace's Uncle Joseph Lettice also lived with them. In 1901 Horace was living at their shop where he continued working as a grocer. Lewis Dan worked as a gardener (not domestic); Mary Ethel, Joseph Horace and Victoria Maud all lived at home. Their brother Harry was a boarder with Martha Carrett who lived along Oundle Road in Fletton. Harry was a grocer's assistant. Horace and Sarah had been married for thirty-four years at the time of the 1911 census and had five children all of who had survived. Victoria Maud was the only sibling living at home.

Horace and Sarah's son Joseph Horace, a grocer, was a boarder with Thomas and Harriet Heath at 123 Owen Road in Wolverhampton in 1911. During 1914 Joseph married Maggie C. E. Howard in Wolverhampton. Their children were Douglas, Mildred and Allan born in the Pottersbury district.

J.H. Brudenell Grocery Stores Warmington
Courtesy of Stephen Brudenell

Horace and Sarah's son Harry married Margaret Keen during 1891 in the Oxford district where Margaret was born. In 1901 they lived in Middlesex but had moved to Amersham by the time of the 1911 census with their daughter and son Edith and William, Harry was a railway station master.

John and Elizabeth's son Walter married Mary Ann Mitchelson during 1893. At the time of the 1901 census Walter and his wife shown as Pollie, from Lincolnshire, living along Church Street where Walter was a butcher working from home. They had a daughter Edith Muriel. They continued with the butchery business in Warmington ten years later.

John and Elizabeth's son John Arthur married Ellen Coulson during 1897. By 1901 they had made their home along East Street in Kimbolton where their son John Edgar Hugh and their daughter Elizabeth Melba were born. John ran his own butcher business from their home. Ten years later they had moved to 96 Queen Street in Leamington Warwickshire. John had moved on from the butcher business and was shown as being in the furniture and cycle business. John Arthur was a Gunner in the Royal Garrison Artillery in the First World War.

Brudenell's delivery van Courtesy of the late Philip Brudenell

The late Philip Brudenell, son of John Edgar and Eleanor spoke to me about his family. Job and Elizabeth Brudenell were Philip's Great gt, gt, gt, gt grandparents. He told me his great Uncle Walter moved to Oundle around 1911 where he had a small holding and was the butcher in the town. John Arthur went into partnership with his brother before the 1st World War. Later John Arthur took over until eventually Philip stepped in to carry on the family business.

The BUNNING families

Thomas Bunning from Werrington married Ellen Jerman from Oundle on 13 October 1627 at St Peter's parish church Oundle.

At Oundle, on Sunday last, Mr. Wm. Ball, draper of that place, to Mrs Margaret Bunning, his housekeeper for some years. *Stamford Mercury 12 October 1821*

Thomas Bunning from Oundle married Elizabeth Bowland, of the parish of Northampton, at Stamford All Saints on 25 November 1822. Their children were John, Mary, Emma, Thomas, James, Elizabeth and George Frederick. Thomas Bunning born in Apethorpe was a painter and in 1841, lived along West Street with Elizabeth and their family. John was seventeen, Emma thirteen, Thomas eleven, James eight, George Frederick three and Robert was eleven months old. Thomas and Elizabeth's son Thomas died in 1844 aged fourteen.

Marriages – May 17, at St Pancras church, London, by the Rev. Robert Barry, Mr Charles Moreton, butcher, of Lubenham, Leicestershire, second son of Mr William Moreton, farmer and grazier, of Marston Trussell, in this county, to Emma, only surviving daughter of Mr Thomas Bunning, of Oundle, in the same county. *Northampton Mercury 19 May 1849*

By 1851 Thomas employed his sons John and James in his painting business. Elizabeth was busy in the home looking after their younger sons George and Robert and William aged eight. Also in the home was Edith Ruff from Middlesex, their servant, Wallis Calcot, a G.P. from Cheltenham and his wife Annie from Elmington lodged with Thomas and Elizabeth.

An article in the Northampton Mercury dated 13 December 1856 showed the following – Corns and Bunions – Thirteen years established – THOMAS CALDWELL – Chiropodist – Kettering Road, Northampton – opposite the entrance to Wellingborough Road – T.C. continues adding weekly to his former LIST of CURES. Great improvements have lately been introduced to accelerate the cure. Relief given by the first operation without pain. At home Mondays and Saturdays. Many people left testimonials to Thomas Caldwell one of which was Thomas Bunning, which read, - 'From Thomas Bunning, Senior Painter and Glazier, Oundle. I certify that Mr

Caldwell has cured two blood corns for me, with which I have suffered about forty years. They were cured without pain. Oundle, November 27th 1856 Thomas Bunning.

In 1861 Thomas, had retired, he and Elizabeth were still living along West Street and only had Robert, a painter, at home. Their son George Frederick, a linen draper, was a boarder with Abel and Caroline Clarson at Tamworth in Staffordshire. Abel was Mayor of Tamworth and a draper. Thomas died during 1866 aged seventy-one.

BUNNING – On the 23rd ult., at Husbands Bosworth, Elizabeth, relict of Mr Thomas Bunning, of Oundle, aged 79. *Leicester Chronicle 3 August 1878*

OUNDLE – Property Sale – The property of the late Mr T. Bunning in Oundle was submitted for sale by auction by Mr S. Deacon at the Talbot Hotel on the 29th inst. Two houses in West-street in the occupation of Messrs. G. Bunning and W. Lenton, jun, were bought by the former for 1200/.; and four cottages in St O'Sythe's-lane were bought by Mr Morton for 225/. *Stamford Mercury 6 September 1878*

Thomas and Elizabeth's son Robert married Elizabeth Waller in the Pancras district of London during 1869. By 1871 they were living along West Street with their two-month old daughter Helena Lottie, Robert was a house decorator. Elizabeth died during 1873 aged twenty-seven. Robert died during 1878 aged thirty-eight. Helena was a pupil at 33 Arundel Square in Islington at the time of the 1881 census. In 1891 Helena was living along North End in Croydon where she was a draper's assistant for James Benrigton.

OUNDLE – July 15, at Colchester, Harry Skingley Chignell, of Carrara, Italy, to Helena Lottie only daughter of the late Robert Bunning, of Oundle. *Stamford Mercury 23 July 1897*

Thomas and Elizabeth's son George Frederick married Martha Everard in the Birmingham district during 1864. Martha was the daughter of Job and Elizabeth from Oundle. In 1861 before Martha married she was living with her widowed mother Ellen Everard at 145 Sand Pitts in Birmingham. George and Martha lived along West Street in 1871 where George was a painter employing five men and one boy. They were still living along West Street in 1891. George was shown as a plumber, painter and glazier.

GENERAL SERVANT (respectable) wanted, with knowledge of cooking. Good references required. Two in family – Mrs G.F. Bunning, West-street Oundle *Stamford Mercury 12 February 1892*

SALES BY AUCTION Oundle Northamptonshire to Plumbers, Glaziers, Painters, Gas fitters and others On Thursday and Friday, 2d and 3d June 1892, on the premises in West-street, Oundle, the property of Mr G.T. BUNNING, who is retiring from business. Descriptive Catalogues may be had six days previous to Sale on application at King's Printing-0ffice, Oundle; the Auctioneer's Offices, Thrapston and Oundle; and at the place of Sale. *Stamford Mercury 20 May 1892*

Sad drowning at Oundle – We regret very much to announce the death from drowning of Mr George F Bunning, of Oundle under circumstances detailed below. Mr Bunning, it would seem, went bathing last Friday afternoon in what is known as Reachlons' Pit, a very dangerous bathing place. Nothing more was seen of him until some ladies and gentlemen in boats picnicing went that way, intending to land there for tea. Seeing clothes on the bank they went further on, and on coming back hours later saw the same clothes. This led to an examination of them, when one of the gentlemen recognised them as belonging to the deceased gentleman. The police were communicated with; the river was dragged and the body of Mr Bunning was recovered late on Friday evening and removed to his home to await an inquest. Much sympathy is felt for the widow in the town, and the event has caused a great sensation. Mr Bunning, an elderly gentleman, was a deacon and trustee of the Oundle Congregational Church, treasurer of the Oundle Temperance Society, a member of the Oundle Improvement Commissioners, and was connected with various other societies and public bodies in the town. – Further details of the inquest can be seen in the *Northampton Mercury 17 June 1892. A more detailed account can be read in the Stamford Mercury dated 17 June 1892.*

Martha died during 1893 aged fifty-eight.

Grave of George Frederick and Martha Bunning
in the town cemetery Stoke Road

OUNDLE – Property Sale – On Thursday week Mr G Siddons sold
by auction, at the Talbot Hotel, Oundle, the valuable freehold estate
consisting of two houses, front shop, and work-shops, owned and
occupied by the late Mr G.F. Bunning, Oundle. The property was
bought by Mr R. Hall, Great Gidding, for 1300/. *Stamford Mercury 23*
June 1893

Thomas and Elizabeth's son John married Frances Pollendine Flack in Westminster during the winter of 1851.

TO BE SOLD BY AUCTION – At the Dolphin Inn, in Oundle on Thursday the 1st day of July 1858 at Six o'clock in the evening – Lot 1 – All that Freehold stone-built and slated Messuage, called the British Queen, situated in the Market-Street, in Oundle aforesaid, with Stables and other Out-buildings, now in the occupation of Mr John Bunning, but of which immediate possession may be had. *Northampton Mercury 26 June 1858* This announcement was also put in the newspaper during February 1859

Nov. 5, at Oundle, of diphtheria, Frances, wife of Mr John Bunning, painter, aged 31. *Northampton Mercury 13 November 1858*

John Bunning, widower whose occupation was a painter and glazier, aged thirty-six, married by Licence to Sarah Jane Baker aged twenty-three at St Peter's parish church on 24 April 1860. Sarah was born at Portloe in Cornwall. Her father was Joseph Francis Baker who was recorded as a Lieut R N. By 1861 they were living along West Street with Thomas aged five, Elizabeth aged three and Mary Louisa aged three months. Susanna Wilson, aged sixteen, was the house servant for John and Sarah, she was born in Oundle.

OUNDLE - Sudden Death – On Wednesday last an inquest was held before W Marshall Esq at Oundle, on the body of John Bunning, a plumber and glazier aged 39, who died suddenly about half past eleven the night previous. Deceased was believed to be a strong healthy man, and appeared well on Monday, and partook of a moderate supper of mutton and bread and beer. He was a man of remarkable abstemious habits. Soon after eleven o'clock his wife heard him moan in his sleep, and, as she could not arouse him she became alarmed and went for Mr Culworth, surgeon, who soon after arrived, but deceased was then either dying or dead. The doctor attributed death to a paralysis on the brain and a verdict of "Natural Causes" was returned. *Northampton Mercury 23 May 1863*

At the time of the 1871 census Sarah, a widow, lived in Portloe Cottage along New Street where she worked as a seamstress. Her children at home were Mary ten and Harry aged eight. By 1881 Sarah was still living along New Street and only Harry was at home, he was a chemist's apprentice. In 1891 Sarah Jane was living at 2 Camden Cottage along New Street with her daughter Mary. Fred Johnson a brewer's traveller lodged with her. Ten years later Sarah was a maker of under-linen, her daughter Mary Louisa was still at home. In 1911 Sarah Jane was living along Rock Road with her daughter Mary Louisa. Sarah died in 1924 aged eighty-six.

John and Sarah's son Harry, a chemist' assistant, was boarding with Susette Rydill and her family at Princes Street in Barnsley in 1891. Harry Bunning married Hannah Elizabeth Stephenson during 1899 at St Peter's parish church Oundle. Hannah's father was George Stephenson. Harry and Hannah lived at 147 Park Road in Barnsley in 1901. By 1911 they had moved to Thorpe Fylingdale, Whitby in Yorkshire, Harry, shown as Henry, was a retired chemist aged forty-eight. They had one child Henry Holland Bunning aged eight.

George Bunning

MARRIAGES - On Tuesday last, at Oundle, (by the Rev. Chas. Hume,) Mr John Bunning, painter, to Miss Ellen Plowright. *Stamford Mercury 24 March 1837.*

In 1841 George Bunning and his wife Mary were living with Mary's mother Mary Plowright along West Street. They had two children John aged three and Mary Jane aged one. A John Bunning died in 1849 aged thirty-eight. (Not sure if John and George were the same person, no record of a George passing away around the same time.) In 1851 Mary Ellen was still living along West Street, shown as a painter's widow, with her children John aged thirteen, Mary Jane aged eleven, Emma aged eight, Anne aged five and Ellen one-year-old. Mary's mother Mary Plowright was also living with the family. Ten years later Mary, shown as Ellen Bunning was living with her mother in Reesby's yard along West Street with her son John a house painter and daughter's Anne and Ellen. Her daughter Mary Jane was a nursemaid living and working at the Solicitor's House along North Street for George and Sarah Edmonds. Mary Jane Bunning died in 1867 aged twenty-seven.

ESTABLISHED 1822 – Plumbing, Glazing, Painting, Gas Fitting and Paper Hanging establishment, West Street Oundle. – Mrs John Bunning begs most respectfully to return her sincere thanks to the inhabitants of Oundle and its Vicinity for their kind and liberal patronage bestowed upon her late lamented Husband, and informs them she has decided on relinquishing the Business to her brother-in-law, Mr George F. Bunning, and for whom she earnestly solicits a continuance of their favours. ALSO – GEORGE F. BUNNING – In succeeding to the above old-established Business, begs to announce that he is prepared to carry on the same in all its branches and trusts by strict personal attention, combined with good workmanship, to merit a continuance of that patronage so long enjoyed by his Father and late Brother. May 27th 1863. *Stamford Mercury 29 May 1863*

George and Mary's son John married Eliza Bright in Luddington on 17 May 1868. In 1871 they were living along West Street with their children Thomas aged seven, William aged two and one month old James. By 1881 they had moved to the Stone Pitt cottages along Benefield Road with William aged twelve, James ten, Arthur six, Edward three and Percy Charles who was ten months old. John died during 1882. Eliza had to support her five children in 1891, James and Arthur were grocers' assistants, Edward was an errand boy, Percy and Mary attended school.

James Herbert Bunning, a shoe hand, son of Eliza and the late John Bunning married Fanny Green daughter of the late Charles Green, during 1894 at St Peter's parish church.

Oundle Petty Sessions – Mr J.G. Hull and Mr W. Lenton, - Arthur Bunning and Frederick Hinman, lads of Oundle were charged with pelting at the walnut trees in the churchyard. P.C. Lyman proved the case and spoke of the complaints received by the police and the risks to passers-by. Mr J.W. Smith, the lay rector, appeared to state that these cases were brought as a caution. The proceeds of the walnuts as well as the personal tithes he gave to the churchwardens towards the cost of maintenance of the churchyard. As neither of the defendants appeared, the Chairman announced that they should be fined 10s. with 4s. Costs and 6d damage each; also, stating that they had the power to send them to prison for three months, or to fine them £5 each. – Several licences in the division were transferred. *Northampton Mercury 1 November 1895*

In 1901 Eliza lived at The Pitts with her son Edward, a groom, and daughter Mary a dressmaker. Ten years later Eliza lived alone along Benefield Road, she was a laundress working from home. It was recorded on the census Eliza had seven children all of whom were alive.

John and Eliza's son Thomas married Charlotte Annie Blades in the Pembroke district in 1889. Thomas Bunning, a groom, signed up to the Royal Artillery at Sunderland in 1886 at the age of twenty-one. He served for twelve years and was discharged in 1898. By the time of the 1901 census Thomas was a caretaker of Sheffield County Court he lived at 62 New Street in Sheffield with his family. Charlotte his wife was born in Elton, their daughter Ethel aged eight was born in Ireland. Thomas' brother Percy Charles also lived with them, he was a boot finisher. Thomas, Charlotte and Mary Ethel were still in Sheffield in 1911.

John and Eliza's son Charles Percy married Susannah Jane Short during 1910. In 1911 they had a son James William aged eight months and were living in Barnwell with Susannah's mother Catherine. Charles was a Chauffer. In 1915 Charles signed up to the Royal Army Corps.

BUNNING families born in Lowick

William Bunning c.1798 was a hawker who lived along St Osythe's Lane in Oundle in 1851 with his wife Susannah and their family. John was a coal merchant, Thomas an apprentice tailor and Elizabeth stayed at home. William was lodging at the Public house along North Street in 1861 and through to 1871 where he worked as a skin dealer/hawker. Susannah lived along West Street where she worked as a milliner with their daughter Elizabeth. Richard Brown, a blacksmith from Oundle was a boarder with Susannah. By 1871 Susannah had moved to New Street where she continued with her milliner's job. William died during 1878 aged eighty. At the time of the 1881 census Susannah was a widow lodging with Elizabeth Hicks, a nurse, along the Benefield Road. Susannah died in 1884 aged eighty-two.

John Bunning married Ann Allestree at St Peter's Parish church in Oundle during 1851. Ann was the daughter of Levi Allestree a carpenter who lived along the Market Place with his children in 1841. Ann's mother was Sarah, nee Pitts, who died during 1841 aged forty-three. From 1861 to 1891 John and Ann were living in New Street at the Red Lion Inn where John was a Licensed Victualler. They employed servants and took in lodgers. In 1881 Ann's niece Sarah Allestree aged twenty-three from Wisbech was working as a Barmaid for John and Ann.

OUNDLE NARROW ESCAPE – On Saturday last, Mrs Bunning, landlady of the 'Red Lion' inn was cleaning out the parcel room, when she had an occasion to take down a gun which hung up. Almost directly she had it in her hands it exploded, the contents going through the ceiling. Fortunately, she had hold of the breech end. Had it been otherwise the consequences must have been serious. *Peterborough Advertiser 17 October 1874.*

The BURROWS families

John Burrows married Mary Nightingale in 1776, they had the following children, John born and died 1780, Martha, John c.1785, Susannah born 1788, died 1789, Rosannah born and died 1794, William c.1795.

John and Mary's son John married Sarah Stimson during 1806. At the time of the 1841 census they were living at Nassington with their family, Rose, Martha, Mary, William and George.

John and Mary's son William married Sarah Bird during 1819. Their two sons were Frederick and William. In 1841 Sarah was a charwoman living along West Street with her son William an agricultural labourer. William and Sarah's son Frederick was a prisoner in the County Gaol Northampton during 1841. Sarah was a parish relief at the time of the 1851 census and had her granddaughter Mary aged four living with her.

William and Sarah's son William married Louisa Landan in 1849. (Louisa was born in Peterborough and at the time of the 1841 census was living with her mother Mary, her four brothers and two sisters in Wellington Street Peterborough.) By the time of the 1851 census when they were living along West Street Louisa was shown as Lucy. They had a daughter Susannah aged one and William Gray aged seven, nephew to William, living with them.

Oundle Petty Sessions July 17 – Thomas Coles and William Burrows, labourers, were committed for one month's imprisonment each, for stealing a quantity of peas, from a field in the occupation of Mr J.A. Newton, of Fotheringhay, on the 15th inst, - Constable Bennett said as he was going along the road about one a.m. he saw the prisoners cross the road from Mr Newton's field and throw something in the hedge, which excited his suspicion, and on examination found a bag and slop belonging to the prisoners full of peas. He took them into custody, when they admitted their guilt, and begged to be liberated. *Northampton Mercury 21 July 1860*

In 1861 William worked as an agricultural labourer he and his family lived in Beales Yard West Street. Since the last census Sarah and Louisa had been born. By 1871 their daughters' Susannah and Sarah were working as domestic servants, Louisa was eleven, Annie nine,

Mary six and Emily aged two years was shown as their granddaughter. At the time of the 1881 census William was a widow, Susannah worked as an agricultural fieldswoman, Mary was a servant in a public house then the children at home were Emily, William aged nine and Mary Ellen aged four. Susannah Burrows, single woman, had a son Mark William Thurlby Burrows baptised 1882. William senior died during 1890.

William and Sarah's daughter Susannah married George Cottingham during 1883; George was the son of William and Sarah who lived in Oundle. (See Cottingham family details).

Mary Ellen Burrows death was recorded in the *Northamptonshire Mercury dated 22 December 1899*. BURROWS - Dec.18. At Oundle, Ellen Mary Burrows, 22.

Susannah's son Mark William Burrows signed up to the Northamptonshire Regiment in 1899. His army records show his conduct was good and was a hard-working soldier and intelligent. He received the Queens medal consisting of 5 clasps in 1902. Due to his misconduct, he had to relinquish them. Mark married Susannah Pheasant on 3 July 1909. Susannah, born in Polebrook during 1891, was the daughter of George and Ellen Pheasant from Barnwell. Not long after they married Mark was convicted of felony. He stole one silver sugar basin value of two pounds and was sentenced in the court of Oundle to one calendar month's hard labour. In 1911 Mark and Susannah were living in Bakers yard along the Market Place in Oundle, they had a son George William aged one. Mark was then able to continue his army career when he was re-engaged to the Army reserves in 1911. Mark's records show he then was re-enlisted to the Royal Fusiliers in April 1919 of the same year. He served in South Africa, India and France.

William and Sarah's son Frederick lived along St Osyths Lane in 1851 with his wife Elizabeth born in Tansor and their son Robert aged two. By 1861 they had moved to Clarkes Yard in West Street. Frederick was an agricultural labourer their daughter Mary was an outdoor servant and Robert was an agricultural labourer. (Not sure when Elizabeth died). Frederick married Sarah Meadows in 1866, he was over twenty years her senior. In 1871 Frederick and Sarah continued to live at Clarkes yard with their two sons William Meadows aged eleven and Thomas John Meadows aged six who was recorded as having lost one eye, their daughters' Rose Ellen three and Emily one month old. Frederick and Sarah had moved to North Street in 1881 with Rose, Emily, Eliza seven and Annie aged three who all attended school, also William Meadows a coal porter and his brother Thomas an agricultural labourer. Frederick died 1882 aged sixty-two. Rose Ellen Burrows single woman had a daughter, May, baptised 1884. By 1891 Sarah was a charwoman and lived along North Street with her daughter Annie and granddaughter Mary aged six. Henry Afford a gardener from Oundle lodged with Sarah. Sarah died in 1898 aged fifty-six.

Frederick and Elizabeth's son Robert Baxter Burrows married Eliza Armsby, daughter of William, in 1874. By 1881 Robert, a brewer's waggoner, and Eliza lived along North Street in the Havelock cottages with their four-year-old daughter Fanny. Ten years later they continued to live along North Street Fanny was a dressmaker's apprentice.

Death of Mr R Burrows – We regret to announce the death of Mr Robert Burrows who has been in the employ of Messrs. Smith & Co.'s brewery for the past thirty years. Deceased was well known and respected in the town. He was a fireman and Church bell ringer. He has been attending the Infirmary at Peterborough for some time past. The funeral took place on Tuesday, when the members of the Fire Brigade followed. The deceased was 50 years of age. The muffled peal was rung in the evening. *Northampton Mercury 21 July 1899.*

In 1901 Eliza and Fanny were still living along North Street. Fanny married Thomas Hugh Walter Seamark during 1906 at Oundle. Thomas, a butler working at Biggin Hall in Benefield, was the son of the late William, a schoolmaster, and Elizabeth Seamark. In 1911 Fanny was living at 10 Brooklyn Road in Shepherd's Bush with her daughters Vivian aged three and Margaret seven months old. Eliza her mother was also living there.

NINETY-NINE - Our congratulations to Mrs Robert Burrows who although not now living in Oundle spent the greater part of her life here, on attaining the great age of 99, and according to her present health bids, fair to pass the century. Born in Denford in 1843 she was married in 1874 at Oundle parish church to Mr Robert Burrows whom many of our older readers will remember. He died in 1899. Mrs Burrows can recall the days when ladies went in to the old Town

Hall in Sedan Chairs carried by two men. When the curfew bell rang at 8pm the shops had to close. On bonfire night, huge fires were ablaze in the Market Place with dancing and games. Mrs Burrows is intellectually bright and takes great interest in current affairs. She now lives with her daughter Mrs Seamark whose husband is Butler at Trent College Nottingham. *Peterborough Advertiser 12 February 1943.*

Mrs Robert Burrows formerly of Oundle, and now living with her son-in-law and daughter Mr and Mrs Seamark at Trent College Long Eaton, celebrated her 100th birthday on September 25th and is enjoying good health. She received a telegram of congratulations from H.M. the King and Queen and a host of others from many friends. *Peterborough Advertiser 15 October 1943.*

OUNDLE – The funeral took place at Oundle on Monday of Mrs Eliza Ellen Burrows, widow of Mr Robert Burrows, who died 45 years ago. Mrs Burrows, who celebrated her 100th birthday on September 25, 1943, had lived with her son-in-law and daughter, Mr and Mrs W. Seamark at Trent College, Long Eaton, leaving Oundle 30 years ago. A service at Mr and Mrs Seamark's home conducted by the chaplain of Trent College, was attended by the head-master and his wife (Mr and Mrs Ikin), one of the governors, and three prefects. The flag was flown at half-mast from the college. The service at Oundle was conducted by the vicar, the Rev. J.L. Cartwright. *Northampton Mercury 30 June 1944.*

Grave of Robert and Eliza Burrows in the town cemetery Stoke Road

The CHAPMAN families

Edward Chapman, of Lord Robt. Manners Regiment, quartered in the parish of Oundle, married Susanna Snary from Oundle in 1782. (As per the UK Parish Register transcriptions).

John Chapman born in Oundle signed up to the 10th Royal Regiment of Hussars during 1795. He served the regiment for nineteen years and ninety-three days. Due to rheumatism contracted during the Corunna retreat in 1808 John had to be discharged from the Regiment in 1814 at the approximate age of thirty-seven.

In the course of Saturday night last the garden of Mr John Chapman, victualler, of Oundle, was robbed of a large quantity of fruit; the thieves not content with this broke and destroyed a considerable portion of the garden fence. An entry in the Deaths column. Last week, much respected, aged 66, Mr John Chapman, landlord of the Ship Inn, Oundle, and an eminent farrier. *Northampton Mercury 16 October 1830*

Samuel and Sarah Chapman

Samuel Chapman born at Laxton c.1793 was a baker, and his wife Sarah born at Collyweston c.1793 had three daughters, Ann, Elizabeth and Sarah and a son Samuel. They lived along North Street during 1841. Samuel and Sarah's daughter Elizabeth, shown as being 'under age' married John Prentice in 1841, he was a carpenter. (See Prentice family details)

In 1851 Samuel, had changed his occupation to a butcher. He continued to live along North Street with Sarah and their six-year-old granddaughter Sarah Chapman Prentice. Her mother was Elizabeth Prentice, nee Chapman, who died at during January of 1850 aged twenty-nine. Sarah's four-year-old brother Samuel Prentice was living with their father John Prentice at the time of the 1851 census. Samuel Chapman senior died in 1853 aged sixty. By 1861 Sarah, a widow and retired baker lived along North Street with Sarah Chapman Prentice aged fifteen who was an assistant draper. Sarah senior died in 1863 aged seventy.

Samuel and Sarah's daughter Sarah married William Knibb in Kettering during 1849 they were both born in Oundle. In 1841 William Knibb and his twin brother Joseph were living with

Benjamin Knibb aged seventy along the Market Place. William and Joseph were drapers. William and Sarah continued to live along Market Place at London House in 1851 where William employed William Paine as a draper's apprentice and Caroline Gee was their house servant. By 1861 William and Sarah had a young family, they were Benjamin nine, Joseph eight and William aged three. Sarah died during the summer of 1864.

An entry in the SITUATIONS column of the Stamford Mercury 26 August 1864 reads - To Parents and Guardians – WILLIAM KNIBB, Draper, Oundle, has a vacancy for an Apprentice, or a junior Assistant. *Oundle* Aug. 23.

Samuel and Sarah's son Samuel married Charlotte Broughton in Oundle during 1832. Samuel and Charlotte lived at St Osythe Fields in 1841. They had a daughter Ann Elizabeth. By 1851 Samuel, aged forty-two from Benefield was a letter carrier, he lived with Charlotte aged forty-seven and their daughter Ann aged nine from Oundle.

An inquest was held at Oundle on Saturday last, on the body of Saml. Chapman, postman of Oundle to Kates Cabin, who died suddenly on the previous Wednesday night. Verdict - apoplexy. *Stamford Mercury 30 March 1855.*

Charlotte Chapman, a widow by 1861, lived along St Osyths Lane with her daughter Ann, they were both dressmakers.

Commitments to the Northampton County Gaol – Charlotte Chapman and Hannah Plumb, for 14 days' hard labour each, for wilful damage, at Oundle. *Northampton Mercury 23 April 1864.*

In 1871 Charlotte, a postman's widow was still living along St Osyths Lane. She died in 1880 aged seventy-seven.

Thomas and Charlotte Chapman

In 1861 Thomas and Charlotte lived at 2 Poplar Row along West Street with their family, Elizabeth thirteen, John I eight, Rose A six and Mary M aged two.

Rose Ann Chapman

Rosanne Chapman, c.1821, was the daughter of John and Elizabeth from Upper Benefield, John was a shepherd. In 1851 Rose Ann Chapman from Benefield was a house servant for Elizabeth Wright, aged sixty-one, who was an Innkeeper and farmer of 120 acres and lived along New Street in Oundle. By 1861 Rose was living in New Street at the Talbot Hotel where she worked as a chambermaid for William Wright. He was the Innkeeper and farmer employing three men and one boy. At the time of the 1871 census Rose was cook at the Angel Hotel along Bridge Street in Northampton. By 1881 Rose was living at Biggin Hall in Oundle where she worked as a charwoman/laundress. In 1891 Rose, her daughter Ann Elizabeth aged thirty-one and Rose Annie Chapman aged four, both born in Oundle were living back in Benefield, her brother's John and David also lived with them. (At the time of the 1881 census Rose's daughter Ann Elizabeth lived in Benefield with her uncles John and David.) Rose Chapman senior died in 1899 aged seventy-nine. By 1901 David, John and Annie continued living at Benefield.

John and Elizabeth Chapman

John and Sarah Chapman's son John married Elizabeth Basford during 1865. In 1871 John Chapman, born in Benefield, a butcher employing one man, lived with his wife Elizabeth, from Buckinghamshire, along West Street with their family. Arthur L aged four, Florence Dell aged two, Frederick John aged one and William Archibald three weeks old. They employed Elizabeth Barwell from Oundle as their domestic servant. Sarah A Basford was visiting at the time of the census and was sister to John. By 1881 John had become a master butcher he and his wife lived at Setchells Yard with Florence, John, William, Elizabeth May seven, Albert six, Charles Jonas four and Blanch ten months old. John and Elizabeth were living along West Street in 1891. Their son John was working with his father as a butcher, May, Charles, Blanche and Grace Eleanor who was nine stayed at home. Ten years later John and Elizabeth had only Charles also a butcher and Grace a dressmaker living at home. In 1901 Blanche was a domestic servant for Mary Holt, a printer and stationer who lived at 69 High Street Sutton near Epsom. By 1911 Blanche was a domestic servant for Elsie Eveline, a draper, who lived at 1 Mafeking Terrace High Street in Purley Surrey.

Drunk – Elizabeth Chapman, Oundle, married woman, was summoned for being found drunk in Oundle on the 3rd inst. – Inspector Scotney said at midnight on the date in question his bell rang violently, and on looking out he saw defendant in a drunken state, and she staggered across to the church yard. When he got down she had gone. The same evening at seven o'clock she came to the station and made a complaint about her husband and son. She was then in a drunken state. – Fined 10s and 4s costs. – Unable to pay, defendant was removed in custody. *Northampton Mercury 6 October 1905*

James and Dinah Chapman

James Chapman, widower, married Dinah Steers, widow of George, in 1858. By 1861 James and Dinah were living along Benefield Road with their family John aged twelve, Henry six from Shelton (sons of James and his late wife Sophia), Herbert one year and eleven months from Oundle. Also, living with the family were George Steers aged eight, son of Dinah and George, and William Negus aged seven from Oundle and John Negus aged two from Middlesex were Dinah's nephews. In 1871 James and Dinah still lived along Benefield Road with Henry, Herbert, Mary Ann eight and Rosetta aged five. Ten years later, James continued to live along Benefield Road, with his daughter Mary a domestic servant. James wife Dinah was a nurse (S M) and was lodging with Frederick Ward his wife Alice and their family in Benefield. James Chapman died in 1885 aged sixty-seven. By 1891 Dinah aged sixty-nine, a widow, lived along Benefield Road in 'Cunningtons' cottage' with her three-year-old granddaughter Catherine from Oundle. Dinah Chapman died in 1896 aged seventy-five.

James Henry Chapman

In 1891 James Henry Chapman, six years old, was living with his Uncle Alfred and Aunt Emma Smith who lived in Ashton. Ten years later Kate Chapman, a year younger than James also lived with Alfred and Emma Smith. James Henry Chapman married Annie Shrives from Oundle in 1905. By 1911 they lived along North Street with their family Herbert Alfred five, James Henry three, Eva Maud two and their Uncle Alfred Smith a widower from Ashton lived with them. James senior was a steam waggon driver in a brewery. James and Annie had two more children Reginald Arthur in 1912 and Ida Margaret in 1914.

James Henry Chapman, a motor driver, was enlisted in the Royal Army Service Corps in 1915 and initially based at Avonmouth. James served the country for four years. Details can be found in James Henry Chapman's army records. The Royal Army Service Corps. was responsible for ensuring the British Army was supplied with various provisions.

Photographs courtesy of Norman Hanna

Families unknown. Photograph courtesy of Norman Hanna

The COALES/COLES families

Various spellings have been found over the census recordings and parish transcriptions of Coles, Coales and Coals within the same family. There were families living at Oundle, Ashton, Armston, Polebrook, Barnwell, Nassington and Kings Cliffe.

James and Mary Coles children were William c.1785, Stephen c.1787, Mary c.1789, Samuel born in March and died in April 1792, Charlotte c.1793 and Thomas c.1796.

James and Mary's son William married Mary Ann Nightingale during 1816. In 1841 they lived at Nassington with John fourteen, Thomas seven and Mary Ann aged fifteen, William was an agricultural labourer. By 1851 they had moved to Fotheringhay with their sons John and Thomas. William and Mary Ann had moved again by 1861 to Tansor.

James and Mary's son Stephen Coals married Elizabeth Eaton during 1815 at St Peters church in Oundle. Some of Stephen and Elizabeth Coles children were James c.1816, John c.1819, Stephen c.1821, Michael c.1827, Mary Ann c.1829 and Phoebe c.1834.

An entry in the Oundle deaths column read – On the 27th ult., at Cossington, of consumption, Ann second daughter of the late Mr Stephen Cole of Oundle, and niece of the late Lieut. Col. W. F. Hulse. Hulse, of the Leicestershire Militia. *Stamford Mercury 11 March 1831.*

In 1841 Steven Coles, a gardener and his wife Elizabeth lived along North Street with their family Steven a baker, Michael, Mary and Phoebe. At the time of the 1851 census Stephen and Elizabeth only had their son Stephen a baker, and daughter Phoebe at home. By 1861 Stephen and Elizabeth's family had all left home.

At Oundle on the 20th ult., Elizabeth wife of Stephen Coles, aged 82. *Stamford Mercury 2 September 1870.*

Stephen Coles aged ninety-five was living at the Laxton Alms-houses along Church Lane at the time of the 1871 census.

A CENTENARIAN – An inmate of Latham's Hospital, named Stephen Coales, celebrated his one hundredth birthday, on Monday last. Considering his great age, the old boy is the most nimble of the six inmates. On Monday, he was in good health except as he said he had "got a touch of the screws," and for which reason he did not have a hand at cards, a game he occasionally enjoys. He is a non-smoker, but not a teetotaller, generally taking two glasses of beer daily. He talks of trimming the grape vine again, which he has done for some years, and he likes to fix the ladder himself, not caring for any help. *Northampton Mercury 6 February 1886*

A CENTENARIAN SPORTSMAN – Mr Stephen Coales, of Laxton Hospital, who exceeded his hundredth birthday some time ago, took a journey round the Town Hall on a tricycle on Whit-Monday. This was indeed the novelty of the day. *Northampton Mercury 4 June 1887*

AN OUNDLE CENTENARIAN – At Oundle a centenarian may almost daily be seen taking his walks abroad. His name is Stephen Coales, and he is an inmate of Laxton's Hospital, an almhouse founded by Sir William Laxton, a London grocer, who died in 1556. There is some doubt as to his exact age, though he states that he is 105. That he is over 102 is proved by the following entry in the Oundle Baptismal Register: - "1787, Mar. 7, Stephen, son of James and Mary Coals," and he says that he remembers being taken by his parents to be baptised. He attends church regularly, walking to and fro without an attendant. He suffers slightly from deafness and his memory is impaired, but he talks intelligently of events in his childhood, and he has not had an ache or pain for years. For over fifty years he followed the occupation of a gardener. Coales has a good appetite, and is not limited in his diet, though he has but one tooth, of which he is rather proud. He is in the habit of having half a pint of beer with his dinner and half a pint with his supper, which he greatly enjoys, while as a medicine he occasionally takes a glass of gin and water. He is a non-smoker, and says that he could "never manage a pipe." *Northampton Mercury 14 September 1889.*

OUNDLE – Death of the Oundle Centenarian – We regret to have to announce the death this week of the Oundle centenarian, which took place on Saturday last. His name, as many of our readers well know, was Stephen Coals. His age was somewhat doubtful, but up to the time of his death he persisted in saying that he was 105 years of age. His birthday was celebrated each year on February 1st. He was an inmate of Laxton's Hospital, a London grocer, who died in 1556. The following is a copy of the Oundle Register of Baptisms recording his baptism: - "1787, March 7th, Stephen, son of James and Mary Coales."

He said he remembered being taken by his parents to be baptised, so that he must have been over 102 years of age. Up to a day or two prior to his death he had a daily walk without any attendant. He had had no pain or ache for many years before his death, he had a good appetite, and was in the habit of taking two glasses of beer daily. He was a non-smoker. The day before his death he fell asleep, and never woke again, so that his frame was apparently completely worn out. *Northampton Mercury 19 October 1889.*

Thomas and Mary Ann Coales

In 1834 Thomas Coales married Mary Ann Burton in Oundle after their Banns were read. At the time of the 1841 census Thomas and Mary lived along North Street with William six, Louisa four and Emma two, Robert Coles aged twenty also lived with them. By 1851 Thomas, a cooper, and his wife Mary Ann, a laundress, had moved to Benefield Road where they lived with their family. Louisa aged fourteen also a laundress, Elizabeth eight and Robert six attended school, Thomas Burton Coales four and John George two years old. Their son William Burton Coales aged fifteen was a cooper, he lived with his grandfather Thomas Burton, a widower who also lived along Benefield Road. In 1861 Thomas and Mary Ann had moved back to North Street with Elizabeth a laundress, Robert and Thomas both agricultural labourers, John twelve, Emma nine and Christopher their grandson aged two born in Oundle. Living along North Street in 1871 was Thomas and Mary Ann's daughter Emma who was a domestic servant for Edward Scarsbrick, a teacher of music, and his family.

Thomas and Mary Ann's son William Burton Coales married Harriet Mason, daughter of Isaac Mason, during 1856. In 1861 William, a general labourer, and Harriett lived along West Street with William Mason, stepson, aged nine. Harriet died in 1869 aged thirty-nine. William Burton Coales, widower, married Jane Kirby during 1868 she was the daughter of William Kirby a brewer's labourer. In 1871 and 1881 William and Jane Coale were living at Tynemouth where William was recorded as being a parcels agent. William died in 1890 aged fifty-eight at Tynemouth. At the time of the 1891 census Jane was still living at Tynemouth with their nine-year-old daughter Georgina.

Oundle Petty Sessions April 26 1869 – Robert Coales of Oundle, was charged with creating an obstruction on the pavement in front of Mr. J. Beal's shop in the Market-place, on the 22nd ultimo. – For months past an intolerable nuisance has existed through the assembling of great numbers of loungers, whose language was of anything but a delicate nature. – Defendant was a fitting subject to be made an example of, so said the Chairman. Penalty and costs, £1. 9s. 6d.
Northampton Mercury 1 May 1869

In 1871 Robert Coales, son of Thomas and Mary Ann lived along North Street with his sister Elizabeth a laundress, Christopher twelve, recorded as Robert's son, and his nieces Louisa seven and Ann one-year-old.

Robert married Betsy Carr during 1881, they lived along St Osyths Lane with Charles Carr aged eleven and Herbert Carr aged eight. Betsy was the widow of Henry Carr; they lived along North Street in 1871. Robert was shown as a general labourer out of employ. By 1891 Robert, a brickyard labourer, continued living along St Osyths lane with Elizabeth. Frederick Afford from Oundle lodged with them.

Thomas and Mary Ann's daughter Elizabeth married Thomas Rippin, a merchant's labourer from Southwick during 1879. By the time of the 1881 census they were living along North Street with Elizabeth's children Christopher aged twenty-one, Louisa seventeen and Ann Coles ten, and their own daughter Minnie Rippin aged nine months. Elizabeth died in 1890 aged forty-nine. By 1891 Thomas Rippin had moved to West Street, not far from the Old Hind Inn, with Annie Coales a Housekeeper, Minnie Rippin ten and Thomas Rippin aged nine.

William and Eliza Coles

William Coles from Thurning married Eliza Ward from Boston during 1857. In 1861they lived along West Street with their daughter Mary Ann aged four months. By 1871 William was a coachman/domestic servant he and his wife Eliza continued to live along West Street with their daughters Charlotte nine and Annie aged five. William had changed his occupation in 1881 and was a gardener; he and his wife Eliza Ann, a laundress, lived along Mill Lane with their daughters Charlotte and Annie.

Petty Sessions Oundle – William Coles, Oundle, gardener, was summoned for a breach of the Poaching Prevention Act, on the 17th

July. Inspector Alexander said on the morning in question, about four o'clock, he saw defendant beating a hedge in a barley field, in the occupation of Mr John Brighty, on the Glapthorne-road. Defendant had a gun, and when he saw witness he turned aside. Witness followed him and took the gun. It was a double-barrelled one, one barrel of which was loaded, capped, and cocked. Witness asked defendant if he had any permission to be there. Defendant said "No." Witness left him, and about an hour after he saw him on the Glapthorne-road. He had the gun under his arm. He charged him under the Poaching Prevention Act, and took possession of the gun, which he found charged with powder and shot. There was game in the hedges. Defendant said he had permission to shoot over Mr Hill's land adjoining. There were several previous convictions against him, and he was now fined 30s., and 9s. 6d. costs. *Northampton Mercury 5 August 1882*

James and Elizabeth Ann Coales

James Coales, from Polebrook, was a solicitors' general clerk and lived with his wife Elizabeth Ann in the Camden Cottages along North Street in 1871 with their family. William Weekly Coales aged three, Annie E aged two and James H five months old. Martha Weekly aged twenty-one from Crowland was cousin to James also lived with them.

October 17th at Oundle, William Weekly eldest son of James Coales aged 4 years and 6 months. *Northampton Mercury 21 October 1871*

ACCIDENT – On Saturday, the son of Mr James Coales, New-street, broke his leg while skating on the Biggin pond. Under the treatment of Mr Calcott, he is progressing favourably. This is the first serious skating accident in the neighbourhood during the winter. *Northampton Mercury 7 February 1880*

By 1881 James and Elizabeth Ann had moved to New Street with their family Annie Elizabeth and James Henry. Elizabeth died during 1885. James Coales, a widow in 1891, lived along the Market Place next to the Crown Inn with Annie twenty-two and James twenty, a solicitor's clerk like his father.

OUNDLE – It is with regret we record the death of Mr James Coales, who passed away on Monday evening at his residence in the Market, at the age of 72. Mr Coales was managing clerk for Messrs. Pooley and Maudesley, solicitors, Oundle, a position he had occupied for many years, and he died in harness, being at business up to a few hours of his death. He was a man of upright principles and of a sympathetic nature, always ready and willing to help any good cause. He had been a chorister in the Parish Church Choir for a number of years. Some time ago he was seized with a stroke from which he apparently had never recovered. He had been a widower for many years, and leaves a son, Mr H Coales, solicitor, Aylesbury and Miss Coales, daughter. *Northampton Mercury 31 October 1913*

John and Sarah Coles

In 1871 John Coles lived in Nassington with his wife Sarah, both from Fotheringhay, with their family James fifteen, George eleven, Stephen nine, Robert six and Mary two. Steven and Elizabeth Coales son Steven was lodging at the Montague Arms in Barnwell he was a mason's labourer.

John and Sarah's son Stephen Coales married Elizabeth Brinsley during 1889, by the time of the 1891 census they were living along Benefield Road. In 1901 Stephen, a gravel pit labourer had moved to 11 Rose Lane in the Australia Terrace row of houses in Woodstone with his family, Elizabeth his wife was a laundress and their son James Stephen aged eight. Stephen's brother Thomas also lived with them and worked as a gravel pit labourer, he was twenty-one. By 1911 Stephen had changed his occupation to a labourer's gardeners domestic and had moved back to Oundle with his family. They lived along Poplar Row in Benefield Road with their children Gladys six and Ronald Lewis aged three. Stephen's brother Thomas also lived along Poplar Row he was a boarder with them. Stephen and Elizabeth's son James Stephen was living at the Talbot Hotel along New Street where he worked as a billiard marker. William Austin Curley, from Benefield, was the Hotel keeper and his wife Agnes Annie from Woodnewton assisted him in the business. Stephen and Elizabeth went on to have two more sons George and Percy.

The COTTINGHAM families

In 1841 Ann Cottingham c.1827 was living at Tates Row in Oundle and working for John and Jane Steers as a servant. By 1851 Ann, born in Wadenhoe, was working as a general servant for Henry Roper, a druggist living along West Street in Oundle.

Thomas Cottingham born in Aldwinkle c.1824 was an agricultural labourer, he married Mary Starsmore from Fotheringhay during 1848. In 1851 they were living along Benefield Road with their one-year-old daughter Sarah. By 1861 they had all moved back to Aldwinkle with Sarah, Lucy aged eight, Joseph aged three and Watson five months old.

William and Ann Cottingham lived at Wadenhoe in 1841 with their family Ann and Thomas twins, Elizabeth and William. At the time of the 1851 census Elizabeth, unmarried, was recorded as being deaf and dumb living in the Oundle Union Workhouse along Glapthorne Road and was shown as a pauper. She was still there in 1861 but shown as an idiot and dumb. There was also an Elizabeth Cottingham recorded next to her aged seven and William aged three both born in Ringstead. By 1871 Elizabeth continued to live in the Workhouse also listed with her were Sarah Cottingham aged thirty-eight, a domestic servant and Eli Mark aged nine both were born in Wadenhoe.

At the Union House, Oundle on the 31st ult., Elizabeth Cottingham, Wadenhoe, aged 58. *Northampton Mercury 20 January 1872*

William and Ann's son William married Sarah Smith in 1850. By the time of the 1851 census they were living along St Osyths Lane in Oundle. No trace of them on the 1861 census

In 1871 they were still living along St Osyths Lane with their young family William and Thomas who were both born in Wadenhoe then George born in Oundle. Ten years later they had moved to Drumming Well Yard George worked as an Agricultural labourer, William and Sarah's grandson Harry Lee age two was in the household on the night of the census. By 1891 William and Sarah were living on their own the family had all moved. Sarah worked as a Laundress.

William and Sarah's son George married Susannah Burrows during 1883. Susannah was the daughter of William and Louisa. By the time of the 1891 census George, a general Labourer and Susannah a charwoman were living along Drumming Well Yard. Also, living with them were Susannah's sisters' Emily Burrows, a domestic servant, Mary Ellen Burrows, her brother Mark William Burrows who had been born a few months after the 1881 census, Frederick Cottingham aged eight and George Cottingham aged six. Susannah's brother William Burrows was a boarder and finally Harold Cottingham aged two was shown as George's grandson. Mary Ellen Burrows died during 1899 aged twenty-two. By 1901 George and Susannah were living along Binders Row with George, Frederick and Edith aged seven. At the time of the 1911 census they were living along St Osyths Lane, George was a general labourer with the building trade, George Thomas was a bricklayer's labourer, Frederick Harry was a gardener's labourer and Edith May was at home. George and Susannah had been married twenty-seven years had six children five of whom were still alive. Susannah died not long after the census was recorded aged sixty-three.

William and Sarah's son William married Louisa Burrows during 1884. Louisa was the sister of Susannah. In 1891 they were living along St Osyths Lane. They had four children William aged six, Mable four, Louisa two and Ernest eight months old. By 1901 they had moved to East Road their family had increased with the arrival of Leonard in 1893 and Charles F in 1895. William was a mason's labourer and Louisa was a charwoman. William the oldest child was a horse driver for a corn contractor. Ten years later still along East Road William was a general labourer in the building trade, William junior was a bricklayer's labourer, Louise a mother's help, Leonard was an assistant in armoury (Grocers Company) and Charles was a domestic gardener.

ACCIDENT IN OUNDLE – On Monday evening a man named William Cottingham had one of his legs broken through being run over by a wagonette, in which were Lord Burghley and others, who had taken part in a Conservative meeting. *Northampton Mercury 1 July 1892*

The COTTON families

Follow the journey Robert Charles Cotton's ancestors took from Turkey in Bedfordshire to Robert Charles who set up the family business in Oundle. The shoe maker business was carried through the generations of Cotton families.

Ruben Cotton and his wife Rachell lived in Turvey with their seven children in 1841. They were Jonathan, James, Charles, John, Jonna, Ann and Mary. In 1851 they lived along the High Street in Turvey, Reuben, Charles and their grandson Henry aged nine were agricultural labourers, Joanna and Mary were lace makers.

Reuben Cotton was summoned as a witness in the case regarding the 'Right of fishery – Higgins v. Battams' a Special Jury case – Mr Keane Q.C. stated the case to the jury - Reuben Cotton's statement reads as follows – 'Reuben Cotton: I am 73 years old, and have lived in Turvey all my life; so long as I have been able to work I have worked for Messrs Higgins of Turvey Abbey. It was a part of my duty to look after the cobs in the river, and by Mr Higgins direction I let two of them to Mr Battams. I have been about when bow nets were laid between the cobs and the left bank. Have seen the river fished and dragged by direction of Mr Higgins, and have helped to drag it myself. In my time, I have known two of the tenants of Snelson before Mr Battams, first Mr Bithrey and then Mr Chandler, and although they both talked to me while about my work, they never interfered with me. I have worked about the cobs 50 years, and during that time have often seen the rushes cut. I have gone processing (perambulating) down the Buckingham side of the river, and we have gone through the garden at Snelson in Mr Bithrey's time. I recollect another processioning in Mr Chandler's time. Have heard old men who are now dead say many a time that the Ouse was in the parish of Turvey and county of Bedford. Have often seen Mr Higgins go on to his cobs by means of planks and rushes put down.' Full report can be seen in the *Bedfordshire Times and Independent 16 March 1867*.

In 1841 William Cotton and his wife Sarah were living in Turvey, Bedfordshire, with their five children, George twelve, Charles ten, Reuben five, Louisa four and Emma aged one. In 1851 William and Sarah were shown as living along Carlton Street in Turvey with their family. Charles was nineteen, Reuben seventeen, Louisa thirteen,

Emma eleven, Ann nine and Hannah seven. William was an agricultural labourer as were his sons. Sarah was a lace maker as were her daughters apart from Hannah who attended school. By 1861 William and Sarah had moved to 12 Stockers End in Turvey. William and Sarah's son George, a widower, lived with them as well as their three daughters Emma, Anne and Hannah who were all lace makers.

William and Sarah's son Reuben married Maria Osborn from Buckinghamshire in 1853. By the time of the 1861 census Reuben, a shoemaker, and his wife Maria lived at 15 Chapel Place in Turvey. Their children were Robert Charles aged six, Reuben aged four, William aged two and Anne aged one. Ten years later they had moved to High Street in Lavendon near Newport Pagnell. Their children were Charles, Reuben, William, Fanny, Albert and Frederick George. Reuben and Maria moved again by the time of the 1881 census and were living at 30 Bridge Street in Thrapston where Reuben continued with his work as a shoe maker. Only Fanny, Albert, a shoe maker and eight-year-old Sarah lived at home. They had moved again by 1891 to the High Street in Thrapston. Living with Reuben and Maria were Fanny a machinist and Fred a shoe maker. Still living along the High Street in Thrapston in 1901 was Reuben and Maria with only their son Fred at home. Maria died during 1905 aged seventy-three. In 1911 Reuben, a retired tradesman, lived along Bridge Street in Thrapston with his son Fred, a boot maker, and had been deaf since childhood. Annie Butcher was their house-keeper. Reuben died in 1916 aged eighty-three.

Reuben and Maria's son Reuben married Emily Rivett in 1878 in the Wellingborough district. In 1881 they lived along the Bedford Road in Lavendon with their daughter Florence. Reuben was a boot and shoe dealer. They were shown to be living along the Turvey Road in Lavendon by 1891; Florence had a brother Herbert R and a sister Margaret F. Ten years later the family had grown with two more sons Bernard and Joseph and a daughter Nellie. Reuben and Emily had five of their children at home in 1911, Herbert was a carpenter and joiner, Margaret and Ellen did housework, Bernard assisted in the family business and Joseph attended school.

THRAPSTON – A Smash – On Tuesday afternoon a young man, a butcher, names Yeoman's, of Woodford, whilst turning a light cart in front of Mr. Reuben Cotton's shop for the purpose of putting the horse in the shafts, had the misfortune to run the shafts into the shop window, completely smashing a large pane of glass. *Northampton Mercury 17 May 1901*

Reuben and Maria's son William married Sarah Holmes in Buckinghamshire during 1876. In 1881 they lived along North Street in Oundle with their children. Christopher aged four and Laura was three months old. William was a boot and shoe maker. William and Sarah had gone back to Newport Pagnell to live by 1891. They had three daughters at home, Laura, Gladys and Renee.

Reuben and Maria's son Robert Charles married Annie Maria Cunnington towards the end of the year in 1879 at Oundle. Annie was the daughter of Thomas and Matilda Cunnington who lived in Reesby's Yard in West Street. Robert, Annie and their daughter Annie M.M. (Alice Maud M.) lived next to Robert's brother, William in North Street in 1881. I have not been able to locate the whereabouts of Robert and his family in the 1891 census. However, in 1901 Robert Charles Cotton, shoemaker, was living along Market Place which was his family home and business place. Robert's wife Annie was busy with their family Maud aged twenty, May eighteen, Fred twelve, Hector ten, Fanny nine, Milly seven and Phillip aged seven months. Robert continued with his family business where they lived along the Market Place in 1911. It was recorded on the census Robert and Annie had been married for thirty-two years and had seven children all of who were still alive. At home with Robert was Annie Maria his wife, Evelyn Ethel Blythe their widowed daughter with her children Daisy Kathleen aged six and Violet Milly aged four, their son Albert H. aged twenty a shopkeeper (bootmaker), their daughter Edith M aged seventeen and their son Phillip aged ten.

Robert and Annie's daughter Fanny Elizabeth was staying with Thomas and Harriett Mills at 29 Collyhurst St Rochdale Road in Manchester in 1911. They were Fanny's Aunt and Uncle; Harriett was born in Oundle around 1841. Fanny had a one-month old son Kenneth Arthur and she was recorded on the census as assists mother on housework.

FUNERAL OF MR R.C. COTTON – Canon Smalley Law conducted the funeral on Monday, of Mr R.C. Cotton, whose death at the age of 77 caused much regret among his friends. *Northampton Mercury 12 August 1932.*

FUNERAL OF MRS EMILY COTTON – A section from the obituary states – The funeral took place on 8th January of Mrs Emily Cotton, wife of Mr Reuben Cotton, the well-known boot and shoe traveller. *Bedfordshire Times and Independent 17 January 1936.*

FUNERAL OF MR. REUBEN COTTON – A section from the obituary states – 'The funeral took place on Monday of Mr Reuben Cotton, the well-known boot and shoe retailer who died suddenly on November 9th at the age of 82 years. Mr Cotton was well known over a very wide area, where he had travelled in his trade for over 60 years. He retired about three years ago soon after the death of his wife. The business is now carried on by his two sons'. *Northampton Mercury 18 November 1938.*

Reuben Cotton's great, great granddaughter Jacqueline told me the history of the family business.

'Robert Charles Cotton, a practical boot and shoe maker, set up business in North Street in 1877, in a shop that was then to become Hornes' the butchers. Shortly after his marriage to Anna Maria Cunnington Robert moved his home and business to where Johnsons butchers is now. However, it wasn't long before Robert Charles was ready to move again. This time he had his eye on a property right in the middle of the market place, number 7. In 1902 Robert Charles Cotton was successful in purchasing the entire estate which included 7 Market Place and the Coach House on Church Street. When the young family moved in to Market Place it was in a very poor state of repair. Robert and Annie worked many long hours to restore it. There were seven bedrooms and a large drawing room and dining room upstairs. Many features of their restoration can still be seen, including a wonderful fireplace and the original, very faded but obviously once beautiful wallpaper. The youngest of the family was Jacqueline's grandfather Philip George, or Phil as many will remember him.

Robert and Annie's eldest son Charles Frederick went to farm locally. Their second son Albert Hector, known as Hector or Hec, was the first to join his father in the business. They employed three full-time workmen, primarily making heavy workboots called 'watertights'. These were chiefly worn by local farmworkers and cost the equivalent of 60p per pair. One of these workmen was Ben Walton; he used to walk to work each day from Lower Benefield, bringing up his family on a wage of 21 shillings a week. His son, Eb, carried on working for

Cotton's for 20 years, then left to set up his own shoe business in the town. During the 1914-1918 war Eb cycled around the local villages during the late evening collecting and delivering repairs. He became known to all as "the midnight cobbler".

In 1915 circumstances forced 15-year-old Philip to leave school to help in the business. Philip had attended Laxton School where the fee was one pound per term. His brother had been enlisted into the army and his father Robert had tripped and fallen on the platform at Oundle railway station and badly broken his leg. Due to many shortages in the war years repairing became the mainstay of Cottons. Incredibly they were taking in around 250 pairs of boots and shoes each week for mending. Eventually Philip was called up for military service and went to Crystal Palace to train as a wireless operator. He remained there until the end of the war in 1918.

After the deaths of Robert and Annie the estate was inherited by Hector, father of Jack Cotton, and Philip George Cotton. Hector and Philip ran a tight ship, with no lunch hours, and stayed open until 7 or 8pm on Saturdays. R.C. Cotton & Sons Ltd is now the oldest established business in Oundle'.

Golden wedding celebration from left to right, Maud, May, Hector, Fred, Philip, Fanny, Millicent. Robert Charles and Annie Marie sitting at front. Courtesy of Jacqueline and Anne (nee Cotton)

The CUNNINGTON families

In 1811 John Cunnington married Ann Wiles, widow of William Wiles.

On Sunday, the 14th inst., during the time of evening prayers at the Methodist chapel, some thieves made free with the poultry belonging to Mr J Cunnington, of Oundle, with which they got clear off. - The poultry of Mr Thos. Ball of same place also fared a similar fate. Fortunately for the inhabitants of Oundle and its vicinity, four of the most notorious fellows as sheep, pig, and fowl stealers, &c. are now in Peterborough gaol. *Stamford Mercury 26 December 1823*

In the night of Thursday, the 19 inst., an Out-house of Mr John Cunnington, of Oundle, was broken into, and a quantity of leather of the value of 12/- stolen. *Stamford Mercury 27 March 1829*

In 1841 John and Ann were living along West Street, their daughter Fanny aged twenty-one and Alfred Whiles aged five also lived with them. John died in 1842 aged fifty-five. By 1851 Ann, a widow; was still in West Street where she worked as a laundress. Her daughter, name changed to Frances, also worked as a laundress. Mary Patchett aged ten lived with them and was Ann's granddaughter.

John and Ann's daughter Frances married Joseph Palmer from Glapthorn at the end of the year in 1851. By 1861 they were living at 34 West Street where John was a brick maker. They had three children Emma eight, John six and Clara three. They had moved to Benefield Road in 1871 where they made it the family home. Joseph was a labourer and Frances a laundress.

At the time of the 1841 census there were a few Cunnington families living in Oundle. The oldest was John aged seventy-two and Elizabeth Cunnington aged thirty-nine. They were shown as living along West Street near Elmington.

Another family was William Cunnington born in Benefield c.1810, and his wife Elizabeth c.1801, from Yarmouth. At the time of the 1841 census they lived along West Street, William was a labourer and Elizabeth was a needle-woman, their children were Elizabeth aged three and John was ten months old. In 1851 William and Elizabeth's children attended school. William died during 1855. From 1861 to

1871 Elizabeth, a widow, lived in Danfords Yard along West Street and worked as a seamstress.

Thomas and Matilda Cunnington

The Cunnington family I have followed is Thomas born c.1816. He married Matilda Pickering during 1839 and by the time of the 1841 census they lived along West Street in Oundle and had a daughter Harriett who was born just prior to the census. Thomas was a shoemaker. In 1851 they had moved to Reesbys Yard in Oundle, Thomas had changed his occupation to a general labourer. Their children were Harriett aged ten, John Thomas eight, Mary A six, Alfred five and Emily was two years old. Ten years later they continued to live at Reesbys Yard but Thomas had changed his occupation again to a baker. Their family had increased with Kate aged nine, George Dudley six, Martha Dudley three and Hannah was one-year-old. Mary and Alfred worked as general servants and Emma (Emily) was a dressmaker. By 1871 their address was shown as Beebys Yard, Emma was working as a machinist in the boot and shoe trade, and then there was Martha and Annie (Hannah) at home. George was living along Church Street at the Grammar School in Oundle where he worked as a knives and shoe cleaner. At the time of the 1881 census the family had moved again to Setchells Yard where Thomas was still a baker. Their daughter Emma married Henry Sewell, a Railway Porter just before the 1881 census was recorded, and they lived with Emma's parents. In 1891 Emma and her husband, Henry Sewell were living at 5 Rock Road in Oundle with their family. Albert Cunnington, a tailor's apprentice was shown as Stepson to Henry. Their other children were Florence, Ethel, Thomas and Alice.

Thomas and Matilda's son George Dudley Cunnington married Eliza Ann Creed in the Marylebone district during 1887. By the time of the 1891 census George a butler and Eliza a cook, were living at Endmoor in Westmorland where they worked for John Weston, a gunpowder manufacturer, and his wife Kate. In 1901 George, a butler, and Eliza, a cook was both working for Edmund Trevor, a solicitor and his family. They lived at the Lodge in Byfleet Surrey where they employed eleven members of staff to help run the household.

Thomas and Matilda's son Alfred married Selina Wills during 1867 Selina was the daughter of William and Sarah Wills who in 1861 lived at Danfords Square in West Street. In 1871 Alfred, a painter journeyman, and Selina were living at Inkerman Square with their sons Alfred aged two and Arthur was one-year-old. By 1881 still at Inkermans Place they had five more children, Kate aged nine, William seven, Sarah six, John four and Albert was two years old. At the time of the 1891 census Alfred and Selina's (shown as Ann) family had increased with the births of Charles Frederick aged ten, Rose and Lilley seven (twins) and Percy was four years old. Alfred and Ann's son Arthur was a groom and his brother William was a baker's apprentice. By 1901 Alfred and Selina were living at 13 Inkerman Place with Charles, Lily and Percy. Charles worked as a painter like his father and Percy was a butcher.

Inkerman Place. Photo courtesy of Arthur Ball.

OUNDLE DIVISIONAL PETTY SESSIONS – Conies – Percy Cunnington and Alfred Brinsley, both youths of Oundle, pleaded guilty to being on trespass in search of conies on land in the parish of Wadenhoe, - Geo. Watts, assistant keeper to Lord Lilford, saw defendants near Bearshank Wood. They had two rabbits. – Defendants said they were searching for work and as they saw the rabbits they took them. They gave them up to the keeper directly he asked for them. - Both defendants stated that they had been out of work for some months, and pleaded for a lenient fine. They pleaded guilty to giving the keeper wrong names. – The Bench inflicted a fine of 5s., and costs 3s., at the same time reminding them that they had been fined several times for a similar offence. A small fine had been imposed on account of their having no work, but if they should appear again they would not get off so easily. *Northampton Mercury 27 January 1905*

Alfred and Selina's son Arthur married Alice Nicholls during 1895. Alice was the daughter of David and Mary Anne who lived at Hemington. Arthur and Alice lived at number 14 next door to Alfred and Selina in 1901. Arthur, a brewer, and Alice had two daughter's Hilda aged four and Margaret was one-year-old. By 1911 Arthur and Alice continued living at Inkermans Place with Hilda and Maggie and their six-year-old sister Amy. Arthur and Alice had been married for fifteen years, had four children one of whom had died.

Alfred, a painter and paperhanger, and Selina, shown as Ann Selenia were also still living next door to Arthur. Percy was their only son living at home but they also had their granddaughter Margie aged ten living with them. Alfred and Selena had been married for forty-four years and had eleven children all who had survived.

One of Oundle's oldest residents, Mr Alfred Cunnington, has died aged 84. He was a bellringer at the church for sixty years. *Northampton Mercury 28 February 1930*

Alfred and Selena's son Charles Frederick married Ruth Morris in 1906. By 1911 they were living at Danfords Square along West Street Oundle. Charles was a house painter. They had a son Charles Morris who was born in 1911 and a daughter Ruby Sophia born in 1915. Charles Frederick signed up for the Royal Engineers Regiment in 1915 for the duration of the war. At the time of enlistment Charles lived along Benefield Road.

The CURTIS family

On Tuesday, last, aged 59, Mr John Curtis, landlord of the Cross-Keys public-house, Oundle. *Stamford Mercury 19 August 1831*

On Wednesday, Mr Geo. Barnes, baker, of Harringworth, eldest son of Mr Barnes, baker, of Oundle, to Mary eldest daughter of Mrs Curtis of the Cross Keys Oundle. *Stamford Mercury 24 August 1838*

At the time of the 1841 census Mary Curtis, widow of John Curtis was a publican living along West Street with her daughter Elizabeth. Elizabeth's sister Mary Barnes, and her daughter Emma Barnes aged one also lived with Mary Curtis. In 1851 George Barnes and his daughter Emma were visiting Thomas and Ann Barnes along New Street. Thomas was a baker and maltster employing his son Thomas and one man. Mary seems elusive to the 1851 census as did George in the 1841.

In the Affairs of Mrs Curtis, deceased. All persons having a Claim upon the Estate of the late Mrs Mary Curtis, of the Cross Keys Inn, Oundle, are requested to send particulars thereof forthwith to Mr William Ball, West-street, Oundle, the Executor. *Stamford Mercury 12 September 1856*

WEST-STREET, OUNDLE, Northamptonshire. To INNKEEPERS and Others. To be sold by Auction, by Deacon and Son. On Friday, the Tenth day of October, 1856, on the premises of the late Mrs Mary Curtis, Cross Keys Inn, Oundle. All the neat and useful Household Furniture, Glass, China, Stack of superior Hay, and Effects – Sale to commence at Ten o'clock. For particulars see catalogues. *Stamford Mercury 3 October 1856*

John and Mary's son William Curtis, born in Oundle during 1806, married Sally Sismey at the beginning of 1829 in Oundle. John was a drover and in 1841 he lived in Aldwinkle with Sally. They had five children John B, William, Marianne, Joseph and Lucy. Hannah Phesant aged fifteen was a servant for them. In 1851 they were still at Aldwinkle with Thomas, Lucy, Joseph, Mary and Susannah. Their sons eighteen-year-old John Curtis, a solicitor's clerk and his sixteen-year-old brother William a brewery clerk were boarders with James Bell a baker living along West Street. At the time of the 1861 census the family had moved and were living at The Ship Inn, Oundle where

William was the Innkeeper. Their daughter's Lucy twenty, and Susannah aged eighteen were Innkeepers assistants. Sally was recorded as Sarah.

Included in the Bankrupts list as reported in the Yorkshire Gazette 15 March 1862 – W. Curtis, Oundle, publican.

On the 19th inst., at Oundle, Northamptonshire, Samuel, son of Henry Pike, of Broome, to Susan, youngest daughter of Wm. Curtis, of Oundle. *Bury and Norwich Post 26 November 1867*

By 1871 William and Sarah lived along West Street where William had returned to his drover's occupation.

William and Sally's son William married Annie Ball during 1860; Annie was the daughter of William Ball, a draper. His widowed mother Margaret lived in North Street Oundle where she was a draper employing three men. In 1861 William and Annie were living along St Osyths Lane where William was a brewing manager. Rebecca Chapman from Glapthorne lived with them as a domestic servant. By 1871 they had moved to Vine Cottage along West Street and had five children William Henry aged nine, Tom eight, Florence five, Edward four and Rosa (Lucy Rosa) was two years old. William's wife Annie died in 1874 aged forty-three.

Melancholy Death – The first day in the new year was marked by the shocking death of Mr. Wm. Curtis, who shot himself early that morning in the skin drying shed of Mr. Mays, fellmonger. Deceased had been employed as a clerk in the brewery of Mr. Paul Durrans, and by this fearful act leaves seven children, Mrs Curtis having died only a few months since. The particulars will be gathered from the evidence at the inquest, which was held the next day at the Waggon and Horses, before Wm. Marshall, Esq. deputy coroner, and a jury of which Mr. H. Wells was foreman. The jury having viewed the body which presented a ghastly appearance. Supt. F. J. Noble, stationed at Oundle, said that he lived next door to the deceased, who was a brewer's clerk, and had known him for sixteen years; he was 39 years of age, and had been a man of cheerful disposition up to about three or four months ago; since that time, he had appeared to be low spirited and to have a great weight upon his mind. He lost his wife about two months since and apparently made great trouble of it. He (witness) had heard deceased say "I shall not get over the loss of my wife". He had left seven children and had been drinking a great deal.

Witness had spoken to him upon it. On Thursday afternoon witness went to see deceased who was ill in bed. He appeared in a low desponding way, and said he never felt so ill before. He had medicine from Dr Calcott. That was the last time he saw him alive. About 7 0'clock the next morning he was sent for by Inspector Evans and went to Mr Mays's yard directly, and there saw the body of deceased who was quite dead. Nearly the whole of the head had been blown away, and a gun lay between his legs. W.B. Calcott, Esq., surgeon stated that he had known the deceased for many years, and had also been his medical attendant, and attended him within the last fortnight. He was suffering from drink, and his mind was affected at times by it. About seven o clock yesterday morning I was sent for to Mr Mays's yard, and on-going found the deceased lying in the drying room quite dead, but not cold or stiff. He was on his back on some skins. There was a gun between his legs also a stick in his hand, those being produced. One barrel of the gun had been discharged the other was loaded and at full cock. Witness examined deceased and found the whole of the skull and greater part of the face blown away, the brains being scattered about.... Mr Calcott said there was no doubt it was deceased's own act....' The jury after some consultation returned a verdict of "temporary insanity accelerated through drink." *Peterborough Advertiser 9 January 1875*

William and Annie Curtis' children

Florence was a pupil at The New Orphan houses, Ashley Down in Gloucestershire in 1881. By 1891 Florence was a domestic help for William and Emma Brown who lived along Denmark Street in Watford. Florence's sister Lucy Rosa died during 1876, in Gloucestershire, aged seven.

In 1881 Tom was a draper's assistant at Messrs Tarns Establishment at Newington in London. Joseph Haines was the House steward.

At the time of the 1881 census Edward was a scholar at the British Orphan Asylum in the parish of Upton-cum-Chalvey in Buckinghamshire. In 1901 Edward John, a chief officer in the merchant service, was visiting Charles Henry Berry, a caterer (coffee house) and his family who lived in Birkenhead.

William and Annie's son William Henry, a merchant's clerk and lodged with Elizabeth Richards a widow, who was recorded as being an Independent lady who lived along West Street in 1881. Ten years later he was lodging with William Lenton jnr and his wife they lived along St Osyth's lane. In 1893 William Henry Curtis married Emma Baylis. Emma was the youngest daughter of the late John Baylis of Egleton. William and Emma were living along West Street in 1901 with their young family, Hilda Isabel and Harry Neville. William's sister Florence also lived with them. In 1911 William was a cake seed merchant they had another daughter Sybil Helen and continued to live along West Street.

Obituary – The death occurred on Sunday of Mrs Emma Curtis, wife of Mr W. H. Curtis, the well-known cake, corn and seed merchant of Oundle. A native of Oakham, she had been many years at Oundle and was an enthusiastic church worker. She had been ill only a few days, and her death came as a shock. She was 76 years of age. The funeral service is to be on Wednesday at the Parish Church at 2p.m. *Northants Evening Telegraph 1 November 1939*

William Henry Curtis' obituary included the following details. Mr William Harry Curtis, aged 90, and well-known in the agricultural world used to attend the markets regularly at St Ives, Spalding, Stamford, Peterborough, Thrapston and Oundle. His main interest was his business, although in his younger days he was a tennis player and fond of boating. He was a life member of the Oundle Rowing Club. He was the last surviving partner of that club's scratch pairs held on August 6 1879. A pewter mug is inscribed with names of M. Thompson, J. H. Smith (stroke) W. H. Curtis (cox). During the 1914-18 war, he served as a special constable. A native of Oundle he started his career with Messrs. E. Lenton and Son agricultural merchants and in 1909 took over the cake, seed and manure side of the business and was active in his business until the time of his illness about seven weeks ago. His son Henry Neville was killed while serving with the R.F.C. in 1917. *Northampton Mercury 12 January 1951*

Henry and Alice Curtis from Uppingham

Another Curtis family who eventually made their home in Oundle was the descendants of Henry Curtis from Uppingham and his wife Alice. They had three sons Thomas, William and Joseph. By the 1861 census they were living along the High Street in Uppingham, Henry was a collar maker for horses as were his sons William and Joseph.

Henry and Alice's son Joseph married Mary Ann Emblow in the Peterborough district during 1867 and by the time of the 1871 census they were living at North Bank in Wisbech with their children Charles Henry, George William and three-week old Fanny. Ten years later the family had moved to Eastgate, Horn Cottages Peterborough in the St Johns parish. Joseph was a harness maker and tripe dresser. Their children were Charles Henry, George William, Fanny Alice, Minnie and Arthur Joseph. By the time of the 1891 census Charles Henry, a painter, was lodging with Peter and Jane Ireson along West Street in Oundle. Joseph, a harness maker, and his wife Mary Ann finally moved to Oundle by the time of the 1911 census where they made their home along Rock Road.

Henry and Alice's son Charles Henry married Charlotte Elizabeth Richards in the Oundle district during 1893.

Accident – The shop window of Mr Curtis, painter, etc., in New-street, was on Monday smashed under peculiar circumstances. A lamb got loose from the premises of Mr North's butchery adjoining, and entered Mr Curtis's house at the back. It made its way in a terrified state to the front of the shop, and made a jump at the window, which was of course smashed into fragments. *Northampton Mercury 6 July 1894*

In 1901 Charles and Charlotte lived along the Market Place and had a daughter Clara May aged five. Charles occupation was plumber/decorator. By the time of the 1911 census they had moved to North Street. Their children were Clara May, Honor Irene and Winifred Maggie. Maggie May Fletton aged twenty-one was living as a boarder with them and worked as their nursemaid. The other people boarding there were Hilary Malcolm Brown aged five and Kenneth Binfield Brown both born in Oundle.

Death of Mr C. W. Curtis – Much regret has been caused by the death of Mr C. W. Curtis, who passed away on Monday after an illness of over 12 months. He was 57 years of age and has left a widow and four daughters. *Northampton Mercury 17 July 1925*

The DANFORD families

An entry in the 'Married' section of the Stamford Mercury dated 1 December 1826 reads - On Tuesday last, at Barnwell, (by the Rev. Dr. Roberts,) Mr. Wm. Danford, of Oundle, to Sophia eldest daughter of Henry Crofts, Esq. of Barnwell Mills. William and Sophia had two children, William Ashley Danford born 1827 and Sophia born 1829. Both children died within a year of their birth.

A very serious and nearly fatal accident occurred on Wednesday morning near Oundle Bridge. Mr Danford, an eminent grazier, and a friend, were proceeding in a gig drawn by a spirited pony the property of the former gentleman, to the fat stock market at Peterboro', when in consequence of some imprudent young men who were on the road holding up their hands, the animal plunged furiously, and running the gig amongst a quantity of timber lying on the road side, smashed it nearly to atoms. Mr Danford himself was very seriously injured in the right knee. *Stamford Mercury 08 May 1835.*

Grave of John Danford in St Peters church-yard

To be sold by auction by Samuel Deacon – Lot 2. All that Plot, Piece, or Parcel of PASTURE LAND, situate in St Sythe's field, in Oundle aforesaid, containing 3A.0R.0P. () bounded on the north, by the private road in St Sythe's field; on the east, by an allotment to the late

Robert Sherard, Esq; on the south, by lot 3; and on the west by the Basford road; now in the tenure or occupation of Mr William Danford. - LOT 3. All that Plot, Piece or Parcel of MEADOW or PASATURE LAND. Situate in St Sythe's Meadow in Oundle aforesaid, containing 3A.1R. 0P. (more or less), bounded on the north, by the last lot; on the east, by an allotment to the said Robert Sherard; on the south and part of the west, by the river Nene; and on the remaining part of the west, by the Basford road; now also in the occupation of the said William Danford. *Huntingdon, Bedford & Peterborough Gazette 18 June 1836*

North Northamptonshire Oundle, Wednesday Evening, Half-past Seven. - Decision as to age – The following judgement was given in the case of Mr William Danford, who claimed for copyhold property, but was objected to as being under age at the time of registration:- "In the case of William Danford, who claims for a copyhold close in Oundle parish, the question for consideration was whether this gentleman, having put his claim at the proper period-viz., before 20th of July, but not having arrived at the age of twenty-one till the 24th of July, could be allowed to remain on the register". *A long debate took place taking into account the 37th section of the Reform Act, followed by the 38th section and 42d clause. The final paragraph reads as follows:* - "The sense then, to be given to the words 'persons who may be entitled to vote,' in the 37th section, is evidently prospective, and refers not to the time of the claim, but to the time of completion of the making out of the lists, namely, the last day of July. It is hardly necessary to say, that the grammatical construction of the words is such as to bear out this; had it been otherwise, the words used would have been 'are then' and 'at that time entitled to vote;' not, contingently, may be at some future time entitled to vote. I, therefore, decide that his name must be retained." *London Evening Standard 7 October 1837*

William Danford, the grocer in Oundle died in 1839 aged forty-eight.

William and Mary Danford's family were William, John, Robert, Ann, Matthew, Rebecca, Sarah,

William and Mary's son Matthew Danford, a mason, married Jane Paine during 1815 in the Oundle district. Matthew died during 1836 aged sixty-two.

During 1841 William Danford, was a Yeoman and lived along West Street in Oundle with his mother Jane aged.

Notice is hereby given, that the partnership lately subsisting between us, the undersigned WILLIAM DANFORD and STEPHEN EAYNOR, carrying on business as post-masters at Oundle, in the county of Northampton, was this day DISSOLVED by mutual consent. – Dated this 14th day of July 1843. William Danford. Stephen Eaynor. Witness Leond. J. Deacon, Clerk to Mr Richardson, solicitor, Oundle. *Lincoln, Stamford and Rutland Mercury 21 July 1843*

William, aged thirty-four, and his mother Jane aged sixty-seven, continued to live along West in 1851. William was a proprietor of houses. Sarah Wilson aged thirteen from Oundle was a servant for William and Jane. Ten years later William and Jane employed Emma Rycraft aged fourteen from Kings Cliffe as their house servant.

At Oundle, on the 15th inst., Jane, relict of Mr Matthew Danford, aged 80. *Northampton Mercury 23 January 1864*

Matthew and Jane's son William married Mary Ann Ball, the widow of George Ball from Oundle, in 1864. Mary's father was Thomas Clarke, a farmer. Mary Ann died aged fifty-four just before the 1871 census was recorded. William, a widow, was still living along West Street in 1871. Emma Clarke was living with William; she was shown as his sister but possibly was sister to William's late wife.

Estate sale – The following property, being the estate of the trustees of the late Mr W.L Fisher, situate in Oundle, was sold last week at the Talbot Hotel, by Mr Samuel Deacon. Lot 1 a slated messuage known as the Plough Inn, was purchased by W Danford Esq., for £450. *Northampton Mercury 9 May 1874.*

Oundle Presentation – On Friday week a meeting of parishioners was held in the Town Hall, for the purpose of presenting to William Danford Esq., a very handsome eight-day chiming clock, bearing the following inscription; - "Mr William Danford, by the ratepayers of Oundle, as a mark of their appreciation of his services as a guardian during a period of upwards of 30 years July 1877". A pair of silver candle-sticks were also presented, and were accompanied with a book containing the names of 120 subscribers. The articles were purchased of Mr Thomas Beal of Oundle. The chairman (The Rev C Hopkins) called upon J.D.W. Russell Esq., to make the presentation. - Mr G.M. Edmonds, Thomas Willson Esq., chairman and Mr R. Richardson, clerk to the Board, also testified to the value of Mr Danford. *Northampton Mercury 11 August 1877.*

In 1881 William, aged sixty-four, a widower, continued to be a proprietor of houses, and lived along West Street not far from Danford's yard. He died during 1885 aged sixty-eight. William was the last member of the Danford family recorded on the Oundle census.

The DENTON/NICHOLS families

The Denton families lived in Oundle and the surrounding villages of Warmington, Fotheringhay, Kings Cliffe and Glapthorne. The Nichols families lived in Oundle, Nassington, Southwick, Kings Cliffe, Wadenhoe, Hemington and Lutton.

William and Jane Denton's family included Rebekah, William, Mary, Anne, John, Sarah, James and George. Their children were born between the years 1793 to 1811.

Sarah Denton, widow, married Stephen Eaynor, a blacksmith, in Oundle during 1840. Sarah was the widow of James Denton who died during 1836 aged twenty-eight. By 1841 Stephen and Sarah were living along West Street with William Denton aged eight and Stephen Eaynor was one-year-old. Stephen junior died during 1843.

William and Jane's son John, an agricultural labourer, was living along North Street in 1841 with his wife Mary and their family. Jane was fourteen, George twelve, William eleven, Sarah Ann seven, John five and Christopher two years old. By 1851 John and Mary had moved to Ashton with their family George, Christopher, Emma eight, James three and Eliza was three.

William and Jane's son George, a horse breaker, married Ann Bellamy during 1836. George died in 1839 aged twenty-eight. In 1841 Ann Denton was living along West Street with her son William Bartholomew aged four, also living with her was John Cook a stonemason, his wife Priscilla and their son William aged one.

Ann Denton, widow of George, married Daniel Nicholes during 1848. In 1851 they made their home along West Street with their joint family. William Denton fourteen a butcher, John Thomas Denton aged nine, George Denton aged seven, Caroline Nichols aged three and Selina Nichols three months. By 1861 Daniel and Ann, still along West Street at the Old Hind Yard lived with their family John Thomas Denton aged nineteen a blacksmith, George Denton seventeen was a servant to a chemist, Caroline Nichols thirteen, Selina eleven and Thomas seven. Levi Bellamy aged seventeen was Daniel and Ann's nephew born in Oundle and was a general servant for them.

Daniel and Ann's son Thomas signed up for the Army during 1874 in the Royal Regiment of Artillery. He moved through the ranks from a driver, Bombardier, and Corporal until he became a Sergeant in 1879. Thomas spent nine years in India. On his discharge, in 1911 at Falmouth, he held the position of Company Sergeant Major and was awarded the George Cross for Long Service. He completed twenty-six years and one hundred and eighty-three days.

In 1871 Daniel and Ann only had Caroline at home along West Street. Daniel died in 1880 aged fifty-eight. By 1881 Ann, a widow, lived along Danford's Yard with her son George Denton a general labourer and Elizabeth Sharpe who was visiting. In 1881 Ann's daughter Caroline, a laundress, was living along Redheads Yard near West Street, with her Aunt Elizabeth Barnard, a Recipient and Parish Relief. Caroline married Frederick Abbott from Polebrook during 1890. Frederick was the son of Samuel and Elizabeth from Polebrook. At the time of the 1891 census Ann Nichols lived along West Street. Ann also had her sister Elizabeth Sharpe aged eighty-one from Ashton, her son-in-law Frederick Abbott aged twenty-six a general labourer from Polebrook and Caroline Abbott nee Nichols her daughter aged thirty living with her. Ann died in the spring of 1891 aged seventy-eight. By 1901 Caroline and Fred were living along the Angel Yard in St Osyth's lane.

George and Ann's son John Thomas married Sarah Anne Fitzjohn in 1864. Sarah was the daughter of Jno' and Mary from Woodnewton. In 1871 John and Sarah lived along West Street with their three children William five, Mary A four and Selina one-year-old.

ACCIDENT – On Saturday an accident, which at first was reported with a fatal result, happened to John Denton, of this town, in the employ of Mr Wise, plumber, at Weldon. It appears the unfortunate man was fixing some spouting, when his ladder suddenly snapped in the centre, precipitating him with a great violence to the ground, and from which he sustained a broken wrist, and other serious injuries, but under medical treatment is progressing favourably. *Northampton Mercury 12 April 1879*

John, a whitesmith, and Sarah were living along Loveday's Yard just off West Street in 1881, their son William was an Inn servant, Mary, Selina, Emily and Mary attended school. By 1891 John Thomas, a blacksmith, was still living along West Street with Sarah and their daughters Selina a dressmaker and Nellie fourteen. John Thomas died in 1892 aged fifty. Sarah Anne Denton, a widow in 1901, lived in Danfords Yard where she worked as a laundress.

George and Ann's son George married Catherine Ruff in 1881. Catherine was the daughter of John and Mary Ruff from Oundle. (In 1851 Mary was shown on the census as a coachman's widow she lived along Church Lane with her daughter's Catherine and Elizabeth and grandson Thomas. William Roughton, widow, and her granddaughter Elizabeth Roughton also lived there. By 1861 they had moved to New Street, William Roughton and his daughter Elizabeth continued to live with Mary. By 1871 William Roughton lived in the Angel Inn yard, Catherine was his housekeeper). At the time of the 1891 census George and Catherine lived along St Osyth's lane.

At the Petty Sessions held in Oundle against five people who had not paid the District Rate and costs, as ordered by the Bench. One of these was George Denton, Oundle, 17s. 6d., adjourned on account of defendant's illness. *Northampton Mercury 22 March 1895*

George's wife Catherine died in 1899 aged seventy-three. By 1911 George Denton aged sixty-seven, a widow, was an inmate at the Workhouse along Glapthorne Road. It was recorded on the census George was formerly a bricklayer's labourer and had been married for eighteen years. He died in 1917 aged seventy-three.

THE DONEGANI FAMILIES

JOS. DONEGANI. Silversmith, Jeweller, &c. Returns his most sincere thanks to the Inhabitants of Northampton and its vicinity, for the Patronage he has so long enjoyed, and begs to inform them he has Removed from George Row to the East side of the Drapery, near to the Post Office, where he hopes to receive a Continuance of their Favors. Drapery, Northampton, January 15 1830. *Northampton Mercury 16 January 1830*

On the 26th January, at Birmingham, Sarah, wife of Joseph Donegani, of this town, aged 47. *Northampton Mercury 6 March 1841*

In 1841 Joseph Donegani, a silversmith, was living along Crispin Street in the St Sepulchre parish of Northampton with his three sons Austin, William and John.

A report in in the Petty Sessions column stated *Lynch Law* – A man named Weed, with his face tied up, applied for a warrant against one Donegani. Both parties are costermongers, fishmongers, or anything' and on Saturday last, as Weed was walking down Abingdon Street, Donegani walked up to him and knocked him down. There was no doubt that the complainant had been brutally assaulted. Police sergeant Smith said he did not see the assault, but he came up just as Weed was picking himself up. But instead of coming towards him and giving his assailment into custody, he ran off in the opposite direction, "as if he meant putting up with it." Smith added, that Donegani justified the assault on the following grounds. Some time ago Weed was hard up in Thrapston. Donegani took him in, housed, and fed him, in return for which recourse to the law, promised to punch the ingratitude out of his head wherever he met him, bided his time, and on Saturday kept his word. Donegani is supposed to be in Oundle, and Weed on being told that he must pay for the warrant and the expense of catching his man, took time to consider. *Northampton Mercury 5 January 1850*

Joseph Donegani died during 1850, at Northampton, aged sixty-six.

Joseph and Sarah's son Austin married Elizabeth Howe in Oundle during 1851 in Oundle. Elizabeth was the daughter of George and Mary Howe from Wadenhoe. At the time of the 1851 census

Elizabeth was a general servant for Henry Roper, a druggist, and his wife who lived along West Street in Oundle.

OUNDLE – A Novelty – Mr Donegani, fishmonger of this town received a consignment of tortoises on Thursday last which were sold at good prices. *Peterborough Advertiser 8 August 1857.*

At the Oundle Petty Sessions on August 16, - A licence to deal in game was granted to Mr A. Donegani, fishmonger, of Oundle. *Stamford Mercury 20 August 1858*

By 1861 Austin and Elizabeth were living in the Market Place, Oundle where Austin was a fishmonger and game dealer. They had three children Austin six, Sarah A two and Alfred one-year-old. Mary Howe aged twenty-one from Hemington was a general servant for the family.

OUNDLE – Christmas Cheer – The butchers of this place have again set forth, for public approbation, a splendid selection of meat of all kinds; and while the quality of the article runs so "level" throughout the town, comment on individual enterprise would be invidious. The show of game, poultry, &c., was limited to Mr. A. Donegani, who had one of the finest displays in the county as regards quality. The grocers also contributed their quota of Christmas temptations arranged in a most tasty manner, the fruits being very fine. *Stamford Mercury 25 December 1868*

Austin and Elizabeth continued to live along the Market Place during 1871 with their children, Austin sixteen, Sarah Ann twelve, Alfred Howe Donegani ten and Charlotte Elizabeth seven years old all were born in Oundle. Their niece Charlotte Weldon aged twenty-two born in Thrapston also lived with them.

ACCIDENT – Mr Austin Donegani, fishmonger, of this town, met with rather a serious accident on Friday last, at Weldon. It appears whilst endeavouring to get into the cart the horse shied out, and the cart coming into contact with a bank at the side of the road, overturned falling on Mr D. Fortunately no bones were broken, but he nevertheless sustained serious injuries about the legs, beside being severely shaken from the fall. *Northampton Mercury 27 March 1875*

Oundle Petty Sessions – Fowl stealing – Charles Ling, a tramp, was brought up in custody charged with stealing a dead fowl from the establishment of Austin Donegani, poulterer, Market Place Oundle, on the 2nd instant. Alfred Howe Donegani, the son of the prosecutor, deposed that about six o'clock on the evening of the day named he placed seven dead fowl on the slab in the front window of the shop, and in a few minutes, he noticed one fowl had disappeared; he valued it at 3s. A boy named George Martin said he was playing with some boys near the Town-hall, when he saw prisoner remove a fowl from the shop of prosecutor, and put it under his arms. He informed Mr Donegani. The witness afterwards identified prisoner as the thief at the tramp ward in the Union Workhouse. P.C. Hinds charged him with the theft, which he denied, but admitted being in the town at the time. The fowl had not been found; Prisoner pleaded Not Guilty, and was committed for trial at the Quarter Sessions. *Northampton Mercury 7 December 1878*

In 1881 Austin was shown as being a fish, fruit and game dealer, still in the Market Place with Elizabeth and their family. Austin and Alfred were both assistants in the family business, Sarah Ann was a governess and Charlotte attended school. Still in the Market Place in 1891, Austin's occupation was shown as fish, fruit, poulterer and game dealer. Sarah and Charlotte were both governesses, Alfred was an assistant for his father.

Austin senior died during 1893 aged sixty-six. Elizabeth died the next year in 1894 aged sixty-seven.

While engaged in building operations at Mr. Donegani's house on Monday, Mr Henry Howe had the misfortune to slip on the scaffolding and fell to the ground on his head. Fortunately, the injuries were not serious. *Stamford Mercury 6 July 1894.*

Wanted, for Fish, Fruit, Poultry, and Game Trade, a respectable young Man, 18 to 20, having a little knowledge of the trade. – Apply A. Donegani, Oundle. *Stamford Mercury 12 October 1894*

Austin and Elizabeth's son Austin married Sarah Maria Stacey during 1882 at Ware in Hertfordshire. In 1891 they were living along St Osyths Lane with their children Evelyn May was seven and Percy Austin Stacey Donegani aged three. By 1901 Austin had taken over his father's business where he lived with his wife Sarah and their son Percy aged thirteen. Austin junior died during 1909 aged fifty-five. Sarah died during 1940 aged ninety-four.

Austin and Sarah's son John married Clarrice Lillian Johnson during 1922 in the Peterborough district. Their granddaughter Jean (nee Donegani) told me there were three children, her father John, his brother Austin and sister Joan. John owned a garage along East Road.

John Donegani taken in East Road in the 1950's.
Photo courtesy of Jacqueline (nee Cotton)

Austin and Elizabeth's daughter Charlotte was living along South Road in the Hayden Terrace where she 'Let rooms and was a Teacher of Music' in 1901. Ellen King a widow aged seventy-two, Emma Samons aged forty-nine both from Lancashire living on their own means and Sidney Dring aged twenty-one and ironmongers' assistant from Grimsby all boarded with Charlotte. By 1911 Charlotte only had Florence Alice Morehen, her domestic servant, living with her.

The death has occurred at Northampton Hospital of Miss Charlotte Donegani, daughter of the late Mr Austin Donegani, a well-known Oundle tradesman. She was 60 years of age. *Northampton Mercury 1 March 1929*

Charlotte's sister Sarah Ann died in 1945. LAID TO REST AT Malvern Hills. Emma Samons died 17 December 1934. FRIEND OF SISTERS. (As recorded on headstone in Oundle cemetery, eastern side of chapel).

OLDEST CATHOLIC FAMILY – A popular feature of the Northampton Mercury is the extracts from the Mercury of 100 years ago, and one of these, published last week referred to a robbery at the silversmith's shop of Mr Donegani, of Gold-street, Northampton. It is interesting to know that two granddaughters of old Mr Donegani, the Misses Donegani, are living at Oundle, where his son, Mr Austin Donegani, was in business for forty years; and two grandsons, Mr B. Madden, of 38 St. Michael's-road, and Mr Joseph Madden, who played for the Catholics and Northamptonshire at cricket, are living at Northampton. Four other grand-daughters are alive. Mr B. Madden claims that the family is the oldest Catholic family in Northampton. His ancestors were, as his grandfather's name suggests, Italian. *Northampton Mercury 15 October 1926*

The FOX families

There were many lines of the 'Fox' families living in Oundle and surrounding villages mainly Ashton and Warmington. Listed below are only a handful of them who at some stage settled in Oundle.

William Fox and his wife Eleanor were married in Oundle in 1740. Their children were John c.1743, William c.1745, Elisabeth c.1755, Mawley c.1759. William was a farmer, they lived in Ashton.

William and Eleanor's son John, a gardener and his wife Ann's children were Mary, John, William, Thomas, Morley.

John and Ann's son William married Rebekah Richardson in January 1794, Rebekah died in July 1794. William then married Hannah Christian during 1796 in Oundle. Their children were William c.1796, Hannah c.1797 and Charles c.1799. Hannah gave birth to three more sons George c.1801, Christopher c.1803 and another George c.1805 they all died while very young. Hannah also died in 1805 and was buried in St Peters churchyard with her children. William, Hannah and Charles were the only surviving children of William and Hannah.

William and Hannah's daughter Hannah married Anthony Rippiner on 4 November 1823 in Oundle. (See Rippiner family details.)

On Monday last, Mr William Fox, farmer, of Oundle, met with a singular and terrible accident. He was attending the unloading of some timber, when a tree was drawn from off the carriage so near him as by its rebounding from the ground to strike him under the chin. The force was so great as to break Mr. Fox's jaw, and knock out several of his teeth; placing him in a situation of great misery; and it is even feared his life is endangered by the accident. *Stamford Mercury 2 April 1824*

A report in the 'Deaths' column in the Stamford Mercury 9 September 1831 – On Saturday last, aged 35, Mr William Fox, of Oundle Lodge.

William Fox senior was in the Laxton's hospital along North Street in 1841 where Susannah Ragsdale was matron. He died during 1846 at the Laxton hospital aged sixty-eight.

William and Hannah's son Charles married Harriet Pierce during 1820 in Oundle. Harriet was the daughter of Solomon and Susannah. In 1841 Charles, a farmer, and Harriet were living in the Oundle Lodge not far from Chapel Lane with their children. Harriet aged fifteen, Frederick fourteen, Sarah eleven, John seven, Rebecca five and George aged three. Elizabeth Freeman aged twenty, Samuel Horspool aged forty, William Norris fifteen, John Warner fifteen and Elizabeth Tate also fifteen all apart from Elizabeth Freeman were employed as servants living in the Fox house-hold. By 1851 Charles, a farmer of 225 acres employing nine labourers lived with Harriet at Fox's Lodge with three of their children, Rebecca aged fifteen, George aged thirteen and Elizabeth aged eight. Sarah Swann from Benefield was a house servant, both William Langley from Oundle and William Beasley from Glapthorne worked for Charles Fox as indoor labourers, all three were seventeen years old. William and Harriet's son John was a draper's apprentice living in the Market Place with Thomas Norburn, a draper, and his family.

TO BE SOLD BY AUCTION – By Deacon and Son. On Wednesday, the 30th day of March 1853, on the premises of Mr Charles Fox, Oundle Lodge, who is changing his Residence; Comprising 7 very useful cart horses, sound and in good condition; nag horse, five-year-old, quiet in harness; useful pony, six-year-old, quiet; 8 two-and-a-half-year-old steers, heifer, heifer in calf, 3 stirks, 8 large store hogs (very fresh), 20 lambhogs. Harness for 8 horses, scuffler, 8 sheep troughs, 3 sheep cribs, 2 turnip cutters, horse-hoe, roll, 4 wood ploughs, iron plough, pair of gate harrows, 2 pair small ditto, pair seed ditto, pair twin ditto, gig, double-ridge manure turnip drill, ten-coulter Suffolk drill, nine-coulter ditto, broad-wheel waggon with double shafts, narrow-wheel ditto with iron arms, 2 broad-wheel carts, narrow-wheel ditto, 5 boarded cribs, horse-power chaff cutting machine, capital six-horse-power thrashing machine by Hornsby, capital dressing machine by Blackwell, weighing machine and weights, bean and malt mills, ladders, stack cloths and poles, 12 bullock chains, barn tackle, waggon and cart ropes, hand turnip drill, corn screen, fan, draining tools, 3 hay drags, quantity of netting, tools in lots, old iron, stone garden roll, 3 ale pipes, 2 hogs-head casks, 3 half-hogshead casks, and other effects. – The Company are requested to meet the Auctioneers at Eleven o'clock, when Refreshments will be provided, and then proceed to sale. *Stamford Mercury 25 March 1853*

Charles and Sarah Fox's family from Ashton

Charles and Sarah's son George married Mary Ann Gray, widow, during 1847. By 1851 George a baker and Mary Ann lived along West Street with their family, Charles Gray fifteen, Nathaniel Gray thirteen, George Gray eleven, John Gray eight, Alfred Gray six, William Morley Fox aged one. Ann Newton from Stoke Doyle was the house servant. In 1861 George, a porter to a wine merchant, and Mary Ann had John a cooper's apprentice and Alfred a shoe maker apprentice at home as well as William eleven and Elizabeth aged eight. Ten years later George and Mary had moved to Benefield Road and only had William, a butcher, at home.

George and Mary Ann's daughter Elizabeth married Arthur Howitt during 1876. (See Howitt family details)

George and Mary Ann's son William married Sarah Ann Dexter during 1871. By 1881 they were living in the Albion cottages along Benefield Road with Thomas George eight, Martha Ann six, James four and William mother Mary Ann. In 1891 William and Sarah Ann had moved to Kettering with their family. In 1891 Mary Ann was living with her widowed daughter Elizabeth Howitt. Mary Ann died in 1894 aged eighty-four.

George Fox's father Charles died in 1881 and George died in 1884 aged fifty-five.

Charles and Sarah's son Charles married Harriet Lane during 1859. Charles was the son of Charles and Sarah from Ashton. Charles and Harriet were living along Hubbard's Yard in Stoke End when the 1861 census was recorded, they only had one daughter Ellen aged one at home. At the time of the 1871 census Charles was an

Charles and George Fox' grave in the town cemetery Stoke Road

agricultural labourer, he lived at No 3 Clarke's Yard along West Street with Harriet and their family. Ellen aged eleven, Ruth nine, Sarah seven and Joseph five. James Fox aged fifteen from Ashton who was a visiting them at the time of the census. In 1881 Charles, a gas stoker lived along Drumming Well Yard with Harriet, and their family. Ruth nineteen, Joseph fifteen, Arthur eight, Marcus six and John aged two. By 1891 Charles and Harriet continued to live along West Street in Drumming Well Yard with their family. Marcus aged seventeen was a carpenter, John twelve, Charles nine and Frank seven were all scholars.

A boy named Frank Fox, of Oundle, narrowly escaped death from drowning on Monday. He was playing near the pit in a field on the East Backway, when he fell into the river. He disappeared under the water twice, and was then pulled out by a fellow playmate named Binder, who rescued him with a fishing rod. *Northampton Mercury 11 September 1891*

Charles and Harriet's son John signed up for the Northamptonshire Regiment in 1897. His records show he was a labourer working for C Binder prior to being enlisted. John served his country for eight years.

Charles and Harriet's son John married Mary Ann Horn during 1900. They were living along West Street in Hawes Yard at the time of the 1901 census, Maud Horn aged four was shown as a visitor. John was a fishmonger's assistant. By 1911 John Fox aged thirty-two was a farm labourer and lived along West Street with his wife Mary Ann and their children. Edith aged nine, Winifred Ruth aged four and Violet Muriel aged one year. John and Mary Ann had been married for ten years, had four children but one had died.

Charles and Harriet's son Charles was enlisted to the Northamptonshire Regiment in January 1901. Charles' military records show he served his country for fourteen years having been to South Africa, India and France. Charles married Gertrude Hutchins in 1912.

At the time of the 1901 census Charles and Harriet had two sons at home, Marcus was a solicitor's clerk and Frank was a grocer's assistant. Eleven-year-old Lucy Harding was visiting them; she was born in London. In 1911 Charles was shown on the census as an Old Age Pensioner formerly at the Gas Works. He lived along the Stoke

Road in Oundle with Harriet Lane Fox who he had been married to for fifty-one years. They had two sons at home Marcus Fox was an estate clerk and Charles was a fishmonger's assistant. Charles and Harriet had eleven children three of whom had died.

FUNERAL – the interment took place in Oundle Cemetery, on Monday of Mrs Harriet Fox, who passed away at the home of her daughter at Northampton, at the age of 87. Mrs Fox was the widow of the late Mr Charles Fox, for many years an employee at the Oundle Gas Works, who died in 1912. The service took place in the Cemetery Chapel, the Rev. J. Cooper, Wesleyan minister, officiating. The mourners present were: Mrs Richardson, (Northampton) Mrs Ashley (Romford) daughters; Mr Arthur Fox (Weybridge) Mr Marcus Fox, Mr John Fox, (Oundle) sons; Mr J Richardson, and Mr F.W. Ashby'. *Northampton Mercury 18 February 1927*

Charles and Harriet's son Joseph married Elizabeth Fair in Ossett Essex during 1885. Joseph, a groom, and his wife Elizabeth were living at the cottage at the Mill in Boughton Northants in 1891. They had two children Laura and Arthur. By 1901 they had moved to 25 Park Street in Northampton with their family, Arthur eleven, Ethel eight, Charles six, Marcus four and one-year-old Herbert. Joseph and Elizabeth had moved to Oundle by the time of the 1911 census. Their family at home were Charles Joseph and Marcus both grocer's assistants, Herbert Lane Fox, William James nine, Alfred Ernest six and Frank George three years old.

Charles and Harriet's son Frank married Edith Helena Streather in 1908. They were living along East Road in 1911. Frank was a grocer's assistant. They had two children Sylvia Pauline and Douglas William.

OUNDLE – A pretty wedding took place at St Peter's on Saturday when Mr Herbert Lane Fox, son of Mrs Joseph Fox, late of Oundle, was married to Miss Winifred Rose Bamford, Oundle, youngest daughter of Mr and Mrs W. Bamford, Oundle. The bride has been a prominent member of the Operatic Society, taking leading parts for several years, and also a member of St Peter's church choir. *Northampton Mercury 25 April 1930*

William and Mary's son James married Sarah Rowlett, from Ashton, in 1854. By 1861 James a railway porter aged thirty-one lived at Gann's Yard in St Osyths Lane with his wife Sarah. In 1871 they were living in Ashton. At the time of the 1881 census James and Sarah were back in Oundle, living along Stoke Road in the Cemetery Lodge where James was the Curator of the cemetery. In 1891 James aged sixty was the cemetery keeper and lived in the Cemetery Keepers house with Sarah. James died in 1892 and Sarah died in 1899.

CEMETERY – Mr Rhymes, of Ashton, has been appointed to succeed the late James Fox as Cemetery keeper. *Northampton Mercury 16 December 1892*

William and Mary's son Thomas at the age of thirty-three was a farmer of 144 acres employing 1 labourer and 1 boy in 1871. He lived along West Street with his wife Emma and their family, Charles aged four and Mary aged ten months. Thomas was a wine and spirit porter in 1881, he and Emma had moved to Glapthorne, their family had increased with Charles and Mary then Agnes, Frederick, Florence and Edis. In 1891 Thomas, a wine merchant's porter had moved back to Oundle, along New Road, between Glapthorne Road and Rock Road, with Emma. Their son Charles was a brickyard labourer, Florence aged fourteen a dressmaker's apprentice and their thirteen-year-old daughter Edith (Edis). By 1901 Thomas had become a gardener he and Emma only had Florence at home she worked as a dressmaker. Eliza Mary Friars a teacher from Surrey and Harry Chapman a railway clerk from Rutland boarded with the family. Thomas died in 1908 aged sixty-nine. Emma continued living in the family home at the time of the 1911 census, it was recorded she had been married for forty-two years had eight children three of whom had died.

OUNDLE-NONAGENARIAN – The funeral took place on Wednesday, of Mrs Emma Fox, who died on the 13th inst, at the residence of her daughter, Mrs A Tebbutt, Gordon-road, at the age of 91 years. The interment was in Oundle Cemetery, the first portion of the service taken in the Parish church, Canon Smalley Law officiating. The chief mourners were: Mr Charles Fox, Mr Frederick Fox (sons), Mr C. Gray, Peterborough (nephew), Mr A Tebbutt (son-in-law), Mrs Stapleton, and other friends. There were several beautiful wreaths. *Northampton Mercury 18 February 1927*

Thomas and Martha Fox

Thomas Fox, a brazier, married Martha Negus in 1847. She was the daughter of Francis and Sarah Negus who lived along St Osyths lane. Thomas born around 1820 in Addington Northants lived along St

Scythes lane he was a tin plate worker. At the time of the 1851 census the lane was written as St O Scythes lane, Thomas, a journeyman tin man, and Martha had two sons John aged two and William three months. In 1861 the lane was recorded as St Osythes lane where Thomas continued to live with Martha. Their family had increased John, William, John (Tom?) seven, Emma four, Martha two and George under one year. Ten years later all children apart from John were still at home. William was a gas-house labourer, Tom a gentleman's gardener's assistant, Emma was a dressmaker's assistant then Maria and George attended school. In 1881 Thomas, a tinman and brazier his wife Martha was a shopkeeper (General) Tom was a blacksmith's labourer and George was a tailor, the lane name was recorded as at St Oscythes lane.

Thomas and Martha's son Tom married Martha Jane Woods during 1885. In 1891 Tom, a railway shunter lived along St Osyth's Lane with Jane and their four-year-old son Cecil. Tom's parents also lived with them.

Death of Fire Brigade Man – The members of the Oundle Fire Brigade performed a sorrowful duty on Tuesday last, viz. attending the funeral of one of the oldest members, Mr Thomas Fox, who died at the age of 71 a few days previously. The men under the command of Captain Knight, presented a smart appearance, and bore the coffin to its last resting place. *Northampton Mercury 3 July 1891*

At the meeting of the Oundle Urban District Council on Monday 4th September 1899 the following was agreed – 'Out of the applications for Cemetery porter, they selected that of Tom Fox, of Oundle, for the post, and on the motion of Mr Willson, seconded by Mr Coombs, this was confirmed.' *Northampton Mercury 8 September 1899*

By 1901 Tom had changed his occupation to a cemetery curator. He lived with Jane and son Cecil in the Cemetery House along the Stoke Road. Jane died during 1904 aged fifty-two. In 1911 Tom was a caretaker for the Oundle Urban council and lived in Oundle with his son Cecil who was a gas stoker at the Oundle Gas Works. Tom's mother Martha was an inmate at Latham's alms-house along North Street. Martha died in 1905 aged eighty-eight.

Thomas and Martha's son William Francis Fox married Emma Whittington in 1878. By the time of the 1881 census William, a railway labourer lived along St Osyth's lane with Emma and their one-year-old daughter Beatrice. In 1891 William was a gas manager and lived along Station Road with Emma and their children. Beatrice Sarah was ten, Mable six, Ethel five and Jessey was three years old. Ten years later William was a manager of the Gas Works and lived along East Road in the Gas Cottage with Emma and their family. Mabel A was a confectioner's assistant, Ethel aged fifteen, Jessie thirteen, Thomas was nine, Gladys aged five and Reginald three. In 1911 William still lived in the Gas Cottage with Emma and their children. Gladys aged fifteen was a draper's assistant and Reginald aged thirteen was a scholar and grocer's errand boy. May Thompson from East Haddon was a school teacher boarding with the family. William and Emma had been married for thirty-two years had seven children but one had died.

The FRANCIS families

There were 'Francis' families living in the surrounding villages of Oundle including Ashton, Nassington, Polebrook, Woodnewton, Aldwinkle and Blatherwycke.

William Francis from Ashton married Harriet Wade, a widow from Oundle, during 1822. In 1841 they were living along West Street in Oundle with their sons Charles eight and Samuel William six years old. William senior was born in Ireland and Harriet in Northampton. By 1851 they continued to live along West Street William was a labourer and Harriett a straw bonnet maker. Their sons were both tailors.

William and Harriet's son Samuel William married Mary Jane Jones during 1858. Mary Jane was the daughter of James Jones who was also a tailor. By 1861 Samuel and Mary Jane were living along the Market Place in Jones Yard where Samuel was a clothier and Mary Jane a milliner. They had a daughter Gertrude Miller Francis.

William and Harriet were living at 2 New Street in Oundle in 1861 Harriet was doing very well with her bonnet making business she had two young girls living and working with her. Georgina Penny was an assistant and Jane Redhead an apprentice learning the business. Harriet Holmes aged eleven and Tom Eaton aged fifteen and working as a shoemaker were grandchildren to William and Harriet. William died during 1867 aged sixty-nine. At the time of the 1871 census Harriet, a widow and milliner/ straw bonnet maker was still living along West Street. Her daughter in law Mary Jane was also a widow working and living with Harriet as a milliner's assistant. Mary Jane's daughter's Gertrude and Agnes also lived with the family. By 1881 Harriet had her granddaughter Gertrude living and working with her. Mary Jane and her daughter Agnes lived along St Osyths Lane with her mother Elizabeth Jones, also a widow. Harriet continued living along West Street in 1891 and Gertrude was back with her grandmother working as a dressmaker. Harriet died during 1893 aged ninety-six.

Samuel and Mary's daughter Agnes married Alfred Henry Goldsmith during 1892. In 1901 Alfred and Agnes were living at Gungreen, Hawkhurst Kent where Alfred was a Prudential Assurance agent. Their family were Gertrude May six, Frederick four and Henry was two years old.

Mary Jane Francis was living on her own at the time of the 1901 census along St Osyths Lane where she continued to work as a milliner and dressmaker. In 1901 Gertrude Miller Francis, still single was living along Chaplin Road Hendon, Wembley and was shown as a retired dressmaker. Mary Jane died in Hendon during 1909 aged seventy-one, possibly at the home of her daughter Gertrude.

By 1911 Gertrude's address was May Villas, Chaplin Road. Gertrude's relatives John Douthwaite an umbrella manufacturer working in the city, John Percy Douthwaite a warehouseman in the umbrella manufactures and Gertrude May Goldsmith aged fifteen born in Oundle were living with her. Gertrude May was the daughter of Agnes, who was sister to Gertrude Francis. (Recorded on the 1891 census the Douthwaite family were living at Woodlands Brightside in Lewisham. John senior the umbrella manufacturer married Louisa Pickering Jones from Oundle in 1875; they had a son John Percy. Agnes Francis lived with them and was their niece continuing to work as a dressmaker).

Joseph and Charlotte Francis from Norfolk

Joseph and Charlotte were visiting James Cattermole, from Norfolk, who lived in Polebrook during 1851. Joseph and Charlottes children were Emma aged two and John was four months old. In 1861 Joseph was a horse-keeper, he and Charlotte's family had grown with Arthur aged eight, George six, Benjamin three and Charlotte one-year-old. By 1871 they lived at Polebrook Lodge with John an agricultural labourer, Benjamin a farm boy, Charlotte, Amy eight, Robert six and James four all attended school, the youngest was Eldred aged two. Joseph and Charlotte had moved to Armston by 1881 with three of their sons. Robert was a groom, James an agricultural servant and Joseph aged nine attended school. Joseph and Charlotte's friends James Cattermole and his sister-in-law Maria lived next door to them. Joseph, a yardman on a farm, and Charlotte were living at Polebrook Hall with their son Joseph and grandson Arthur who were both grooms at the hall in 1901. Charlotte died during 1909 aged eighty.

Joseph and Charlotte's son George married Mary Rebecca Owen during 1875, and were living next door to George's parents in 1881 with their four-year-old daughter Emma.

Joseph and Charlotte's son Robert married Elizabeth Ann Burton in the district of York during 1896. By 1901 they were living at 40 Swann Street in York with their sons John R aged two and George aged one month. Robert and Elizabeth had moved by the time of the 1911 census and were living at Armston with their son John Ronald aged eleven. Robert's father Joseph, a widow and old age pensioner also lived with them. Joseph died during 1912 aged eighty-five.

Joseph and Charlottes' son John married Mary Ann Hopper during 1873. By 1881 they were living at Armston near Oundle with their family, Arthur six, Clara five, Ralph two and Helen was seven months old. John was a widower in 1891, he lived at Armston with Arthur sixteen, Clara fifteen, Ralph twelve, Helen ten and John Tom was seven. In 1901 John was a farm stockman, he had moved to Polebrook and lived at the Duke's Head with his daughter Sarah and son John Tom an errand boy. John's son Ralph was working as a servant (his occupation was shown as lunatic attendant) at the Asylum in Ilford Essex.

John and Mary's daughter Helen married John Gascoigne during 1910. At the time of the 1911 census they were living with Helen's father in Polebrook, they had a two-month old son called Douglas Francis Gascoigne.

John and Mary's son Ralph married Mary Ann Wright in the Honiton district during 1908. By 1911 Ralph, a domestic man servant, and Mary Ann were living at Armston. They had three children, Victor John, Harold Steven and Dorothy. Mary Ann died during 1916. Ralph joined the Army in the 2nd Life Guards Regiment at the end of 1916.

Ralph and Mary's son Harold was a motor mechanic in the 1930's. He married Mary Jane Chester during 1943 in the Thrapston district.

Joseph A Marshall, son of John William and Ailey from Warmington married Phyllis M Chester during 1947 in the Thrapston district. Phyllis and Mary Jane were sisters.

Virginia Francis (nee Burgess) told me the following. Harold Francis and Archie Marshall (Joseph A.) went into partnership. Archie used to repair radios and televisions in part of the building and Harold did repairs to cars. Later they bought the site along Benefield Road which once was St Ann's in the Grove Infant school. With lots of rebuilding Francis and Marshalls garage slowly developed. At some stage Archie had a shop along West street where he repaired televisions and sold electric goods.

Harold Francis in his workshop. Photo courtesy of Virginia Francis.

The HINMAN families

Thomas Hinman born at Melton Mowbray c.1818 married Ann Giddings born in Oundle c.1821, just after the 1841 census was recorded. Ann was the daughter of William and Mary who lived along Church Lane in Oundle, William was an ostler. At the time of the 1851 census Thomas, a currier, and Ann were living in Warkton near Kettering and had three children Edward eight born in Oundle, Mary four and Harriet one-year-old both born in Warkton.

Death column – Sept. 24, suddenly, Mr T. Hinman, of Wellingborough, aged 42. *Northampton Mercury 29 September 1860*

By 1861 Ann, a widow, was living along St Johns Street in Wellingborough where she worked as a grocer to support her family. Martha Ellen aged fourteen and George aged nine were both shoe worker's, Martha seven and Nathan two were scholars. Martha Grimond a visitor aged sixty-five was a charwoman. In 1871 Ann continued to be a grocer, her children worked, Harriet was a fitter of uppers, Martha a machinist, Fanny a grocer's assistant and George was a clicker in the shoe trade as a cutter of lowers. By 1881 Ann only had Fanny at home and her granddaughter Lilley Laughton aged nine living with her.

Thomas and Ann's son Edward was an apprentice cabinet maker in 1861 living with John Gann a cabinet maker and upholsterer in the Market Place in Oundle. By 1871 Edward was living with his wife Elizabeth and their son George Edward aged one in St Osyths lane, Edward was a cabinet maker.

At Oundle on 14 July 1874 George Edward son of Mr Edward Hinman aged 3 years and 11 months. *Stamford Mercury 31 July 1874*

In 1881 Edward and Elizabeth lived in the Ganns Cottages, East Backway along the Ashton Road. They had two daughters Jessie and Maggie.

The following reports were taken from the Northampton Mercury:

Conservatism – Mr Edward Hinman, a Conservative working man, was, on Thursday, presented with a silver inkstand, and a purse containing £20. The inkstand bore the following inscription: - "Presented to Edward Hinman, by Conservative friends May 1886"

The purse was of blue silk with primrose fringe and bore the words: - "Oundle Conservative Association, presented to Edward Hinman, May 13th 1886. This was the work of some ladies." A full report can be found in the newspaper dated 22 May 1886.

RESIGNATIONS – On account of his appointment as Relieving Officer, Mr E. Hinman has resigned office as secretary to the Oundle Conservative Association. Mr Hinman's resignation as No.1 fireman of the Oundle Fire Brigade has also been received. *16 October 1886*

OBITUARY – It is our painful duty to record the death of Mr Edward Hinman, which took place on Saturday. Death was due to inflammation of the lungs; deceased having been confined to his bed since Christmas-eve. He was appointed Relieving Officer for the Oundle and Fotheringhay districts in September of last year, previous to which he had worked at his trade as a cabinet maker for over 30 years. He was a staunch Oddfellow, and was secretary to the Loyal Providence Lodge for more than twelve years. He was also a member of the Fire Brigade (acting as their secretary since the re-organisation some eight years since), a member of St Peter's ringers, and secretary to the conservative Club. *26 February 1887*

COFFEE TAVERN – The business of the Oundle hotel and Coffee Tavern Co. (Limited), North Street, has been disposed of to Mrs Hinman, late manageress for the company. *12 April 1890*

In 1891 Elizabeth, a widow, was described as the coffee tavern keeper. Her daughter Jessie also lived with her along North Street. At the time of the 1901 census Elizabeth was living by her own means along New Street. Alfred Browning a bank clerk boarded with Elizabeth. By 1911 Elizabeth was living along the Market Place; she had another lodger, Madelwihyasta Benson, a fifty-year-old married woman born in Guernsey.

Alfred Hinman and family from Rutland

In 1841 Alfred Hinman, born in North Luffenham, aged fourteen was an apprentice for the wheelwright Robert Pepperday at North Luffenham in Rutland. He married Alice Nicholls, born in Kings Cliffe during 1850, and by the time of the 1851 census they were living with Alice's widowed mother Elizabeth, a schoolmistress and her sons. Alfred was then a carpenter journeyman. During 1841 Alice's father William Nicholls was a schoolmaster. By the time of the 1861 census Alfred, a wheelwright, and Alice had moved to North

Street in Oundle. Their three children Caroline and John Henry both nine and William seven were all born in North Luffenham. In 1871 Alfred and Alice still lived along North Street, with John Henry eighteen, William sixteen, Alfred ten, Ruth seven and Edward four years old. Their daughter Caroline was lodging at 6 Windsor Road in Ealing where she worked as a domestic servant for George Balderson, a butcher, his wife Eliza Ann and George's eighty-five-year-old mother. Alfred died during 1876 aged fifty. Alice Hinman married Henry John Bath during 1878.

Neglect of School – In the case of John Henry Bath, painter, Oundle, for neglecting to send his step-son, Edward, to school, an order was made, with costs, 4s. *Northampton Mercury 17 April 1880.*

By 1881 they were living along North Street with Alice's son Edward aged fourteen, her mother Elizabeth Nicholls and a lodger Thomas Whissell a watchmaker from Warwickshire. Henry Bath was a house decorator born at Guildford in Surrey.

Alfred and Alice's daughter Ruth married Weston Nicoll Robinson during 1887 in the district of Prestwich in Lancashire.

At the time of the 1891 census Henry and Alice continued to live along North Street, Alice's daughter Ruth and her one-year-old son Harold also lived with them. In 1901 and 1911 Ruth was living with her husband in Prestwich. Alice died during 1891 aged fifty-nine. In 1901 Henry was a boarder with Henry Hudson who lived in Glapthorne.

Alfred and Alice's daughter Caroline

In 1881 Caroline, at the age of twenty-seven, was the head attendant at the Asylum at Caterham in Surrey. Between 1891 and 1901 Caroline was the assistant matron at the Institution. By the time of the 1911 census Caroline was living at Barrowden in Rutland with William and Elizabeth Nicholls who had been married for thirty-one years and had no children. They were Caroline's grandparents, although the census shows Caroline as being their niece.

Alfred and Alice's son Edward signed up for the Northamptonshire Regiment during 1888. During his thirteen years' service, he went to India and South Africa.

Alfred and Alice's son John Henry Hinman married Annie Gilby from Thurning during 1879. By 1881 John, worked as a wheelwright as did his father, and Annie lived along North Street with their son Frederick Charles aged one. John's brother Alfred lodged with them, he was a butcher. Ten years later Frederick had a brother William Henry aged eight and a sister Ruth Elizabeth who was five. In 1901 John was a carpenter journeyman and Annie a charwoman, Ruth was a dressmaker's assistant then the younger children were Maggie aged nine and Nellie aged six. At the time of the 1911 census John and Annie had been married for thirty-one years and had five children. Ruth was a dressmaker and Ellen (Nellie) a shop assistant both at a drapers/milliner's shop.

John and Annie's son Frederick Charles married Edith Rose Loveday, from Thrapston in 1902.

Wedding – On Easter Monday a wedding took place at the Parish Church of Islip, the contracting parties being Miss Edith Rose Loveday, third daughter of Mr Thomas Loveday, of Thrapston, and Mr Frederick Charles Hinman, son of Mr J. Hinman, Oundle. The bride was given away by her father, was becomingly dressed in electric grey, trimmed with ivory satin and chiffon, and hat to match. The bridesmaids were Miss Maggie Loveday (sister to the bride) Misses Ruth, Maggie and Nellie Hinman (sisters to the bridegroom). They were dressed in royal blue with cream silk, and hats to match. They each wore a brooch and necklace, the gifts of the bridegroom. The best man was Mr W. Hinman. The marriage service was performed by the Rector (Rev. A. C. Neely), and the presents numbered over 50. *Northampton Mercury 4 April 1902*

In 1911 Frederic (as spelt on census) and Edith were living at 30 Dale Road, Bournbrook in Worcestershire with their daughters' Mary aged seven and Maggie aged three. Frederic was a cycle polisher for a cycle manufacturer.

John and Annie's son William Henry married Eliza Ann Hill in 1911. It was recorded on the 1911 census that they had been married for seven weeks. They lived along Benefield Road, William was a manager baker.

John and Annie's daughter Ruth.

WEDDING - A pretty wedding was solemnised in the Parish Church of Bournbrook, Birmingham, on Thursday week between Mr. Claude Francis Copley, of Wadenhoe, Oundle and Miss Ruth, eldest daughter of Mr J. Hinman, Rock Road Oundle. Mr W. Copley, brother of the bridegroom, was best man. The bride, who was charmingly attired in a tailor-made costume of saxe blue and hat to match, was given away by Mr. F. Hinman, her brother. Miss M. Hinman, sister of the bride, and the Misses Mary and Maggie Hinman, nieces, were the bridesmaids, and were all prettily dressed in green, with white hats. The presents numbered over 50. The bridegroom's father, Mr J.W. Copley of Wadenhoe, was amongst the guests. The illness of the bride's father was the cause of the wedding being celebrated away from home. *Northampton Mercury 23 February 1912*

John Henry Hinman died during the winter months of 1912 aged sixty.

Obituary – The death occurred on Sunday at Oundle of Mrs J. Hinman, widow of Mr John Hinman, Rock-road, at the age of 77. She was a respected church-woman and member of the Mother's Union, being one of the first to join in Oundle. Two sons and two daughters, Mr F. Hinman, Oadby, Mr W. Hinman, Oundle, Mrs C. Copley, Desborough, and Mrs J.W. Smith, Burton Latimer, are bereaved. *Northants Evening Telegraph 24 January 1939*

The HOWITT families

Isaiah and Sarah Howitt lived in Spalding during 1861 with their children Arthur thirteen, Ann ten, Elis nine, Lucy seven, Albrick five and John was two years old.

Isaiah and Sarah's son Arthur a saddler, born 1848 in Spalding was lodging with Charles Vessey and his family in New Street Oundle during 1871. Charles was a whitesmith. Arthur married Elizabeth Fox during 1876. Elizabeth was the daughter of George and Mary Fox who lived along West Street. In 1881 Arthur, a master saddler, and Elizabeth Ann were living in New Street where they made it the family home. Their children were Arthur, Edith and George. Arthur senior died later in the year of 1881 aged thirty-three. By the time of the 1891 census Elizabeth, a widow, worked as a saddler, her son Arthur was a saddler's assistant, Edith and George attended school. Mary A Fox mother to Elizabeth also lived with the family.

There are reports in the Northampton Mercury throughout the 1890's with regards to A. Howitt's involvement with sport, listed are a few of them. He belonged to Oundle Town football team. At the 19th annual meeting of the Oundle Athletic Club on Easter Monday 1890 A. Howitt came 2nd in the Quarter Mile Flat Race for Oundle boys under sixteen. At the Oundle twenty-seventh annual sports festival in April 1898 he came 1st in the Half Mile Handicap, 1st in the Quarter-mile Handicap,

In 1901 Elizabeth Ann continued the family business as a saddler, her son Arthur was a saddler and her daughter Edith was a milliner working from home.

Smashes – On Friday three squares of glass in one of the windows in Mrs Howitt's saddler's shop in New-street were smashed, and a short time after one of the casements fell from an upper window at the post office, one or two pedestrians having narrow escapes. *Northampton Mercury 27 December 1907*

Elizabeth recorded on the 1911 census that she had four children, one of whom had died. Amy Helen Marsh a draper's assistant from Pitsford and Richard Stanley Harradine a stationer's assistant from Ramsgate were both boarders with Elizabeth.

Arthur and Elizabeth's daughter Edith married Nathan Egbert Dixon on 1 September 1908. Nathan was the son of Mr Nathan Edwin and Elizabeth Dixon who lived at Rose Cottage along Glapthorne Road during 1901. Nathan Edwin was a surveyor.

Wedding – A wedding took place on Tuesday, the contracting parties being Mr Nathan Egbert Dixon, second son of Mr N. E. Dixon, of Rose Cottage, Glapthorne-road, and Miss Edith Howitt, only daughter of the late Mr Arthur Howitt and Mrs Howitt, New-street, Oundle. The bride, who was prettily attired in a dress of white Swiss embroidery and white lace hat, and carried a bouquet, was given away by her brother Mr Arthur Howitt. Her maids were Miss Nellie and Miss Alice Dixon, sisters of the bridegroom, who wore pink hats and sashes. Mr A. G. Dixon, the bridegroom's brother, Conservative candidate for south Lincolnshire, acted as best man. The Rev. William Smalley Law officiated. There was a large array of presents. The happy pair left by an afternoon train for Colwyn Bay, where the honeymoon is being spent. *Northampton Mercury 4 September 1908*

At the time of the 1911 census Nathan, a railway clerk, and Edith were living along Herne Terrace in Oundle with their daughter Edith Eleanor aged one.

Isaiah and Sarah's son Eli, a tinman, born 1850 in Spalding was lodging with Priscilla Blackwell, a widow, and her family in St Osyth's Lane during 1871. Eli Howitt married Selina Afford during 1874. Selina was the daughter of George and Elizabeth who lived along Benefield Road. In 1881 Eli and Selina lived along West Street with their family Harry, Fred, Sarah and Albric. By 1891 Eli and Selina were still along West Street with Harry, seventeen a printer's apprentice, Fred fifteen a baker's apprentice, Sarah thirteen, Albric eleven, Emily nine, Florence six, Annie five, Sydney one and Charles was two months old.

FRIEND-IN-NEED-CLUB – The annual dinner of the Friend-in-need Club was held at the Crown Inn on Friday last, about 80 sitting down to an excellent spread, provided by Host Cunnington, treasurer of the club. Mr Eli Howitt presided. After dinner, the usual toasts were duly honoured. Songs and other amusements concluded an enjoyable gathering. The club is in a flourishing condition as after experiencing a heavy year of sickness a dividend of 11s.1½d was returned to each member. There are now 88 members. Mr Hancock has been elected secretary in place of Mr W. Glenn who has left the town. *Northampton Mercury 4 January 1901*

Eli and Selina had moved to Benefield Road by 1901 where Eli was a whitesmith. Their family at home were Florence an assistant dressmaker, Annie a domestic nursemaid, then there was Sydney eleven, Charles ten and Charlotte eight years old. Their sons Harry and Fred were living at 104 Church Street in Gainsborough where they both were bakers. They were boarders with Thos' Sowerby, a tailor, and his family. In June 1901 Sidney, (spelling as shown in report) Howitt from Benefield Road was awarded a scholarship to proceed to Secondary School. *Northampton Mercury 12 July 1901.*

Eli and Selina's son Sydney was a student training at St Peters College in Peterborough during 1911.

<u>Evening School</u> – Sydney Howitt was successful in obtaining certificates in examinations under the East Midland Educational Union: - Model drawing (first class) Geometrical drawing (second class) Sydney Howitt. *Northampton Mercury 10 October 1913*

Eli and Selina were still along Benefield Road in 1911, they had been married for thirty-seven years, had eleven children one of whom had died. Florence was a dressmaker at home and Charlotte was a draper's shop assistant. They also had their granddaughter Kathleen Green aged seven living with them. Eli died in 1916 aged sixty-four. Selina died in 1936 aged eighty-one.

Funeral of Mrs S. Howitt – Many Mourners at Oundle – The funeral took place at Oundle of Mrs Selina Howitt, of 35 Benefield-road, Oundle, who died on Friday at the age of 82. The first part of the service was at Jesus Church conducted by the vicar, the Rev. J. L. Cartwright, the curate, the Rev. T. P. Pigrun, reading the lesson. There was a wreath from women members of the parish church choir. A full list of mourners can be seen in the Northampton Mercury 17 January 1936.

Eli and Selina's son Harry married Rose Hannah Redhead during 1901. Rose Hannah was the daughter of David and Elizabeth who lived at the Black Horse in Oundle where David was a tailor and publican. In 1911 Harry and Rose were living in Ilkley Cottage Houghton Road in Dunstable where Harry was a printer's reader. They had a nine-year-old son Edgar Albric.

Eli and Selina's daughter Sarah Elizabeth married Arthur Oliver Green during 1903. By the time of the 1911 census they were living at 47 Mallock Street in Leicester where Arthur worked as a printer's letterpress. They had two children at home Marian aged two and Wilfred Arthur who was under one month old. Their daughter Kathleen was with her grandparents Eli and Selina Howitt.

Eli and Selina's son Arthur married Kate Proud from Huntingdonshire during 1903. Kate was the daughter of Joseph and Martha from Ramsey. By 1911 Arthur, a harness-maker lived along Rock House in Oundle with Kate and their children Arthur aged seven and Jack aged two.

Eli and Selina's son Fred Stephen and his wife Amy were living at 62 Ropery Road in Gainsborough during 1911 with their daughters Iris Eva aged five and Margaret Esme aged three. Fred was a baker/confectioner and Amy assisted with the business. They had been married for six years.

Eli and Selina's son Charles Herbert was a hairdresser during 1911 he lived as a boarder with George Oglesby, a mattress maker living at Ordsall in Nottinghamshire. Charles married Violet M Barnard during the summer months of 1911 in the Peterborough district.

BRUDENELL Butchers shop.
Photo courtesy of Nigel Afford.

R. C. COTTON & SONS.
Photo courtesy of Jacqueline and Anne nee Cotton.

Neville George Ganderton fishmonger.
Photograph courtesy of Peterborough Images.

Photograph courtesy of Peterborough Images.

The KING families

Francis King c.1720 in Glapthorn, married Elizabeth White during 1745. They had five children, Anne, Robert, Francis, John and Sarah. Francis senior died in 1761 which was the year their youngest daughter Sarah was born.

Francis and Elizabeth's son John married Mary Wade at St Peter's church in Oundle in the 1780's. Their children were Francis, Nathaniel, Charity, John, Reuben, Anne, Job, Joseph and Selah?

Yesterday at all Saints church, Mr Nathaniel King, shoemaker of this place, to Mrs Elizabeth Draycott, housekeeper for 23 years to Major Hurst, of St Martin's. *Stamford Mercury 31 October 1834*

In 1841 Nathaniel, a cordwainer, and his wife Elizabeth lived at All Saint's Place in the Stamford Union.

In Truesdale's Hospital, Stamford, on Tuesday last, Nathaniel King, aged 66. He was at church in usual health on Sunday, and took his own dinner to the bakehouse on that day; but was seized with cholera at night, and died early on Tuesday morning. He had been a member of the Stamford Society of Ringers for more than 40 years; the usual tribute of respect was paid at his funeral, by ringing a dumb peal at All Saints church; and it is singular that the articles necessary for muffling the bells were prepared by himself about three months since. His parents are still living at Oundle, and it was their custom to make affectionate enquiries of persons from Stamford about the health of their boy. *Stamford Mercury 7 August 1846*

John and Mary's son Francis married Elizabeth Burgess during 1801 in Oundle. Their children were Mary, John, Charles and Jane.

At the time of the 1841 census John and Mary, both aged eighty-three, lived along West Street where John worked as a shoemaker. Living with John and Mary were Edward Whethers aged sixty-two, a pipemaker, Elizabeth Arnett aged twenty-five and her children William aged three, James two and her baby girl (not named) aged four months. Mary King died during 1846 aged eighty-nine. In 1851 John was living along West Street with Richard Warren, a cordwainer, and his wife Anne. John was shown as a pauper and brother to Anne.

At Oundle, on Thursday the 22nd inst., John King, aged 94, whose corpse was borne to the grave by six married grandsons, and the stools carried by two great grandsons. *Stamford Mercury 30 May 1851*

John and Mary's son Charles married Mary Ann Aspital during 1832. At the time of the 1841 census they were living along West Street where Charles was a cordwainer. Their children were Charles Francis nine and Thomas Burgess King two. By 1851 Charles and Mary were living along St Osyths Lane, Charles was a shoemaker. Their children were Charles, a labourer, Thomas twelve and Sarah Ann nine were scholars, Alice three and Anne aged one. Charles and Mary had moved to Benefield Road by 1861 where Charles continued to be a shoemaker. Their eldest son Charles was still living at home and their youngest daughter Elizabeth aged nine. Their daughter Alice was a domestic servant living in the Maltsters Yard in the Market Place, she worked for James Wilson, a tailor, and his wife Lucy.

In 1871 Charles and Mary were still in Benefield Road Charles had changed his occupation to a painter. Elizabeth was their only child at home. Their grandson Tom aged seven also lived with them. Their daughter Sarah Ann was a cook for Dr Charles Linton, a general practitioner MRCS from Fotheringhay, he lived along North Street at Dryden House Boarding House in Oundle. Mary died in 1874 aged sixty-four and her husband Charles died during 1875 aged sixty-seven.

Charles and Mary's daughter Alice married Edwin Read in 1867. His first wife Maria died in 1866. In 1871 Alice and Edwin were living in Fletton with their family, William, Mary and Annie. By 1881 they were living along Fletton Lane with their children, Annie, Charlotte and Edwin Arthur. Ten years later they lived along Mile End Road, Fletton where Edwin was a railway inspector. Their daughter Charlotte was a teacher and lived at home with her parents. In 1901 their address was shown as Mile End Village St Margaret's Road Old Fletton, Edwin was a gateman (Points) for the railway. Edwin died in 1908 aged seventy-nine. Alice lived at 1 Clifton Villas Queens Walk in New Fletton during 1911 with her daughter Charlotte who was an assistant school teacher. Alice died in 1925 aged seventy-eight.

Ray King from New Zealand passed the following details to me: – 'Thomas Burgess King, son of Charles and Mary Ann, born 25

May 1839 may have attended Oundle Grammar School and then worked for one of the stately homes or for Smiths the brewer as they all had horses. He may have started as a stable hand. At aged 21 his occupation was a groom. He joined the army in the City of Leicester having lowered his age to 20 where he signed up to a 10-year service contract. He was sent for training in Cork. Joined the 14th Reg. 2nd Battalion and then sailed to New Zealand on 23 April 1861 from Queenstown Cork now known as Cobh [Cove] He served in New Zealand then sailed on 15 October 1866 to Melbourne, Australia. While in New Zealand Thomas married Mary Baker c.1862 to 1863. A daughter Sarah Annie Burgess known as Annie was born 1864. While in Melbourne two more children were born. Mary Elizabeth 10 November 1867 and William Thomas 24 January 1870. Thomas occupation was now a coachman. Thomas, Mary and family sailed for England 28 October 1870. He obtained his 10-year army discharge. After the discharge, they may have stayed with Thomas's parents in Oundle. While in England two more children were born. George Henry in November 1871 and Arthur Edward in January 1894. No trace of birth certificates'.

At the time of the 1871 census Thomas Burgess King, his wife Mary and their children Sarah Ann and Mary Elizabeth both aged eight and William Thomas aged one were visiting Harriett Paine at the Royal Oak in Great Bowden in Leicestershire. Harriett was the publican.

Ray King's records include the following – Thomas and family returned to New Zealand in 1875. Thomas died in 1875 while in the Auckland Harbour. A month later 19 September 1875 Mary's son George Henry died aged 3 years 3 months. Her son Arthur Burgess died 17 March 1879 aged 4 years 9 months. Her daughter Sarah Annie Burgess married Joseph Christopher Spinley. Her son William Thomas, my grandfather married 6 July 1898 Kate Jackson. He died 31 August 1919 aged 49. William and Kate's children were Arthur Burgess born 1899 died 1949. Winifred Mary born 1900/1901 died 1960. Doris Lillian born 1903 died 1977. Trevor William born 1907 died 2 days old. Elsie Myrtle born 1909 died 1969. George Raymond born 1911 died 1944, George was my father.

John and Mary King's son Reuben

In 1841 John and Mary King's son Reuben and his wife Ann, lived along Church Lane, Oundle with their family William, Reuben,

Elmer and Frances. Reuben senior, William and Reuben junior were all shoe makers and Elmer was an apprentice wheelwright. Reuben's wife Ann died in 1850 aged sixty-one. Reuben, a widower, lived on his own in Church Lane in 1851. A report in the Stamford Mercury on 23 January 1857 stated that Reuben King had passed away on the 9th inst., in the Laxton Hospital aged 65.

Reuben and Ann's son William married Mary Ann Goodman during 1842. In 1851 William, a shoe maker, and his wife Mary a schoolmistress, lived along Church Lane with their family Elmer George, Clara and Mary. Joseph Wilson a widower was an upholsterer from Scotland, he lodged with the family. At the time of the 1861 census William and Mary a dealer in second hand clothes lived along St Osyths Lane. Their son Elmore (change of spelling) was a tailor, Clara was a shoemaker's domestic servant and Mary attended school.

William and Mary's daughter Clara Goodman King married Mark Thurlby during 1869. (See Thurlby family details)

By 1871 William had changed his occupation to a sexton and town crier, his wife Mary Ann was a broker. Lodging with William and Mary Ann was their son-in-law Mark Thurlby, a shoemaker master, his wife, Clara Goodman Thurlby, and their granddaughter Clara King Thurlby aged one. Mary Ann King died in 1874 aged sixty-eight. In 1881 William King, the town crier, lived along St Osyths Lane.

Benjamin Marshall has been appointed town crier in the place of William King, retired. *Northampton Mercury 15 May 1886.*

By 1891 William King aged seventy-seven was living with other residents in the Laxton Alms Houses along Church Street. He died in the Laxton Hospital in 1896 aged eighty-two.

Reuben and Ann's son Reuben married Fanny Black during 1843. In 1851 they were living at Polebrook where Reuben was a school master and Fanny a school mistress. They continued to live at Polebrook. Reuben died in the spring of 1880 aged sixty-two. By 1891 Fanny, a widow, lived on her own along North Street. Ten years later Fanny was an inmate at Latham's Alms-houses along North Street she died during 1904 aged eighty-six.

Reuben and Ann's son Elmer married Sarah Elizabeth Hodson during 1850. By 1851 Elmer, a cooper, and Sarah lived along Drumming Well Yard with their seven-month old daughter Rhoda.

At the time of the 1861 census Elmer King was a cooper and innkeeper living along New Street with Sarah and their family, Elmer, John Nathaniel, William Henry and Charles. Hannah Marshall aged twelve from Oundle was a general servant and Mary Strickland from Peterborough was visiting the family. In 1871 Elmer and Sarah continued to live along New Street at the White Hart where Elmer was the innkeeper. Their children at home were John Nathaniel a clerk, William Henry, Charles Francis and Mary Jane all attended school. Sarah Elizabeth died in 1879 aged fifty-one. In 1881 Elmer, a widower, lived along North Street with his family where he worked as a cooper. Nathaniel was an ironmonger's assistant; William was a grocer's assistant and Charles was a bookseller's assistant. Mary stayed at home and was the house keeper.

Obituary – We have to record the death of Mr Elmer King, of Oundle, which took place on Monday the 26th September, the deceased being 64 years of age. He had been a member of the St Peter's church choir for the past 53 years. *Northampton Mercury 8 October 1887*

Elmer and Sarah's son William Henry married Catherine Chew during 1889 in Oundle. Catherine was the daughter of William and Frances Chew from Polebrook. By 1891 William Henry, a grocer and tobacconist, and Catherine were living with John Chew of the same occupation along the Market Place in Oundle. John Chew was Catherine's brother. Elizabeth Fellows aged seventeen from Stoke Doyle was their general servant. William Henry died in 1893 aged thirty-four.

Elmer and Sarah's son Nathaniel was an ironmonger lodging with Eliza Dakin along North Street during 1891. He married Flora Agnes Storey during 1894 in Oundle. Flora was the daughter of Elijah and Anne Storey who lived along the Market Place in Oundle.

We regret to record the death of Mr Nat King (son of the late Mr Elmer King of Oundle) who died in London on Sunday last. The deceased married the eldest daughter of Mr E. Storey who is left with one son to mourn their loss. The deceased was well known in Oundle where he spent his early years. His age would be about fifty. *Peterborough Advertiser 23 April 1910.*

In 1911 Flora Agnes, a widow, was living at 28 Seward Road Hanwell in Middlesex with her son Victor Gerald aged fifteen, a printer's apprentice.

William and Mary's son Elmer George married Anna Elizabeth Pitts during 1870. Anna was the second daughter of William and Mary Pitts from Church Street in Warmington. William Pitts was a pianoforte tuner. In 1871 they had made their home along New Street in Oundle. By 1881 Elmer George King, a tailor, and Anna had moved to North Street with their family Jessie, Laura, Percy, Ethel and Francis. By 1891 Elmer and Anna lived along St Osyths lane with their children. Laura Pitts King was a pupil teacher as was Percy Elmer King, Ethel and Francis attended school. At the time of the 1901 census Elmer, a journeyman tailor and musician, his wife Anna and their daughter Ethel lived along South Street in Hayden Terrace.

OBITUARY – We regret to record the death of Mrs E. G. King, wife of Mr King, of Hayden-terrace. Deceased passed away on Monday at Stamford, where she had been staying for some time with her daughter. *Northampton Mercury 18 May 1906*

In 1911 Mary Ann King aged sixty-two was a music trader and teacher living at Hayden House along West Street. Her widowed brother Elmer George was a retired tailor and lived with Mary. Elmer George died during the winter of 1913 aged seventy.

FUNERAL OF AN OLD MUSICIAN – The interment of Mr Elmer George King, the old townsman and musician, took place in the Oundle Cemetery, the officiating clergyman being Rev. W. Smalley Law. The mourners were Mr Percy Elmer King (Axminster), son; Mrs Shortland (Woking), Mrs Houghton (Earls Barton), daughters, Miss King (Haydn House, Oundle), sister; Mr Houghton (son-in-law); Miss Maggie King (niece); Mr N.E. Dixon, Mr Hatch. There were a large number of beautiful wreaths. *Northampton Mercury 2 January 1914*

Reuben and Ann's son Francis never married. At the time of the 1851 census he was living in the School house attached to the chapel in the Hamlet of Ashton. Francis was a school master. In 1861, Francis had moved to Oundle, he was living along the Market Place on the East Side where he was an organist and professor of music. By 1871 Francis had moved to West Street where he stayed for the rest of his life. He employed Jane Garn as a domestic housekeeper. Francis

Brockley, a pianoforte tuner from London was visiting Francis. Ten years later Francis had Henry Alfred Walker, a pianoforte tuner visiting from Northumberland and Lucy Haynes from Polebrook was general servant to Francis. In 1891 Francis was an organist and teacher of music, still living along West Street in Hayden House with his nieces Mary aged forty-one a teacher of music and Pearl aged eleven both born in Oundle. By 1901 Francis was shown as a professor of music. His niece Mary Ann King was a teacher of music, his niece Clara Thurlby from Oundle was a domestic housekeeper. Mary Ann Laxton from Thurning was a general servant.

Death of Dr King of Oundle – We regret to record the death of Mr Francis King, Mus. Doc. who passed away at his residence Haydn House, Oundle, on Saturday after a long illness. Dr King, who was for 53 years' organist of the Parish church, showed signs of musical talent very early in life, and at the age of ten was not only able to play the piano, but also to compose music. As a boy, he appeared in the Oundle Town Band more than 60 years ago, and among the interesting experiences he was wont to recall were occasions when at Parliamentary contests at Northampton, the band was engaged to play for three weeks at a time for 10s a member and extras. Master Frank alternated with the flute and the drum, and was in addition a bellringer. When hardly out of his teens he opened a school in Ashton, being a proficient penman, writing a beautiful hand, and at one time had about thirty scholars, sons of farmers and other middle class patrons. Afterwards he was appointed Writing Master to the Latham's hospital (Blue coat) school, a position he held for many years, in fact till about fifteen years since, when the masterships, for there was also a resident master, were withdrawn. Appointed organist on the resignation of Miss Reasby, one of the deceased gentleman's greatest ambitions was to attain his jubilee in the post, and in this he was gratified. About five years ago there being signs of failing health, he retired, and was then presented by the parishioners with a purse containing nearly 100 sovereigns. From that time the deceased was more or less unwell, but occasionally rallied and seemed much better till last week, when there were unmistakable signs that the inevitable end was approaching. Dr King was a fine player on the organ, piano, viola and cello, the viola being his favourite instrument, especially in chamber music, of which he was very fond. He was for some year's music master at the Oundle School, and some thirty or forty years ago was conductor of the flourishing Choral Society. The deceased gentleman was also a talented composer. He was buried on 19 June 1901 in Oundle cemetery. *Northampton Mercury 21 June 1901*

At the County Court on Monday before Mr E.P. Monkton, Deputy Judge - A Phonograph – Miss Mary Ann King, music warehouse, Oundle, v William Brackley snr, labourer of Ashton. – Claim for £1 3s 9d., balance of account for phonograph. – The defendant's wife appeared and admitted she ordered the instrument for her son to amuse him, as he was ill, and he had since died. The original piece was £3. 0s 3d. The instalments paid were from the son's wages which were allowed him during his illness by the Hon. C.N. Rothschild. The instrument had since been sold for 10s. – An order was made for 2s. a month. *Northampton Mercury 19 November 1909*

We regret to record the death of another old resident, Miss King, Haydn Terrace, which occurred in the early hours of Sunday morning. The deceased lady, who was 74 years of age, was the niece of Dr King, for many years' organist at the parish church. Miss King had been a great sufferer the last few months. The interment took place in Oundle cemetery on Wednesday. *Peterborough Advertiser 7th August 1920*

Alfred King from Wiltshire.

Alfred King, a bookseller's assistant was the son of Alfred and Ann from Chippenham, Alfred senior was a retired jeweller. Alfred King of Oundle married Louisa Long, only daughter of L. Long Esq., of Richmond Surrey, on 15th July 1862 at All Saint's church in Norwood. *Stamford Mercury 25 July 1862.*

Alfred King, a printer and bookseller/master, who employed one man and four boys, and his wife Louisa, lived along New Street Oundle in 1871. Their children were Clara Letitia Dyson King aged seven, William Timbre King aged five, Fanny Louisa King aged four and Maud Isabel King aged one. Betsey Lovell aged forty-six from Cotterstock was their general domestic servant, Emma Cottingham aged fifteen from Glapthorne was their nursemaid. In 1881 Alfred King, the bookseller and printer continued to live along New Street with his wife Louisa and three of his children Clara, William and Maud. Betsy Lovell was still their general servant and was joined by Sarah Ann Walton from Finedon. Louisa died during 1889 aged fifty-two. By 1891 Alfred King, was a bookseller and printer also a stationer living along New Street. His daughters at home were Clara, Fanny and Maud. Alfred's sister Charlotte King was also living with them. Caroline Drinkwater from Gloucestershire was their general servant.

KING – Feb. 24 at Oundle, Northamptonshire, Alfred King, formerly of Chippenham, Wilts, aged 98. *London Evening Standard 27 February 1891*

Ten years later Charlotte's brother' Alfred, a widow, who was still living along New Street continued with his bookseller's business. His daughter Clara Letitia was possibly running the home; Maud Isabel was a school governess. Charlotte Timbrell King lived by her own means in a house along Station Road in Oundle. In 1911 Charlotte's brother' Alfred, a printer bookseller, continued living along New Street with his unmarried daughters Clara, and Maud who was a nursery governess. Eva Jane Ellis from Warmington was a general servant for Alfred. Charlotte Timbrell King, aged seventy-six, was a boarder with William McMichael, a coal merchant who lived in the Tudor House along North Street with his wife and children.

Mr Alfred King, one of the oldest tradesmen of Oundle, died on Monday at the age of 86. *Northampton Mercury 6 October 1922*

OLD BUSINESS CHANGES HANDS – Widespread interest will be aroused by the announcement when it is officially made, that the well-known and old established business of Alfred King & Son New Street Oundle, is to change hands as from Monday next. Miss King, its kindly septuagenarian proprietor, is going into retirement, and it will be carried on by Mr V.E. Leayton, with the present capable and loyal staff. The business was established in 1861 by Mr Alfred King, Miss King's father, who died eleven years ago. It has always occupied the old and picturesque premises in which it is conducted. It was originally acquired from Mr Todd, who worked in a bank and who was, therefore, unable to devote undivided attention to it. Miss King has lived there all her life. Although her well-earned retirement means something of a wrench it has its compensations. She is going to live with her sister in a charming house on the Hurn, and on Wednesday was busily engaged in choosing the papers for decoration. The business which includes stationery, books, printing and fancy goods has long enjoyed a close connection with the school. Both Miss King and her father have long been bibliophiles and could speak with authority upon rare editions. Townspeople will wish Miss King a happy retirement and at the same time congratulate Mr Leayton upon his enterprise. *Peterborough Advertiser 31 August 1934*

The LEATON/LEAYTON families

John Leaton married Jane Prentice during 1753, they both came from Oundle. Their family included Zachariah, Mary, Daniel, Jane, Elisabeth, John 1, John 2, Martha, Thomas, and Sarah. Zachariah, Daniel, John 1 and 2, and Martha died in childhood. John's wife Jane died in 1797 aged sixty-seven. John died in 1814 aged eighty-three.

Thomas Leaton married Catherine Cunnington at Benefield in 1800. Their children were William c.1801, George c.1803, Henry c.1805, John c.1808, and Thomas 1822.

In 1851 Thomas senior, a widow, was living at the Wheat Sheaf Inn at Upper Benefield where he was a pauper carpenter. Living with him was his son Thomas, daughter-in-law Lucy and his grandsons Thomas six, John four and George two. Thomas senior died during 1853.

Thomas and Catherine's son Henry has been difficult to trace through the census years. In 1861 Henry Leaton aged fifty-five was a shoe-maker he lodged with Thomas Allen an innkeeper and blacksmith at the Turks Head in New Street, Oundle. Henry died at the Union house in Oundle during 1873 aged sixty-seven.

Thomas and Catherine's son George married Eliza Wyman from Oundle towards the end of 1840. In 1841 George, a butcher, and Eliza lived along West Street. By 1851 George and Eliza had moved to Benefield Road with their children John Thomas aged nine, Catherine aged seven, Mary five and Joseph was three. George died in 1860 aged fifty-six. In 1861 Eliza worked as a charwoman and lived along West Street in the British School Yard. Her family were Mary aged fifteen who worked as a servant, Joseph aged thirteen a farm servant and Sarah Ann was six years old. George and Mary's daughter Mary died towards the end of the year in 1861 aged sixteen. Eliza married William Walker in 1868. By 1871 they continued to live at Eliza's home, William was a Chelsea pensioner born in Rutland. Eliza's son Joseph an agricultural labourer and daughter Sarah Ann a 'domestic servant out of place' also lived at home. Eliza died in 1875 aged sixty-three.

George and Eliza's daughter Catherine, aged sixteen, was in the union workhouse at the time of the 1861 census. By 1871 she was still in the workhouse, as a farm servant. Ten years later Catherine was a general servant and shown on the census as an 'imbecile', she died during 1888 aged forty-five.

In 1881 George and Eliza's sons John Leaton aged forty-eight and Joseph thirty-three were general labourers lodging at 'The George Inn' along Glapthorne Road on Tilley Hill with the innkeeper/gardener William Hunt. I have had problems finding John and Joseph Leaton on the 1891 census. Joseph died in 1898 aged fifty-one.

George Leaton from Benefield

George, son of Thomas and Hannah, lived with his wife Mary along West Street in 1841 with their family, Mary thirteen, Thomas eleven, George nine, Ann seven, Hannah four and William was one-year-old. Hannah died during 1849 aged twelve. By 1851 George and Mary were still along West Street with their family, William, Margaret eight, Henry three and Herbert was ten months old. Their daughter Ann was a general servant for Richard Price a saddler who lived along New Street. Margaret died during 1859 aged sixteen. In 1861 George, a butcher lived along the south side of West Street with Mary and their ten-year-old son Herbert. Ten years later George aged seventy worked as a butcher journeyman; he continued to live along West Street with his wife Mary and their daughter Mary aged thirty who worked as a barmaid. George died in the June of 1882 aged eighty-one, Mary died the next month aged seventy-five.

George and Mary's son Thomas was a butcher's apprentice in 1871 living in Southwark London.

Charlotte Layton aged seventy-two, born in Oundle, was shown on the 1871 census as an agricultural labourer's widow. She was a patient in the Parson Latham hospital in North Street for eighteen women. Nothing else can be found for her.

William Leayton from Uppingham

William Edwin Leayton married Mary Ward during 1847 in the Uppingham district. By 1851 William Edwin was lodging with John and Christina Wilson at Hog Ley in Kettering where he was an upholsterer journeyman. His children Orlando aged two and William aged one month, were shown as lodging with William and Mary Cooper in Bedford. In 1857 they had a son William Lacey he died during the same year. William Edwin died in 1861 just before the census was recorded. At the time of the 1861 census Mary Leayton, an upholsterer's widow lived in the Blackwell's Yard along St Osyths lane with her family. Orlando was a tailor's apprentice, Montague nine and John aged seven attended school and the youngest child was Eliza aged two. Priscilla Sharpe, shown as a widow and mother in law, who at the age of seventy-one was an upholsteress, lived with Mary Leayton. In 1871 Mary was living along St Osyths Lane in Danfords Yard, she continued with her work as an upholsteress. Living with Mary were her sons Orlando a tailor and John Sharpe Leayton a printer's apprentice, her daughter Eliza Priscilla was twelve years old.

At the Workmen's Club and Institute, Mr Leayton was appointed secretary and librarian, in the place of Mr F.B. Dixon resigned. *Northampton Mercury 30 April 1881*

The Oundle Star Minstrels, just formed, have elected Mr O. Leayton and Mr E.H. Munds corner-men. Mr C. Maddison leader of the band, Mr Browning pianist, and Mr F. Garner hon. sec. *Stamford Mercury 13 September 1889*

The Oundle Star Minstrels made their first appearance in public on Tuesday evening last in the Town-hall, Oundle. The first part consisted of sentimental and comic songs, and the second was of a miscellaneous character. Mr O. Leayton, who is a versatile comedian, and whose local allusions are very smart made a clever "Bones," while Mr E. H. Munds as "Tambo" was excellent, and Mr J. M. Underwood was emcient "interlocutor." The comic sketch Black Justice was an immense success, the characters being well sustained by Messrs. O Leayton, F.W. Garner, J. M. Underwood, E. H. Munds, J. Hinman and G. Berridge. The violin playing of Mr C. Maddison was a musical treat. The entertainment concluded with 'Brannigan's Band, with walk-round. The song was taken by Mr. F. W. Garner. The Troupe were attired in grotesque costumes. Owing to the success of the entertainment it was repeated last (Thursday) night. (All wording as per report) *Stamford Mercury 13 December 1889*

By 1891 Orlando Leayton, at the age of forty-two, was a county court bailiff and lived along North Street. His mother Mary lived with him and was shown as a housekeeper. Orlando married Martha Searle during 1895 in Whittlesey where Martha lived. Martha was the daughter of Tom and Harriett Searle who lived along Gracious Street in Whittlesey. In 1901 Orlando, a bill porter, and Martha were living along North Street in Oundle with their children Victor Edwin aged five and Gladys Lillian aged two years.

Included in a report in the Northampton Mercury dated 1 March 1901 titled - Proclaiming the King at Oundle where the town was bedecked with flags and banners was a report of all who attended including Mr O Leayton Town Crier.

On April 24th, at Walsall, at the home of her daughter, Mary widow of the late William Edwin Leayton, of Oundle, in her 82nd year. *Grantham Journal 28 April 1906.*

The Northampton Mercury had a section for children called The Uncle Dick Society which promoted to be kind to birds and not to be untruthful. In the issue dated 1 July 1910 was an entry as follows – "Mustn't Touch – Dear Uncle I am sending you a very pretty postcard, feeling sure you will like it, for I think it a suitable one for your album of our admirable Society. Mother is very fond of the little birds. There is an old wall in our yard and some sparrows have built their nest there, and it is so interesting to watch the mother feeding them. Love to auntie and yourself. – From your loving Niece Gladys Leayton (No2427) North Street Oundle. – I think the postcard Gladys sends is the very prettiest I have ever seen, and I shall prize it very much. It shows a little girl of two or three standing on a chair peering into a bush at a little nest with two lovely eggs in it. She is so pleased, and looks at the eggs and nest with simple wonder. It says underneath, 'Mustn't Touch' which is just what the Uncle Society stands for." Gladys' brother Victor Edwin became a Captain in the group on 27 May 1910.

By 1911 Orlando had changed his occupation and was a news correspondent, he and Martha and their daughters were continuing to live along North Street. Victor aged fifteen was a clerk in a coal merchants and Gladys aged twelve attended school.

Owing to the slippery state of the paths last week several accidents occurred. Mrs O. Leayton cut her arm. *Northampton Mercury 26 January 1912*

RAVENSTHORPE – WEDDING -The Wedding of Mr V E Leayton, only son of Mr and Mrs O Leayton, of Oundle, and Miss Ivy Edmunds, second daughter of Mr and Mrs Edmunds, of Ravensthorpe, took place at Ravensthorpe Parish church on Monday.

The presents included a silver tea service to the bride from the Cotterstock District Nursing Association, and a cake basket and set of tea knives to the bridegroom from the choir of St Peter's Oundle. Mr and Mrs Leayton will live in Market Place Oundle. This is a section of the report from *Northampton Mercury 7 September 1923*

OUNDLE – Postal Workers Dinner – Oundle postal workers, with their wives and friends and a number of Peterborough colleagues, had dinner together at the Talbot Hotel on Saturday evening, Mr H.H. Markham presiding. Reminiscences of the days when Oundle had only a very small office, proved very interesting, and Mr Orlando Leayton told how, fifty years ago, before postal staffs had fixed holidays, he acted for a day as letter carrier in order that the postman could go to London. Mr Leayton occupied the greater part of the day in the delivery of a little over 400 letters and newspapers. An excellent musical programme was gone. *Northampton Mercury 22 February 1929*

OBITUARY – Much regret has been caused by the death of Mrs O. Leayton, who passed away at Northampton Hospital on Tuesday. Mrs Leayton, who was 65 had been ailing for some time and a few days ago an operation, which was successful, was performed, but complications arose. There is sincere sympathy for the husband, son and daughter. *Northampton Mercury 26 February 1932.*

Mr Orlando Leayton, who has been town crier at Oundle for 35 years, has resigned owing to advancing age. He is 84. *Northampton Mercury 24 June 1932*

Orlando took part in the community in many ways – Veteran Fireman – Tilley Hill Sick Club – Secretary of the Oundle Quoit club – Brother O Leayton of the Loyal Providence Lodge of Oddfellows – Secretary of the Athletic Club.

FAMILIAR OUNDLE FIGURE – DEATH OR MR ORLANDO LEAYTON – CHORISTER FOR 65 YEARS -The death of Mr Orlando Leayton, of Oundle, believed to be the oldest Press correspondent in the country, and one of the oldest town criers, occurred at Grantham on Monday. Mr Leayton, who was 84 years old, went for a holiday to his brother's home in Grantham last Christmas, and was taken ill shortly afterwards. For a great number of years Mr Leayton was town crier at Oundle, and resigned from the position only a year ago. His uniform, similar to that of a naval officer, was familiar to all towns-people and visitors, and Mr Leayton was extremely popular by reason of his courtesy and affability. Mr Leayton was a native of Rutland, but he had lived in Oundle for over 70 years. He was a member of the Oundle Parish Church choir for 65 years, and served in the Fire Brigade for 35 years. He was a well-known Oddfellow (Manchester Unity), and helped to found many lodges. He was also an authority on the history of Oundle. He was a billposter for 40 years, and he once estimated that he had walked 70,000 miles during that time. Mr Leayton's wife died about two years ago, and there is one son Mr V.E. Leayton. *Northampton Mercury and Herald 19 May 1933.*

(Slight difference in Mrs Leaytons year of death according to the report.)

'TYPEWRITERS TODAY are almost a necessity for business and private use and one typewriter, the 'Remington' is of an outstanding quality as will be seen by an announcement in this issue. Mr. V. E. Leayton is making a special window display of Remington's and they are worth seeing. *Peterborough Advertiser Friday July 27th 1934.*

The LEIGH families

The family name of Leigh was very popular in the villages surrounding Oundle, Barnwell, Polebrook, Thurning, Tansor, Nassington and Fotheringhay.

At Oundle, on Sunday last, Mr Saml. George Leigh, Grocer and tea dealer, of Oundle, to Miss Tookey, daughter of Mrs Tookey of the same place. Letitia Tookey was the daughter of John and Rebecca from Oundle. *Stamford Mercury 6 September 1822*

SAMUEL GEORGE LEIGH, Printer, Bookseller, Stationer, and Account Book Manufacturer, Oundle – Begs most respectfully to return his grateful Acknowledgments to his Friends and the Public, for the very flattering Support and Encouragement he has experienced in this as well as the other Departments of his Concern, and assuring them that every possible Attention shall be paid to whatever Commands they may continue to favour him with, hopes by reasonable Charges and expeditious Execution, to merit a Continuance of the same ; also takes this Opportunity of informing them that he has recently purchased a large Assortment of PAPERS, PLAIN and FANCY STATIONERY, and Articles generally useful for Professional and Mercantile Purposes, which he can offer them at reduced and extremely reasonable Prices. S.G.L. has also made an Addition of about 300 Volumes to his Circulating Library, of the most approved and popular Works, recently published, consisting of History, Biography, Travels, Novels, Tales, Romances, &c.&c. including the Works of Scott, Radcliffe, Byron, Galt, De Genlis, Porter, Edgeworth, Rolls, Maturin, Opie, Roche, Latham, Lewis, Morgan, Moore, Crabbe, &c.&c. The third Part of his Catalogue may be had in a few Days: he also intends adding as they are published, Works of the same Class. Engraving, Copper-plate and Letter-press Printing, neatly and expeditiously executed. *Books neatly and elegantly bound.* A great Variety of new and second-hand Musical Instruments; new and popular Music at Half Price. An extensive Selection of the most modern and fashionable Paper Hangings, Borders, &c. Transparent Blinds, &c. *Northampton Mercury 4 November 1826*

Samuel George Leigh's business ended in 1831 when unfortunately, he became bankrupt. A full report of all Samuel's assets can be found in the Northampton Mercury dated 15 January 1831. The report also includes – 'The spacious premises, in which the Business of Grocer and General shopkeeper has been carried on more than half a century.'

In 1841 Samuel Leigh, a grocer, and Letitia lived along West Street with their family John Johnson fourteen, Louisa Letitia thirteen, Mary Rebecca twelve, Isabella eight, and Walter Thomas was four years old. Letitia's mother Rebecca Tookey also lived with them. At the time of the 1851 census Samuel had changed his occupation to a surgeon/dentist (Practising as Dentist) he and Letitia had moved with their family to 99 Portland Crescent in Leeds. John was also a dentist and Walter attended school. Samuel was born in Brigstock.

Enquiries having been made in the neighbourhood of Northampton relating to the relatives of the late William Leigh, Esq. of Overton, Hampshire, any needful information may be obtained of Mr S. G. Leigh, dentist, Portland-crescent, Leeds.

In 1861 Walter was Samuel and Letitia's only son living at home, he was a bookseller. Ten years later living with Samuel and Letitia was Louisa Laxton aged twenty-one. Louisa was the daughter of James and Hannah who lived along Stoke Road in Oundle. Samuel and Letitia continued living along Portland Crescent in 1881. Samuel died later in that year aged seventy-nine. In 1891 Letitia was living on her own means and had Alice Fletcher, a nineteen-year-old from Rotherham as her servant. Letitia died in 1898 aged ninety-four in Leeds.

May 29, aged 44, at Melbourne, Australia, from fracture of the base of the skull through a fall, William Tookey Leigh, eldest son of S. G. Leigh, dentist, Portland-crescent, Leeds, formerly of Oundle Northamptonshire. *Northampton Mercury 21 August 1869*

Samuel and Letitia's son Walter Thomas married Hannah Smith at Leeds in 1862.

FIREWORKS from One Shilling per gross WALTER T. LEIGH'S Stationer, CAMDEN HOUSE, 145 Woodhouse Lane Leeds. *Yorkshire Post and Leeds Intelligencer 30 October 1869*

In 1871 Walter and Hannah were living along Woodhouse Lane with their family, Percival, William, Walter, and Hannah Letitia. Walter was a bookseller and tobacconist and was recorded as partially blind. Ten years later they were at the same address with their five sons and four daughters. The oldest child was Percival Tookey Leigh sixteen then William fourteen, Walter Smith Leigh twelve, Hannah Letitia ten, Ethel Mary nine, Herbert W seven, Emma K five, Thomas Wilson Leigh three and Margeuretta Tookey Leigh was one-year-old. Walter and Hannah had moved by 1891 to Brookfield Terrace in Headingley with Burley near Leeds. Their five children at home were William and Walter both dentist assistants, Ethel was nineteen, Herbert a warehouseman, then there was Thomas who attended school. Walter died in 1900 aged sixty-three.

Walter and Hannah's son Percival was a dentist lodging with a family in Lambeth during 1891. Percival married Blanche Legat Whitaker during 1898 in the Ecclesall Bierlow district. By 1901 they were living at 55 Headingley Lane Headingley near Leeds. Eliza Ann and Susan Russell from Filey were domestic servants for the family. In 1911 Percival and Blanche had moved to 6 Portland Crescent in Leeds. The census records show that they had been married for eleven years and had no children. Percival Tookey Leigh was a Lord Mayor and Alderman of Leeds in 1935. www.leeds.gov.uk *Lord Mayors and Aldermen of Leeds since 1626*

Robert and Harriet Leigh's family

In 1841 Robert Leigh born in Thurning c.1800, an agricultural labourer and his wife Harriet born in Titchmarsh c.1800 were living along Benefield Road with their children John ten, William eight, Catherine five and Robert two years old. By 1851 they continued to live along Benefield Road, William and Robert were agricultural labourers like their father, their other children were Catherine, Rebecca five and Thomas two years old. All their children were born in Oundle apart from William who was born in Titchmarsh. Robert senior died during 1856. Catherine died during 1860. In 1861 Harriet, a widow aged fifty-six, worked as a spinner, her son Thomas was a labourer. They lived next door to William and Eliza Wyles along Benefield Road. Harriet married Charles Bourne who also lived along Benefield Road during 1864. (In 1861 Charles was shown on the census as a widower and worked as a contractor. Living with him was his daughter Maria also a widow and her four children). By 1868 Charles Bourne had died. At the time of the 1871 census Harriet was living alone along Benefield Road. Harriet died in 1875 aged seventy-four.

Robert and Harriet's son Robert was lodging with John and Jane Davies at their home in St Botolph Aldersgate in East London during 1861. Robert was a porter. John Davies was a gold and silver repairer. Robert married Ann Elizabeth Callender during 1862 in the Clerkenwell district, Middlesex. In 1871 Robert and Ann were living in Bermondsey, they had a son Herbert, he was eight. Roberts' brother Thomas, a porter, also lived with them. By 1881 Robert was a widower, Ann died during 1874. Living with Robert was his sons Herbert a butcher and Frank aged eight. Thomas Leigh continued to live with them. At the time of the 1891 census Robert a wharf labourer only had his son Frank at home, he was a butcher.

Robert and Harriet's daughter Rebecca married George Wyles during 1870 he was a shoemaker. In 1871 they were living along West Street in the Shoemakers shop with George's brother William also a shoemaker. Ten years later George was described as a shoe maker master, they had a large family. Eliza Eleanor nine, Louie Margaret seven, Ada Leigh five, Charles William three, George Percy two and Arthur Edward two months. By 1891 George was a boot and shoemaker, he and Rebecca's family had grown. Their children were Eleanor nineteen, Margaret fourteen a schoolteacher, Ada fifteen a draper's apprentice, Charles thirteen, George twelve, Arthur ten, Alfred eight, Willie seven, and Robert three were all scholars. In 1901 their children at home were George a post office telegraphist, Alfred a grocer's assistant, Willie a boot and shoe maker at home with his father then Robert the youngest was not working. (See Wyles family details)

The LIMMAGE families

Researching the Limmage families has brought to light many variances in their birth years and to name changes.

John Limmage born in Washingley c.1823 married Sarah Ann Atkins during 1849. Sarah was born in Elton c.1827. Their family included John c.1850, Ann c.1852 died 1853, Alice Ann c.1854 and Arthur c.1864 died 1865. At the time of the 1861 census John and Sarah were living along Duck Street in Elton with their children John eleven, Ann (Alice) six, James three and George two all born in Elton. By 1871 John Leimage and his wife Hannah (name change) had moved and were living along West Street in Oundle with their children, James, George, Mary seven and Emily five, they were born in Elton and William the youngest aged two was born in Oundle. Their son John was lodging with a family in Wellingborough where he was an ironstone labourer. John and Sarah Ann had moved to Drumming Well Yard just off West Street in 1881 where John was a general labourer. Their son James was a general labourer, Mary and Emily were fields-women then their other children were William twelve, Edward eight and seven-year-old Alfred (born as Albert Leimage).

James Limage, Oundle, was charged with assaulting and beating his father, John Limage, on the 15th inst. – Prosecutor, who appeared with a disfigured face, said he had been in bed three hours, when he heard prisoner quarrelling with his sister. He had knocked her down, and on-going to her protection, prisoner knocked witness down, and kicked him on his right eye. Prisoner was further charged with assaulting and beating Ann King. – As prisoner had been previously convicted, he was now sentenced for the first offence to two months, and for the second to six months' imprisonment. *Northampton Mercury 20 January 1883*

Emily Limage was fined 2s. 6d. and 10s. 6d. costs for striking Lucy Graythorne. *Northampton Mercury 7 July 1883*

John Limmage senior died during 1884 aged fifty-five.

Mary Limmage was charged with assaulting Eliz. Clarke on the 9th inst. This was a neighbours' quarrel, both parties living in Drumming Well-yard, Oundle. Defendant was ordered to pay 12s. *Stamford Mercury 23 April 1886*

INQUEST – An inquest was held on Friday last at the Nag's Head Inn, before Mt J.T. Parker (coroner) on the body of the infant child of Mary Limmage, single woman of Oundle. Sarah Anness deposed that she was fetched at half past ten, on the 5th inst., to go to Mrs Limmage's house in Drumming Well-yard, as she, (Mrs Limmage) was going out to see her other daughter. She told witness her daughter Mary was near her confinement. On the following morning witness sent for the doctor, but he was from home. Soon after she was confined. The child was very black. Witness again sent for the doctor, who had not returned. The child died on Thursday morning about twelve o'clock. As far as the witness knew it died from natural causes. Alice Ann King gave corroborative evidence. Mr C.N. Elliott, M.D., deposed that he was not engaged to attend this case beforehand, and was engaged at Elton when sent for. He went to Mrs Limmage's house about twelve o'clock on Thursday morning and found the child was dead. He examined the body carefully, but found no marks. The cause of death was asphyxia, which is natural with newly-born children. The jury returned a verdict of "Death by natural causes." *Northampton Mercury 15 September 1888.*

By 1891 Sarah, a widow, was living along North Street where she was a dressmaker. Her sons George, Edward and Alfred (Albert) lived with their mother and were all labourers'. At the time of the 1901 census Sarah was living on own means supported by her family along North Street. George was a horse-keeper for a carter and Edward was a drayman for a coal merchant both lived with their mother, also Annie Limmage, aged thirteen, granddaughter to Sarah lived with them.

John and Sarah's daughter Emily married Thomas William Smith, son of Thomas (John) and Sarah from Wadenhoe, on 8th February 1891. At the time of the 1891 census they were living along North Street with their daughter Annie aged two years. Thomas was a labourer born in Wadenhoe c.1856. In 1901 Emily, a widow was a charring domestic and lived in Hawes Yard along West Street with her daughter Emily aged nine and her son Thomas Edward Limmage aged six.

Emily, widow, married John Robert Cranfield during the winter of 1901. By 1911 they were living at 11 South Street in Peterborough with Emily's daughters' Annie Limmage a general servant and Maud

Smith who did factory work, also Emily's granddaughter Dorothy Limmage aged one.

Emily's daughter Annie married John Leonard Tate during 1913. They had two daughters Margaret and Elsie and a son Leonard.

John and Annie Tate (nee Limmage)
Photograph courtesy of Linda Rowton.

John and Sarah's son William married Elizabeth Dunkley at the end of the year in 1890. By 1891 they lived a few doors away from William's mother with their daughter Kaley aged three.

Petty Sessions – Elizabeth Limage, married woman, Oundle, was brought up in custody charged with stealing six shillings, the property of Caroline Abbott. The procecutrix said on the 15th the prisoner came to her to fetch some beer, which she did. She had 6s. 6d. in a tin box in the house in a cupboard on the stairs, and she put some money in it after going to the post. She was away from the house about five minutes when fetching beer. After drinking the beer prisoner went home, and when prosecutrix subsequently went to the cupboard there was no box or money to be found. Nobody other than the prisoner had been in the house in the meantime. She went to Mrs Limage and accused her of taking it. This was met with a denial, and Mrs Abbotts husband informed the police. When under cross-examination by the clerk of the court prosecutrix fainted, and had to be taken out of court. P.C. Lynam proved receiving information of the robbery, and

157

of informing the prisoner that she was suspected of stealing the money. After the usual caution prisoner said "I know nothing of the money I never had it." She then cried and said "I cannot think what made me do it; I will never do so again: I was behind with my rent and took the money to pay my rent with. I took the money out of the box and put the box in an ash tin in the street." The box had not been found. Prisoner continued: "I paid Mr Todd 4s. 4d. out of the money for my rent, I bought a pound of sugar, half a pound of currants, and two eggs at Chew and Kings; some writing paper and postage stamps, and this is the remainder of the money (producing 1s. 2d.)" He then brought her to the station and locked her up. Prisoner fainted at this point in the evidence, but on recovering elected to be dealt with summarily and was fined 5s. with 15s. costs. A month was allowed. *Northampton Mercury 18 May 1894*

In 1901 William, a brewers' drayman, and Elizabeth lived at 18 Inkerman Place with their four children Albert eighteen and Cecil seventeen, both general labourers, Kate fourteen and John eight years old.

In 1891 Cecil Clare Dunkley aged seven was shown on the census as the adopted son of John and Julia Dunkley who lived at Woodwalton.

Elizabeth's son Cecil Dunkley committed suicide by hanging in 1903 aged nineteen. Cecil was not able to do anything owing to an injury sustained over six years ago by being run over. He was a cripple, and at times he suffered a good deal of pain. On Saturday afternoon witness left him in bed whilst she went shopping. She was away 20 minutes and on her return deceased was hanging from the bannister. She ran for assistance. Deceased was undressed. He never threatened to take his life, and was generally cheerful. Deceased was in great pain on Saturday. Dr C.N. Elliott, of Oundle, deposed that he had attended Dunkley since a wagon went over him six years ago. His injuries were incurable, and he suffered great pain at times. Nothing could be done for him. His sufferings might have caused him to be not responsible for his actions at times. The full report can be seen in the *Northampton Mercury 11 September 1903*.

In 1911 William and Elizabeth continued to live at 18 Inkerman Place with their son John Edward, a maltsters' labourer, also Albert Hunt Limmage and Thomas Edward Smith both shown as relatives.

William and Elizabeth's son Alfred Hunt Limmage married Gertrude M Underwood during 1922.

John and Sarah's son Albert married Emily Francis from Nassington during 1896. At the time of the 1901 census they were living at Setchell's Yard in Oundle with their children Frances May aged two and Kate two months old. Sarah Francis aged fifteen, shown as Emma's sister, was living with them and worked as a domestic housemaid. Albert was recorded as Alfred while living with his parents. Emma was born as Emily and liked to change her name. By 1911 Albert and Emma had moved to Church Lawford in Rugby where Albert was a cowman on a farm. Their children still at home were Frances May, Kate Elizabeth, Albert Thomas aged six and Edith Harriet one-year-old.

In 1911 Edward Limmage aged forty-nine and Albert Limmage aged three were living with Samuel King and his wife Alice along Victoria Yard in Oundle. Albert was shown as nephew to Samuel and his Alice. (Edward was possibly the son of John and Sarah as in the early census years their ages varied quite a bit).

James Limage, son of James and Elizabeth from Washingley

James Limage married Sarah Ann Clark during 1872. They were living at Clements Gate Street in Diseworth in Derbyshire at the time of the 1881 census. James was a gamekeeper. James and Sarah had moved back to Washingley in 1891, and were still there in 1901. James was a gardener on a farm. In 1911 they lived at Lutton. It was recorded on the census James and Sarah had two children both of whom had died. James died in 1915 aged seventy and Sarah in 1918 aged seventy-one.

The MARLOW families

John Marlow married Lucy Blackwell during 1808 at Benefield. Their children were James Blackwell Marlow, William, Mary, John, Mary Blackwell Marlow, George and Ann.

In 1841 John c.1786, a groom, and Lucy Marlow c.1791 lived along Drum Well Lane near to West Street with their twins George and Ann aged ten. Their son William Marlow was a male servant for Thomas, a farmer, and Mary Wildash they lived in the Market Place.

John and Lucy's daughter Mary Blackwell Marlow married Robert Quincey during 1845. In 1851 they had three children George, William and Ann and were living with Robert's parents at Hemington. Mary Blackwell Quincey died during the summer of 1851.

John and Lucy were shown as living along Drumming Well Yard in 1851 where John was a hostler, their daughter Ann lived with them. Lucy died in 1857. By the time of the 1861 census John, widower, lived on his own along Shillibeers Yard in West Street.

In Laxton's Hospital, Oundle, on the 15th, John Marlow, aged 84. *Northampton Mercury 1869.*

John and Lucy's son George married Mary Ann Parish during 1856. By 1861 they were living along Harvey's New Road in Spalding. John was a groom and gardener.

John and Lucy's son James married Grace Rowell during 1838 in the St Ives district. Grace was born in Coppingford. In 1841 James, a gardener, and Grace, lived along Mill Lane with Elizabeth aged two and four-month-old William Rowell Marlow. By 1851 their family had increased, Elizabeth and William had been joined by George seven, Robert four, Sarah Ann two and one-year-old Rebecca. Ten years later, living at 14 Mill Lane was James and Grace with their family. George a general labourer, Robert a shoemaker, Sarah, Rebecca, Mary was eight and John aged five attended school. The youngest child was Alfred James aged one.

James and Grace's daughter Elizabeth married William Meacham in 1867.

In 1871 James and Grace's daughter Mary aged eighteen was a servant for Caroline Godfrey, widow, who was described on the census as a 'Gentlewoman'. Caroline lived along Benefield Road and was born in Nottinghamshire.

At the time of the 1871 census James and Grace had the following children at home Robert a bootmaker, Sarah and Rebecca were domestic servants, John was a tailors' apprentice and Alfred attended school.

At the Independent church, Oundle, on the 4th inst., James Cooper, of West Acre, Norfolk, to Rebecca Marlow, of the former place. *Stamford Mercury 15 December 1876.*

On the 1881 census James was shown as James Blackwell Marlow. Living at home with James and Grace was Sarah a parlour maid, Mary a needle woman and Alfred James a shoemaker. Grace Elizabeth Meacham aged five lived with them and was shown as their granddaughter. Grace was the daughter of William and Elizabeth and was born in Buckinghamshire.

James and Grace's daughter Sarah Ann married Edward Allen in St Albans Hertfordshire in 1886. By 1891 they were living along Old Road in St Albans with their two sons Alfred James Marlow Allen aged three and George Edward Marlow Allen was 2 months old. Edward was a railway labourer. In 1901 Edward, a mason's labourer, and Sarah had moved and were living at 12 Mill Lane in Oundle. They had another son Frank aged seven. In 1911 Edward was a labourer for a builder, he and Sarah Ann were still at 12 Mill Lane, Alfred was a general baker, George was a domestic gardener and Frank was a milk seller.

Mill Lane Oundle.
Photograph courtesy of Peterborough Images

Edward and Sarah's son Alfred James Marlow Allen married Ivy Eleanor M Langley during 1914. Ivy was the daughter of George and Sarah who lived at 20 Inkerman Place in 1911.

James and Grace's son Alfred James married Mary Jane Skinner in 1887. By 1901 they lived in one of the London cottages along West Street with Jennie Eva M thirteen, Amy Elizabeth nine, Elsie Rebecca six, and Grace Bessie aged four. They lived not far from William and Ruth Marlow. Jennie Eva died during 1904 aged sixteen. In 1911 Alfred, a town postman, and Mary Jane were living along Stoke Road with their three daughters. Amy Elizabeth was a dressmaker then Elsie Rebecca and Grace Bessie were shown on census as 'at home'. Alfred's sister' Mary lived with them and was a sempstress. Alfred was a keen gardener he was mentioned in the Northampton Mercury on many occasions as taking part in the horticultural shows put on by the Oddfellows of Oundle. He entered his begonia's geraniums, fuchsia's, calceolarias, petunias and many more.

Grace Bessie Marlow became a member of the Uncle Dick Society of the Northampton Mercury. It was listed in the 11 June 1909 issue, Grace was given the membership number 2599 – and was shown as living at Floral Cottage, Stoke-road Oundle; aged 12.

Included in Uncle Dick's children's section was a poem; Birthdays. As your birthday passes o'er you. May it bring you Peace and Love. May hope glide along before you. Blessings reach you from above! Sent by Bessie Marlow, Oundle. *Northampton Mercury 1 July 1910.*

Thomas Marlow married Ann Ruff in 1835. By 1841 Thomas, born during 1813 in Oundle, a shoemaker, and Ann, born 1816 in Stonley Hunts, lived along West Street with daughter Mary Ann aged five and George aged two. George died during 1844. In 1851 Thomas and Ann were living in the British School Yard along West Street with Mary Ann fourteen, Ann aged seven, John four and two-year-old Emma. Family have been difficult to find on the 1861 census. In 1871 and through to 1881 Thomas and Ann had no children at home. Thomas was a shoemaker master. Ann died during 1886 aged seventy. In 1881 Thomas, a widower was living at the Alms-house along Church Street.

Thomas and Ann's daughter Harriet aged eighteen was a servant for Caroline Roper and her sister Mary in 1871. They were both shown as a 'Preceptress'. Their cousin Pattie Eaton Knight, aged eleven, from Titchmarsh was a scholar and lived with them. They lived at Curzon House along West Street. (The definition of a Preceptress is 'A woman who is the principal of a school; a female teacher').

James and Grace's son William Rowell Marlow married Ruth Charlotte Beeby in 1870. At the time of the 1871 census they were living along East Court not far from New Street where William was a jobbing gardener. In 1881 William, a mail messenger born at Stoke Doyle, and his wife Ruth lived in Odys Yard with eight-year-old Henry, George six and William four. Ten years later William and Ruth made their home along West Street with their three sons, James Henry eighteen a solicitor's clerk, John George Atkins Marlow aged sixteen was an articled pupil teacher and William Ernest Edward aged fourteen was a schoolboy.

Petty Sessions Oundle on Thursday 18 July 1889 – "Would screw his nose off" Thomas Hunt, blacksmith, Oundle, was charged with assaulting William Marlow at Oundle on the 5th of July. – Several witnesses were called on both sides, and the evidence was to the effect that defendant put his fist in complainant's face and said "he would screw his nose off." – Bound over to keep the peace for six months. *Northampton Mercury 20 July 1889*

In 1901 William, a postman and Ruth only had their son William at home he was shown as a 'secretary to a limited coy'. May Strickson, from Elton, was visiting William and Ruth. William was a retired postman in 1911, he and Ruth had been married for forty-one years, had three children two of whom had died. They lived at Paynes House in Oundle.

Mr William Marlow, for many years' resident at Oundle, died at Bushey (Herts) on Friday, aged 87. *Northampton Mercury 20 January 1928.*

William and Ruth's son William Ernest Edward married Mary Elizabeth Strickson in 1902.

FUNERAL OF MR MARLOW – In Oundle Cemetery on Saturday, was interred the body of Mr William Ernest Edward Marlow, second son of Mr William Marlow. Deceased was for some year's secretary for the Vince Cycle Works, Elton, and latterly had been in business at Horncastle, where he died on Wednesday week, aged 30 years. The first portion of the service was held in the Congregational Church, the Rev. Ives Cater officiating. The mourners were Mr W. Marlow, Mrs Marlow, Mr G. Marlow, Mr and Mrs R. Marlow, and Mr and Mrs A.J. Marlow, and there were also present Mr R. Knight, Mr C. Rawson, Mr G. Rippiner, and Mr R. Blyth. Deceased being an Oddfellow, the Legal Jubilee Lodge, Oundle, was represented by Bro. H. Sivers, secretary. Deceased leaves a widow and one son. *Northampton Mercury 9 November 1906.*

At the time of the 1911 census Mary, widow of the late William Marlow, was living along Duck Street in Elton with her son John William aged six. Mary was a teacher of music. Mary Elizabeth Marlow married Sydney G. Clarke during 1913.

William and Ruth's son John George married Miriam Rawson Ida Knight in 1910.

SUCCESS – Congratulations are extended to Mr J. G. A. Marlow, customs and excise officer, of this town, on his promotion from second to first class officer, and of his appointment to Wednesbury. Mr Marlow is an Oundelian, and with 15 years' experience has made rapid progress. *Northampton Mercury 12 August 1910*

At the time of the 1911 census John and Miriam Marlow were living at 5 Squires Walk in Wednesbury, Staffordshire where John was a customs and excise officer. Mary Jane Clarke aged sixteen was their general servant. Mary Jane was the daughter of Ernest and Elizabeth Clarke who lived along West Street in Oundle.

James and Grace's son Robert.

MARRIAGE SECTION - At the Zion chapel, Oundle, on the 6th inst., Robert Rowell Marlow to Charlotte fourth daughter of Mr David Kirby, of Nassington. *Stamford Mercury 15 November 1872.*

At the time of the 1881 census Robert and Charlotte lived along Redhead's Yard along the Market Place where Robert was a shoemaker master employing 2 men. Their family were Grace Annie seven, Arthur David five and Frederick was one-year-old. In 1891 Rob Row Marlow, a shoemaker lived along West Street with his wife Charlotte and family, Grace Annie aged seventeen a dressmaker and Arthur David aged fifteen a shoemaker. The younger children who attended school were Frederick eleven, Leonard nine, Mabel Lottie seven, James Alf six, Frances Mary four and Ernest Andrew was two years old.

Leonard Marlow, from New Street, was listed under the Northamptonshire County council competitors who was awarded a scholarship in the 'Class A' examination. *Stamford Mercury 12 July 1895.*

By 1901 Robert Rowell Marlow had changed his occupation to a bootman and a postman, he and Charlotte had moved to New Street with their family. Grace Annie continued with her dressmaking, Arthur David was a bootmaker and postman, Frederick was a painter, Leonard a stationer assistant, Mabel Lottie a draper's assistant, James Alfred a printer compositor, Frances Mary and Ernest Andrew were scholars, the youngest child was Edith Agnes aged nine. Robert, a bootmaker and dealer and Charlotte were living along West Street in 1911 with four of their family. Mabel, James a baker, Frances a dressmaker and Edith was a confectioner's assistant.

Robert and Charlotte's daughter Grace Annie married Samuel Bennet during 1901. In 1911 Samuel and Grace were living at Cottesmore cottage in Oundle with their family, Christine Sarah aged five and Robert Raymond Samuel was seven months old.

Robert and Charlotte's son Arthur David married Alice Mary Slater in 1902. By 1911 Arthur, a postman, and Alice Mary lived along South Road with their three children, Joyce Alice aged seven, Herbert Arthur four and Winifred Mary was two.

Robert and Charlotte's son Frederick married Jane Jinks during 1905. Jane was the daughter of James and Mary from Morborne. In 1911 Frederick, a house painter, and Jane lived along West Street, they had a son Sydney aged four.

Robert and Charlotte's daughter Mabel - At the Zion Chapel on Wednesday the wedding was celebrated of Benjamin John Broughton, of Elkington, Lincolnshire, and Miss Mabel Lottie Marlow, of West Street, Oundle. *Northampton Mercury 4 September 1914.*

The death has occurred at Newark after an illness lasting some years, of Mr Leonard Marlow, a son of the late Mr Robert Marlow, of Oundle. The funeral will take place at Oundle on Saturday. *Northampton Mercury 20 October 1933*

Children living in the Glapthorne Road Union House at the time of the 1881 census were Emily Marlow aged three from Oundle, Mary Ann Marlow aged five and James Marlow aged nine both from Elton. They were all shown as paupers.

In 1891 Mary Ann Marlow was a servant for Joseph, a retired farmer, and his wife Ellen Langham who lived along West Street. Mary Ann died in 1893 aged seventeen.

In 1891 Emily Louisa Marlow aged thirteen born in Oundle was shown on the census as an orphan. Emily was an agricultural labourer and lived with John and Emma Matilda Herson in the village of Southwick. By 1901 Emily was a domestic cook for William Terry, a solicitor and Coroner, and his wife Louisa who lived at 4 Billing Road in Northampton. Emily married Walter Worley during 1903. Walter and Emily were living in Northampton at the time of the 1911 census.

The MARSHALL families

William Marshall, born in Huntingdonshire, married Mary Ann Hill during 1816. Their children were Elizabeth, Mary, John, Ann, William, Lucy and Thomas, Catherine, George and Frederick.

William and Mary's daughter Mary married Robert Brown, an agricultural labourer, during 1838. In 1841 they were living along Church Lane with their two-year-old daughter Emma. By 1851 their family had increased with James nine, Robert seven and Elizabeth one-year-old. Ten years later Robert had changed his occupation to a carter also they had moved to Setchell's Yard, West Street and had five children at home. James was a grocer's assistant, Elizabeth was a servant, the three youngest children were Caroline nine, Hannah two and Lucy was two months old. By 1881 only Hannah was home with her parents.

William and Mary's daughter Catherine was a cook for Robert and Mary Ann Critoph who lived along Portland Place in Leamington Priors in Warwickshire in 1851. Robert's occupation was shown as annuitant and funded property houses land and mortgage. Catherine married Abraham Kershaw, a mechanic from Rochdale, in 1866. They were living at Hare Place in Castleton Rochdale in 1871, Mary Ann White; Abraham's niece also lived with them she was a woollen feeder. Abraham died not long after the census was read in 1871.

William Marshall was living along North Street in 1841 with his children Anne, Catherine, George and Frederick. Mary their mother was not at home at the time of the census. William and Mary Ann's other children were living with the following families during 1841. William was an apprentice wheelwright for Thomas Islip who lived at Yarwell. Thomas was a male servant for Mary Curtis, a publican living along West Street. Lucy was a female servant for Elizabeth Johnson who lived along North Street.

William and Mary Ann continued living along North Street during 1851. They had three children at home Ann, George and Benjamin. By 1861 they were living in Prentices Yard at 1 North Street with their son George aged twenty-seven an agricultural labourer and daughter Ann aged thirty-nine working as a charwoman. Their grandson Benjamin, an agricultural labourer aged fifteen also lived with them. William died during 1866 aged seventy-eight. In 1871

Mary, a widow still had her daughter Ann at home she continued with her charwoman work and grandson Benjamin twenty-five was an agricultural labourer. Mary Ann died during 1874 aged eighty-one. Ann and Benjamin lived along North Street not far from Thomas and Mary in 1881. Benjamin was shown as Ann's son and had changed his occupation to a seedsman's labourer. Ann died during 1884 aged sixty-three.

Benjamin Marshall has been appointed town crier in the place of William King, retired. *Northampton Mercury 15 May 1886*

Benjamin had changed his occupation again by 1891 and was shown as the town-crier he lived with William Bossingham, a coachman, along North Street.

SUDDEN DEATH OF THE TOWN CRIER – Benjamin Marshall, Town Crier, died in a fit about nine o'clock on Monday morning. Deceased had been to the boat-house, of which he was the caretaker for the Town Rowing Club, and on returning fell immediately at hand, and Dr Elliott was soon present, but his services were of no avail. Deceased was a single man, 53 years of age, and held the post of Town Crier for more than a dozen years.

Followed by:

INQUEST – An inquest was held on Tuesday at the Carpenter's Arms before Mr J.T. Parker (coroner), on the body of Benjamin Marshall, the Town Crier, who died on Monday morning. – The first witness was Hannah Bossingham, living in North-street Oundle who identified the body as that of Benjamin Marshall. He had lodged with her for the past 13 years, and was 53 years of age. Witness said deceased had been subject to epileptic fits from childhood. He had had fits on Sunday, and on Monday he went out soon after seven o'clock. He had not recovered from the former fits. He returned and went out again about half-past eight, and soon after he was brought home dead. – William Smith, a carpenter's labourer of Stoke Bruerne, said he saw a man fall on his face and groan, about half past eight on Monday, and he ran for Dr Elliott. Deceased was removed in an ambulance litter and died soon after. Dr C.N. Elliott, of Oundle, deposed to attending deceased on Monday. The cause of death was an epileptic fit complicated by injuries to the head sustained by a fall. – The jury returned a verdict in accordance with the medical evidence. *Northampton Mercury 18 June 1897.*

William and Mary Ann's son William married Mary Gann, born in Lancashire, during 1844. They were living a short distance away from William's parents in 1851 and had two children William was born in Lancashire and Hannah in Oundle. By 1861 William junior and his wife Mary were living in Prentices Yard along North Street with their children William, Frederick and Thomas. Their daughter Hannah was a general servant for Elmer and Sarah King who lived along New Street. At the time of the 1871 census William and Mary were still at the same address with their sons William and Frederick both agricultural labourers.

William, junior, and Mary's son William married Mary Ann White during 1876. In 1881 they lived along Lovedays Yard in Oundle. By 1891 William, a general labourer, and Mary were living with William's aunt Catherine Lawton who lived along Richmond Street Moss Side in Chorlton Lancashire. Catherine was born in Oundle during 1830 and was the daughter of William and Mary (senior) she married Robert Lawton in 1886. Ten years later William and Mary continued to live with Catherine Lawton. William was a manager of a coal yard. Catherine died during 1909 aged seventy-nine in Chorlton. At the time of the 1911 census William and Mary lived at 23 Bickley Street Moss Side Manchester where William was a coal porter. They had no children. His cousin Joseph Brown a widower from Oundle lived with them and was an ironmonger's porter. William and Ethel Ball boarded with the family.

OUNDLE – Another native of Oundle died on the 4th inst., at 25 Bickly-street, Moss-side Manchester – Mr William Marshall, aged 69 years. Although he left the town some years ago, he will be remembered by some, and has some relatives living in North-street. *Northampton Mercury 18 February 1916.*

William snr and Mary Ann's son Thomas and his wife Jane from Lancashire were living along North Street in 1851. In 1861 Thomas was a coal heaver, he and Jane had a daughter Elizabeth aged one and three quarters living along North Street. Elizabeth Ann died during 1862.

OUNDLE – Sudden Death – An inquest was held before W Marshall Esq., county coroner, at the Half Moon, Oundle on Tuesday last, on the body of Thomas Marshall, labourer, aged 38, who died suddenly in the harvest field on Monday morning. Deceased rose early that morning to load wheat, and when he entered the field he complained of a pain at the chest, to which he was subject. This became so severe that he was obliged to leave off work for a time, but about ten o'clock, feeling somewhat better, he resumed his labour, and got into a waggon to load it; but when not more than six or seven sheaves had been pitched in he complained of dizziness, and fell over the side of the waggon. When picked up he breathed very heavily, and there was a gurgling in his throat, and in about ten minutes afterwards he expired. Mr Calcott, surgeon, of Oundle, examined the body and stated that there was no bruise upon it from the fall, neither was he of opinion that this caused or accelerated his death, but that he died from disease of the heart. Verdict accordingly. *Northampton Mercury 22 August 1863.*

William and Mary's (junior) son Thomas married Mary Ann Dean during 1877 she was the daughter of Frederick a labourer. In 1881 Thomas and Mary Ann lived along North Street, which became their permanent family home, they had a daughter Ellen aged three. Thomas, had changed his occupation to a groom by 1861, he and Mary Ann had the following children Alice eight, William six, Kate three and Mary Ann four months. Thomas died in 1898 aged forty-two. In 1901 Mary Ann lived at 1 Hinman's Yard along North Street, she was living on her own means supplied by family. At home with Mary was Ellen a domestic housemaid, William a brewers' labourer, Kate thirteen, Mary Ann ten, Arthur Frederick seven and Thomas Edward four. Ten years later Mary Ann completed the census by using their initials apart from her son – M.A. Marshall aged fifty-three married for 34 years and had seven children all alive at time of census, William twenty-six a brewer's labourer, M.A. daughter twenty domestic worker, A.F. son seventeen brewer's labourer, T.E. son fourteen errand boy.

Tom Marshall from Oundle. Photograph courtesy of Jacqueline nee Cotton.

The MOISEY families

There have been many variants of the surname Moisey throughout the census returns. The following families were mostly born in Oundle.

Henry Moisey was born during c.1792 and was the son of William and Elizabeth from Kings Cliffe. Henry Mowsey married Mary Pridmore during 1812 in Oundle.

In 1851 William (Misoe) b.1813, an Agricultural labourer lived with his wife Mary along St Oscyths Lane. By 1861 then shown as William Miser and Mary lived a few doors away from Henry Moisey along Benefield Road. (William was possibly the son of Henry and Mary) Ten years later the same William Moisey (spelling change) continued to live along Benefield Road, he was an agricultural labourer. William Moisey, a widower, aged sixty-nine, lived in the Alms-houses along West Street in 1881. He died in 1884 aged seventy-two.

In 1841 Henry Moisey, an agricultural labourer, was living along West End in Oundle with his children Elizabeth, Henry, Charlotte, Alice and James. Henry was born in Kings Cliffe, his children all born in Oundle. Henry's daughter Elizabeth, surname shown as 'Miser' married William Asbridge during 1847. By 1851 Henry, (Moyser) a widower, continued living along West Street where he made it his home. His daughter Alice and son James were at home also his married daughter Elizabeth Asbridge and her daughter Caroline Asbridge. There has been no trace of William Asbridge. At the time of the 1861 census Henry was living at 48 West Street with his daughter Elizabeth, a charwoman, and her daughter Caroline. Henry died during 1868 aged seventy-seven.

Elizabeth Asbridge's daughter Caroline married James Ball, a brewer's labourer from Kings Cliffe, in 1865 and by 1871 they were living at Tookey's Row in West Street. They had two sons, James H six and William three. Caroline's mother Elizabeth lodged with them and worked as a washerwoman until she died in 1879 aged sixty-one.

Henrys' son Henry Moisey lived along Benefield Road in 1861 with his wife Mary from Tansor. Their children were Harriet aged eleven, Albert aged three and Harold eight months old. Sarah Plowright aged thirty-two and John William Plowright aged four months from

Oundle were recorded as cousins, they both lived with Henry and Mary.

Oundle – Mary Moysey, of Oundle, was charged with disturbing the congregation, at the Independent Church, on the 31st March, but it appearing from the strange manners of defendant at that and other times, together with a medical certificate, that the defendant's mind was disordered, an order for her removal to the Northamptonshire Lunatic Asylum was granted. *Northampton Mercury 17 April 1869*

Henry and Mary's sons Albert and Harold were in the Glapthorne Road Union Workhouse during 1871. Their name was spelt 'Moyser'. In 1881 Albert was a third hand fisherman on the boat named 'John Bright' in Cleethorpes. Albert married Louisa Ann Whittington in Wakefield West Yorkshire during 1883. Albert died in 1928 aged sixty-nine in Wakefield. Nothing else could be found on the brothers.

Henry senior's son James and his wife Mary lived at Stoke Doyle in 1861 with their son John aged seven months. By 1871 they had moved to Warmington where James was a gentleman's servant. They had four sons and two daughters, John ten born in Kings Cliffe, James Harry nine, Charles six, Annie four, Robert three and Elizabeth was five months old. Ten years later they had moved back to Stoke Doyle where James was a groom and gardener. Charles and Robert were agricultural labourers, Mary E (Elizabeth), Willie eight and Fanny three were scholars.

In 1887 a Leisure Employment Exhibition took place in Oundle. Included in a report in the Northampton Mercury dated 29 October 1887 - The exhibition, indeed, shows what can be done in leisure hours, for the articles in many instances are excellent. Under the section for Children under 12: Knitted Cuffs, 1. Elizabeth Bewick, 2. Fanny Moisey.

By 1891 James, Mary, William and Fanny were living not far from the Shuckburgh Arms in Stoke Doyle. By 1901 Mary, a widow, aged sixty-four, lived along Cabbage Row near to Mill Lane in Oundle. She was born in Fineshade and was a charwoman.

James and Mary's son Charles was a groom for William French, the publican at the Shuckburgh Arms at Stoke Doyle in 1891.

An entry under the headings of 'Places wanted' of the Stamford Mercury 27 August 1897 stated – GROOM-COACHMAN. – Situation wanted by young Man, age 31. Can ride and drive well. 11 years' good reference. - C. Moisey, Stoke Doyle, Oundle.

James and Mary's son Charles married Katherine Gray from Titchmarsh in 1898. By 1901 Charles, a coachman, and Katherine were living at 7 The Drive, Worthing. Ten years later Charles was a general night watchman, they were still in Worthing.

James and Mary's son James Harry from Warmington married Rebecca Jane Hankins from Steeple Gidding during 1880. They made their home at Stoke Doyle in 1891, and were still there in 1901. James and Rebecca's children were James William, Emma Selina, Arthur Edward born in Oundle, Eliza Ethel Mary, Ivy Rose Mabel. Percy Sidney, Gladys Jane Victoria and their eight-year-old grandson Albert who also lived with them were born in Stoke Doyle.

James and Rebecca's son James William married in Caroline Anderson from Whittlesey in 1905. By 1911 they were living at King's Dyke near Whittlesea with their sons James Harry and Arthur Herbert.

James and Rebecca's daughter Emma Selina married Frank Bream during 1909. By 1911 they had made their home in Nassington with their son Hubert Frank who was three weeks old.

James and Rebecca's son Arthur Edward, a groom/gardener married Sarah Ann Plowright in 1913. Arthur Edward was a Private in the Machine Gun Corps Infantry. He was killed in action during 1918 in France.

There were no members of the Moisey families living in Oundle in 1911. They lived in the surrounding villages of Oundle mainly Kings Cliffe or Stoke Doyle, a few families also lived at Warmington.

The PLOWRIGHT families

There were many Plowright families in the surrounding villages of Oundle.

Richard Plowright married Mary Stevenson during 1642, both came from Oundle.

Charles Plowright from Pinchbeck married Mary Arnsby from Oundle in 1815. Charles, a horse-breaker, and Mary had a daughter Mary Ellen. Charles died during 1819 aged thirty-two. Their daughter Mary Ellen married John Bunning, a painter, in 1837. (See Bunning family details re John/George.)

By 1841 Mary was living along West Street where she worked as a confectioner. Mary also had her daughter Mary's family living with her. George Bunning and his wife Mary, and their children John and Mary Jane Bunning. In 1851 Mary was a slater's widow. Her daughter Mary Bunning, a widow, and her children John, Mary and Emma Bunning continued to live with Mary Plowright. In 1861 Mary was still along West Street with her daughter Ellen Bunning and her family John a house painter, Anne aged ten and Ellen eleven attended school. Mary Plowright died in 1864 aged eighty-one.

Thomas and Mary Plowright's children were William c.1824 and Samuel c.1826.

In 1841 Samuel aged fifteen, Sarah thirteen and Mary ten were living at the Oundle Union workhouse. At the time of the 1851 census Samuel, an agricultural labourer, was lodging with John and Rachel Marsh who lived at Pilton, John was a shepherd.

Thomas and Mary's son Samuel married Rebecca Spencer from Ashton during 1853. They made their home in Pilton with their children John Thomas, Ebenezer, Sarah Ann and Henry George Spencer aged twelve, son of Rebecca, also lived with them in 1861. Ten years later their family had grown with the addition of William Spencer Plowright, Elizabeth and Martha Mary, Rebekah's mother Ann Spencer also lived with them.

In 1881 Sarah Ann was a general servant living a short distance away from her parents, she worked for Mary Selby, a farmer of 360 acres in Pilton. By 1891 Samuel was a cottager, their son William was an

Under-game keeper, John their grandson aged thirteen lived with them and was a cow keeper.

Samuel and Rebecca's son John Thomas married Elizabeth Ann Wilson during 1876. By 1881 they were living next to John's brother Ebenezer at Lovedays Yard, their children were Rebecca, Emma and Mary Ann. Ten years later John and Elizabeth were living at Thrapston with their daughter Emma and sons Frederick three and John aged one. By 1901 John and Elizabeth had moved to Wadenhoe with their son John. John Thomas died in the winter of 1901 aged forty-eight.

Elizabeth Ann Plowright, widow of John Thomas, married Frederick Abbott, also a widow, during 1906. Elizabeth died in 1908 aged fifty-six. At the time of the 1911 census Frederick Abbot aged forty-seven, widow, lived along East road with Emma Plowright aged thirty-two, his housekeeper, Emma was Elizabeth's daughter.

Samuel and Rebecca's son William Spencer Plowright married Elizabeth Short during 1898. Elizabeth died in 1899 aged thirty-two. William married Rebekah Dawson Chester at the beginning of 1906. William Spencer Plowright signed up to the Northamptonshire Regiment on 18 April 1906. He was discharged two years later.

By 1911 William and Rebekah were living at Pilton where they had a son John William Chester Plowright aged four. William was a grazier; Mary Ann Chester was visiting the family she was Rebekah's mother.

Samuel and Rebecca's son Ebenezer married Eliza Martha Melton during the summer of 1876. In 1881 Ebenezer was at his parent's home in Pilton. Ebenezer must have had his name entered twice as he was shown also in 1881 as living at Lovedays Yard in Oundle with Eliza and their family John, Jane and Sarah Ann.

Petty Sessions Tuesday February 22 – Before Lord Lyvedes and Colonel Tyron - Ebenezer Plowright and Eliza Plowright his wife, were brought up in custody, charged with stealing a pickaxe, value 3s 6d., the property of Robert Baxter, of Cotterstock. Prosecutor said he was in the employ of Mr Norburn at Cotterstock, and left a pickaxe in the granary. Prisoner had worked for Mr Norburn during the past two or three weeks, and had access to the granary. – P.C. Boulter said he took the male prisoner in custody and charged him. He said "All right, I haven't got the pickaxe, I'll tell you where it is, and you fetch it. It is buried in my allotment." Witness went to the allotment and found the pick buried. – The summons against the woman was dismissed. The man pleaded guilty. - Committed for one month. *Northampton Mercury 26 February 1887*

In 1889 Ebenezer was fined 1 shilling for not sending his children to school. *Northampton Mercury 20 July 1889.*

It has not been possible to find them on the 1891 census. By 1901 Ebenezer and his family had moved to Wadenhoe where Ebenezer was a pitman. Ebenezer and Eliza's daughter Jane was living in Pilton during 1901 where she worked as a domestic servant for her uncle William Spencer Plowright, a widower. Her grandmother Rebecca, a widow also lived with William. In 1911 Ebenezer was an aviary attendant, he and Elizabeth lived at Wadenhoe and had twelve children, seven of whom had died.

Ebenezer and Eliza's daughter Sarah Ann was a general domestic servant for Clement Spurling, his wife Louisa and their daughter Cicely in 1901. Clement was a music master of a public school, they were all born at Camberwell in Surrey. By 1911 Sarah Ann was a servant/cook for Hugh Bryan and his wife Mary, Hugh was the rector at Stoke Doyle. Harriet Louisa Plowright also worked there and was a housemaid. Sarah Ann Plowright married Arthur E Moisey in 1913.

Another 'Plowright' in Oundle during 1861 was Sarah, born around 1829. Sarah lived along Benefield Road with her cousin Henry Moisey born around 1826, also from Oundle. Sarah had a four-month old son John W Plowright. (In 1841 Sarah was in the Workhouse with Samuel and Mary Plowright). By 1871 John W Plowright aged ten was living at Benefield with his grandparents Joseph and Charlotte Preston.

The PRENTICE families

Thomas and Dorothy Prentice lived in Oundle with their children, Biddy c.1783, John c.1784, Susannah was born and died in 1786, Thomas c.1787, Susannah c.1791 and William c.1797.

On Saturday, last, aged 55 Mr Thomas Prentice of Oundle, in this county. He has left a widow and large family to lament his loss *Northampton Mercury 21 May 1808*

One of the Lot's to be sold by auction by Richard Smith at the Turk's Head in Oundle between 6 and 8 in the evening on 22 August was Lot 3. All that Messuage or Tenement, with the Apertenances, in the occupation of Mrs Dorothy Prentice; together with a Piece of Ground near the same, lying at the top of Drumming Well Yard. *Stamford Mercury 7 August 1812.*

This was also advertised in the Northampton Mercury for about three weeks prior to the auction which was held on the 22 August 1812.

Thomas and Dorothy's daughter Susannah married Francis Beaumont during 1813 the witnesses to the marriage were her brother Thomas and sister Biddy. Dorothy died in 1834 aged seventy-six. Biddy died in 1839 aged fifty-six.

Samuel Prentice married Sarah England during 1778 at St Peter's church in Oundle. They lived in Oundle with their family William, Elizabeth, Robert, Samuel, Sarah and John.

Samuel and Sarah's son Robert, a carpenter, and his wife Frances lived in Oundle.

At Oundle, on Monday last, Mr Robt. Prentice, carpenter, after a very long illness; leaving a distressed wife and five small children. *Stamford Mercury 8 March 1822*

Robert was thirty-eight when he died. Frances died in 1828 aged forty-four.

In Latham's hospital at Oundle, on Wednesday se'n-night, aged 70, the widow Prentice, mother of John Prentice, carpenter. It is remarkable that Prentices mother, his wife's mother, his wife's sister's husband's mother, and his brother's wife's mother, all died in one week. *Stamford Mercury 23 December 1825*

Samuel and Sarah's son John lived along North Street in Oundle during 1841 with his wife Mary and their children Elizabeth aged twenty, Samuel fourteen and Thomas was twelve. In 1851 John was a carpenter journeyman, born in Oundle, his wife Mary was born in Harringworth. Their son Samuel was a cabinet maker/ journeyman. John and Mary also had their granddaughter Elizabeth Brudenell aged five born in Oundle and Ann Barnes their niece aged twenty-four working as a servant living with them. In 1861 John was a widow his occupation was shown as a carpenter and retailer in beer, he lived at the Carpenter's Arms along North Street.

John and Mary's daughter Elizabeth married Joseph Cawthorne Brudenell during 1844. A report in the Stamford Mercury dated 30 May 1845 states – 'Died - At Oundle, on Sunday last, Elizabeth, wife of Mr. Jos. Brudenell, tailor, and only daughter of Mr John Prentice, of the Carpenter's Arms.'

Grave of Mary Prentice and her daughter
Elizabeth Brudenell in St Peters churchyard.

On 14th inst at Bushley Worcestershire, Mr Samuel Prentice cabinet maker of Oundle Northamptonshire to Miss Ann Bevan of the former place. *Northampton Mercury 23 December 1854*

Samuel was a cabinet maker and upholsterer, his wife Ann, born in Glamorgan, was also an upholsterer. They had three daughters Mary five, Elizabeth three and Ann two all born in Oundle. In 1861 they all lived along North Street with Samuel's father John. Ten years later Samuel, a cabinet maker and beer seller, employed 1 man and 2 boys. He was living at the Carpenters Arms with Ann and their family Mary fifteen, Elizabeth thirteen, Ann twelve, Charlotte nine, Rebecca seven, Ellen five Sarah three and May was eleven months old. Ann continued with her upholstering. By 1881 still at the Carpenters Arms Samuel was shown as a carpenter and publican. Their daughter Mary was a schoolmistress their other children at home were Elizabeth, Ann, Charlotte, Rebecca, Ellen, Sarah, Mary (May) and Katie was nine. Samuel died in 1881 aged fifty-six. Ann died in 1889 aged sixty.

MUFFLED PEAL – On Monday a muffled peal was rung as a mark of respect to Mr. Sam Prentice, deceased, who had formerly been a ringer. *Northampton Mercury 28 May 1881*

Living along North Street in 1861 was Sarah Chapman Prentice aged fifteen, an assistant draper. She lived with her widowed grandmother Sarah Chapman, a retired baker from Collyweston. (In 1851 Sarah Chapman was living along North Street with her husband Samuel Chapman a baker and Sarah Chapman Prentice lived with them.)

Sarah Chapman Prentice married Edwin Dempsey from Warmington during 1864. By 1871 they were living along West Street with their six children. Edwin was a Commercial traveller Drysaltery. Dry-salters - dealers in a variety of chemical products, some of which are glue, varnish, dye and colourings

Sarah Dempsey died during 1880 aged thirty-six in the district of Aston in Warwickshire.

Samuel and Ann's daughter Ann married Charles Swann from Oundle during 1886. Charles was the son of Christopher and Annie who in 1861 lived along North Street at the Dolphin hotel where Christopher was the innkeeper. Next door at the White Lion Inn was Elizabeth Prentice, a widow and victualler. In 1901 Charles and Ann were living at 53 Louis Street in Sculcoates in Yorkshire, Charles was a master mariner. They had five children Charles thirteen, Annie eleven and Margaret nine all born in Hamburg Germany, Carry was seven and Frank five were born in Hull. Charles sister Charlotte Swann, a governess was visiting. At the time of the 1911 census Ann a widow, was looking after her family. Her son Charles was a ship brokers clerk also there was Annie, Margaret, Carry, and Frank who were supported by their mother. Charlotte Swann Ann's sister in law also lived with them.

Samuel and Ann's daughter Charlotte married George Smith, from Seaton in Rutland, during 1890. In 1891 they were living at Tansor where George was a schoolmaster. They had a son George aged one month.

In 1891 Samuel and Ann's daughters were living along North Street together. Mary the oldest daughter was head of the household and worked as a music teacher, then Elizabeth, Ellen, Sarah, Mary (May) and Kate Bevan Prentice were all living on their own means.

Oundle Choral Society – (Included in this event were) Miss K Prentice was the solo violinist, and Mr. Clement M. Spurling, A.R.C.M., the solo pianist and conductor. The band and chorus numbered eighty performers, first violins Miss Prentice, Miss M Prentice; second violins, Miss N Prentice, Miss K Prentice; viola Miss M Prentice. There was a very large audience, most of the *elite* of the town and neighbourhood being present. It was the most successful concert that has ever taken place in Oundle, and Oundleians have once more established their reputation of being a very musical people. Naturally much credit must be given for the success which attended the affair to the conductor, who filled his post as only such accomplished musicians can. *Northampton Mercury 18 December 1891*

Oundle Science and Art Examination – Magnetism and Electricity; Passes, Mary Prentice, Sarah Prentice, - Fair, Rebecca Prentice – plus other local students. *Northampton Mercury 3 August 1894.*

Oundle Choral Society – The annual Christmas concert took place at the National School last Friday evening under the conductorship of Mr C.M. Spurling, A.R.C.M. There was not such a large attendance as is usual on such occasions, this being doubtless due in great measure to the very unfavourable weather. Taking part in the orchestra were – First violins – Miss Prentice and Miss K Prentice, on second violins included Miss R Prentice. *Northampton Mercury 21 December 1894.*

At the time of the 1901 census Mary Prentice was the head of the household living at 16 Belvoir Street in Leicester, she was a hairdresser working from home. Mary's sisters lived with her, Sarah and May both governess's and Kate Bevan was a hairdresser's assistant for Mary. Henry Hawkins aged twenty-four was also a hairdresser's assistant and lived with them. They employed Sarah Bates from Sutton in Northamptonshire as their general servant.

Also during 1901 Elizabeth was head of household and her sister Ellen, a music teacher, teaching at home, they lived in Jericho Place just off North Street.

On Tuesday and Wednesday evenings an entertainment was given in the Church Street rooms by the pupils of the Misses S and M Prentice. The programme consisted of pianoforte selections, violin solos, and tableaux, the young people giving every satisfaction to the large audiences. The proceeds were in aid of the Waif's and Strays Society and the Misses Prentice deserve all thanks for their arduous efforts on behalf of such an excellent cause, and also their pupils, who while affording pleasure to others, are aiding in this noble work. *Peterborough Advertiser 29 April 1905*

As a result of the concert given by the Misses S and M Prentice, the sum of £2 has been sent to Dr Barnardo's Home and £3.14s to the C.E. Waifs and Strays Society. *Peterborough Advertiser 6 May 1905*

There are numerous entries in the Northampton Mercury of awards and concerts that the Prentice sisters took part in.

By 1911 Elizabeth was living by private means and Ellen was a governess. They had two boarders Edward Ross seven and Stewart Ross five. Elizabeth's sister Mary was living at 175 Shooters Hill, Charlton in London. Her sister Kate married John Webster Raven, a motor engineer during 1901 they were both living with Mary. May was a daily governess for Catherine Wakeford who lived at 2 Sandown Villas in Farnborough.

The RIPPINER/RIPPENER families

Joseph and Mary Rippiner had the following children, Joseph c.1777, Samuel c.1778, Mary c.1782, Robert c.1785, Ann c.1789, Robert c.1792, Elizabeth c.1793 and Anthony c.1796. Joseph Sen., died in 1800 aged forty-six, his wife Mary died in 1818 aged sixty-two.

On Christmas day in 1804 Samuel Rippener married Ann Clark at St Peter's church in Oundle. Samuel was the son of Joseph and Mary. They had the following children although only two survived childhood. Samuel (1) died 1805, Samuel (2) died 1807, Ann died aged nine, Joseph died aged seven and Mary died aged one they were twins, Robert died 1813, John c.1816 and Elizabeth c.1820.

At Oundle, on Wednesday the 15th inst., aged 56, Ann the wife of Mr. Saml. Rippiner, Sen., stone-mason. *Stamford Mercury 24 August 1832*

Lately, at Oundle, Mr Saml. Rippiner, Sen. Stone mason, aged 60. *Northampton Mercury 23 June 1838*

The graves of Samuel and Ann Rippiner and their children in St Peters churchyard.

Samuel and Ann's son John died in 1840 aged twenty-four prior to his second daughter's birth. His widow Mary was living along West Street in 1841, she was twenty-five and had two children Sarah Ann three and Mary one year. Ten years later Mary, a mason's widow, and her daughter Mary were lodging with George and Mary Whyman along the West End.

Ann Rippiner aged forty-five was a housekeeper in 1841 for Thomas Timson, a turnkey, and his wife Elizabeth who was matron at Oundle Bridewel. They were in charge of six prisoners. Joseph Rippiner a mason aged thirty-five, son of Joseph and Charlotte Rippiner, and Sarah a dressmaker and daughter of Anthony and Hannah Rippiner, all lived and worked at Oundle Bridewel. Ten years later Elizabeth Simpson, a widow, had changed her occupation to a broker and lived along West Street. Her sister Ann Rippiner was an assistant broker, as was her niece Sarah, her nephew Joseph was a stone mason. They were all born in Oundle and lived with Elizabeth.

Grave of John and Mary Rippiner in St Peters churchyard.

RIPPINER – At Oundle, on Friday week, Anne Rippiner, aged 63. *Cambridge Independent Press 28 October 1854.*

Joseph and Mary's son Joseph and his wife Charlotte had the following children, Joseph, Samuel, Mary, and Charlotte. Joseph senior died in 1829 aged fifty-two. Charlotte died in 1834 aged fifty-six.

Joseph and Charlotte's daughter Charlotte was living with John and Mary Ann Sanderson at Higham Ferrers in 1851 where she worked as a barmaid, Mary Ann was her sister. Charlotte married Samuel Spencer during 1851, they made their home at Higham Ferrers.

Joseph and Charlotte's son Joseph never married. He lived on his own in 1861 along the Binders Hill where he worked as a stone mason. He lived next to Millin Binder and his family. Ten years later Joseph was lodging with the Binder family who lived at the Hoses on the hill along West Street. (spelling as per census)

OUNDLE – On Tuesday last Joseph Rippiner, stonemason, Oundle, was found dead in his house. The deceased had presented a lost appearance for some time. *Stamford Mercury 24 September 1880*

Joseph and Charlotte's son Samuel married Ann Sismey during 1827. Samuel and Ann lived along West Street in 1851. Samuel was a builder employing two men. By 1861 they had moved to 5a Stoke End. Ann died during 1869 aged sixty-eight. In 1871 Samuel was living with his cousin William Brown and family along Benefield Road. Samuel died during 1874 aged sixty-seven.

Sarah Rippiner lived at 26 West Street where she was a furniture broker in 1861. Her niece Mary Chapman aged twelve from Thrapston lived with Sarah. Rebecca Curtis from Pilton was Sarah's general servant.

Oundle Petty Sessions - Included in cases of unjust and unstamped weights and measures came before the Bench, Inspector Williamson having lately been his rounds – Sarah Rippiner, general dealer, Oundle, some small weights deficient. Penalty and costs 20s. *Northampton Mercury 21 October 1865*

By 1871 Sarah was living along North Street at the Parson Latham's hospital for 18 women. Sarah was shown as a firewoman formerly a broker. She was still at the Alms house in 1881. Sarah died at the beginning of 1892 age sixty-eight.

George Rippiner born 1804 was the son of Susannah Rippiner from Oundle. A George Ripponer aged thirty was recorded in the 1841 census living with George Rowell, a publican, and his wife Sophia at Cowgate in Peterborough. George was shown as being in the Army.

An entry in the marriage section of the Cambridge Independent Press on 31 July 1841 – On Tuesday last, at Oundle, George Rippiner, colour-sergeant of the Royal Marines, to Mary Ann Vye. Mary was the daughter of Thomas and Mary Vye, Thomas was a tailor. In 1851 George Rippiner was an innkeeper and Greenwich Pensioner at the Rose and Crown along the Market Place. He lived there with his wife

Mary, they were both born in Oundle, Sarah White from Oundle was their house servant. The Oundle baptism records show that water from the river Jordan was used in the baptisms of their daughters, Mary Ann in 1851 and Kate in 1853, this was in the Clerk's notes. They also had a son Frank in 1857 and William in 1858, By 1861 George and Mary had moved to Albion Cottage along Benefield Road with their three children Mary was nine, Kate eight and George was four years old. George's mother in law Mary Vye, a widow, also lived with them. At the time of the 1871 census Mary was shown as M.A. Rippiner, a pensioner's wife living along West Street with her daughter Kate a dressmaker's apprentice and son George Thos' a clerk unemployed. In 1871 Mary's husband George was lodging at Derngate in Northampton, he was a recorded as a 'Pensioner Navy'.

At Oundle, on the 5th inst, Mr. Geo. Rippiner, aged 67. *Stamford Mercury 12 January 1872*

9 August 1872 – Suicide at Oundle: Mary Ann Rippiner aged 58 an inmate of Latham's Hospital, cut her throat with a razor. *Stamford Mercury 3 January 1873*

Joseph and Mary's son Anthony married Hannah Fox at St Peter's church in Oundle during 1823. Their children were Sarah, Mary, Eliza, Rebecca and Samuel Anthony. At the time of the 1851 census Anthony and Hannah lived along West Street with their son Anthony aged fifteen, he was a stone mason like his father. In 1861 Anthony Rippiner, formerly a stone mason, and his wife Hannah lived in Setchell's yard along West Street.

At Oundle, on the 30th ultimo, Anthony Rippiner, stone mason, aged 70. *Northampton Mercury 8 June 1867*

Anthony and Hannah's daughter Eliza married John Reed during 1854. In 1861 John and Eliza Reed were living at 1 Victoria Place Oundle with their children Letitia aged five, William three and Henry aged two. By 1871 they were living along Mill Lane with their family. John was an unemployed railway labourer. Their children at home were Letitia a domestic servant, William an agricultural labourer, Harry an errand boy and Charlotte attended school. Eliza's mother Hannah lived with them, she was a widow. Hannah died in 1878 aged eighty-nine.

Anthony and Hannah's son Anthony, a stone mason, married Elizabeth Head, daughter of Thomas Head, during 1860. In 1861 they were living at 5 Danford's Square. They had moved to North Street by 1871 and had three sons, Joseph eight, Anthony six and Thomas two. Ten years later Anthony, a mason/bricklayer master employing 2 men and his wife Elizabeth continued to live along North Street with their family. Joseph was a pupil teacher, Anthony a mason, Thomas, Kate, William and Elizabeth attended school then their youngest child was George aged three.

Anthony Rippiner, stone mason, Oundle was summoned for committing an assault upon his wife, on 21st April 1885. The Chairman: It appears this case was fully heard on 25th September last, and the case adjourned, defendant to be summoned when thought necessary. Mrs Rippiner repeated her former statement to which defendant said "All that's a year and a half ago."-Mr Sherard (magistrates' clerk): You know why it has been so long about, in order to get you to come to some reasonable terms. - Defendant: She has stated more this time than last. Do you think the magistrates would have adjourned the case if she had given the same statements then? – The Chairman: It was hoped you would make some mutual arrangements. This has not been done, - Defendant: I can bring evidence against her. – Mr Monckton: Then, why don't you? – Defendant: If it was such a murderous case, why wait the evidence. – The Clerk: It was only a charge of assault, - The Chairman, in fining defendant 10s., and costs 12s.6d., said if he appeared again he would be more severely dealt with. – The defendant paid the money, and remarked that his wife wanted him to pay 12s.6d. to her and her children. – The Clerk: A cheap way of keeping your family too. – Mrs Rippiner: You have plenty of money. – Defendant: I should have had, only you robbed me for 19 years for keeping your paramour. – Mrs Rippiner: I'll make you prove that. —Mr E.P. Monckton took his seat on the Bench during the hearing of this case. *Northampton Mercury on 28 August 1885*

At the Petty Sessions held on Tuesday October 13th 1885 Anthony Rippiner, Oundle, builder, charged with assaulting his wife on 21st April last, was ordered by the Bench to pay towards the support of his family 12s.6d. per week for seven years, and 10s per week after that period. *Northampton Mercury 17 October 1885.*

By 1891 Anthony was living on his own along North Street. The rest of his family were living apart from Anthony. Joseph, a certified teacher in Elementary school was head of the household living along

Rock Road. Joseph's mother Elizabeth a housekeeper, and his brothers' and sisters also lived with him, Thomas was a stone mason, Kate a dressmaker, William a mercantile clerk, Elizabeth a teacher in an elementary school and George was still at school.

In 1901 Joseph had progressed with his career and was a Head schoolmaster, he lived along Benefield Road at Lime Side. His mother Elizabeth and his sisters Kate a housekeeper and Elizabeth a schoolmistress's assistant continued to live with him. Joseph married Rebecca Prentice in the district of Leicester during the summer of 1901. Rebecca was the daughter of Samuel and Ann Prentice from Oundle. In 1911 Joseph and Rebecca were living along Benefield Road.

Death of Mr J. Rippiner – Joseph, residence in Benefield Road, seventy-nine years a native of Oundle, became Headmaster of the Old British School in 1888, succeeding the late Mr R.G. Roe. The British School became a county council school in a new building and Mr Rippiner continued until 1918 when he retired. Played a prominent part in the public life of Oundle. Fluent speaker and member of the Urban Council since its inception in 1894 and was thrice chairman. Chairman of Latham's Charity Trustee and Oundle Gas Co., since the death of Mr J.M. Siddons. *Peterborough Advertiser 22 January 1943*

George Rippiner

OUNDLE – LOCAL SUCCESS – Mr George Rippiner, pupil teacher at the British School under his brother, the headmaster, Mr Joseph Rippiner, has been successful in obtaining a first-class pass certificate at the examination for scholarships. *Northampton Mercury 9 April 1897.*

Joseph and George Rippiner and teachers at the Council School, West Street.
Photograph courtesy of Joyce Hardick.

On his retirement from the headmastership of Oundle Council School, Mr George Rippiner has been presented with an inlaid bedside table made by members of the handicraft classes, and a gold watch by the scholars, staff and managers of the school. Mr Rippiner was educated at Oundle British School where he became a pupil teacher. After serving some years under the Leicester Education Authority, he returned to Oundle Council School as assistant to his brother, Mr Joseph Rippiner whom he succeeded as headmaster 18 years ago. *Northampton Mercury 22 April 1938*

AN ENVELOPE COLLECTION on behalf of the British Sailors' Society realised £2 15s. The collectors were the Misses Jean Martin, Margaret Cheetham, Dorothy Phillipson, Elizabeth Gale, Joan Palmer and Joyce Richardson. The collection was organised by Mr G. Rippiner. *Northampton Mercury 9 September 1938.*

Anthony and Elizabeth Rippiner's families

Anthony and Elizabeth's son Anthony married Naomi Wright during 1888. By 1891 they lived along Main Street in Bowden Great, Market Harborough where Anthony was a Congregational minister. Ten years later they had moved to 5 Heybrook in Rochdale, Lancashire. Anthony continued with his ministry, they had a son Henry aged nine. They had moved again in 1911 to 1 Green Mount Queen's Park in Manchester. Henry their son was a medical student.

Funeral of Mrs Rippiner – On Friday the interment took place in Oundle Cemetery of Mrs Naomi Rippiner, wife of the Rev. Anthony Rippiner, who died at Manchester on October 20. The body was encased in a polished oak coffin with brass furniture, and the inscription: "Naomi Rippiner born April 30, 1852; died at Manchester October 20, 1914." The deceased was a native of Oundle and a daughter of the late Mr H Wright, master tailor. (more details can be seen in the newspaper report) *Northampton Mercury 30 October 1914*

The Rev. A. Rippiner of Ashton-road Congregational Church, Oldham, has accepted the pastorate of Wycliffe Church, Stockport and will begin his ministry on October 21. Mr Rippiner is an Oundle man well known to Northamptonshire Congregationalists. *Northampton Mercury 14 September 1917*

Anthony and Elizabeth's son Thomas married Mary Ann Willmott from Cotterstock during 1896. In 1901 they were living along Rock Road, Thomas' three-year-old niece Florence Wilmott was living with them. Thomas died during 1904 aged thirty-five. By 1911 Mary still had Florence Willmott living with her, John Curley, an instructor in gymnastics from Bradford boarded with Mary.

Anthony and Elizabeth's son William married Annie Howe in the county of Middlesex towards the end of 1910. In 1901 Annie Howe lived along Rock Road with her parents Henry and Catherine Howe. At that time Annie was a confectioner. William and Annie were living along Glapthorne Road in 1911, William was a builder's manager.

The ROUGHTON families

William Roughton, a pipe-maker, and Mary's family included, William, Ann died aged one in 1816, Samuel, Charlotte, Mary, Ann, Hannah, John, Michael, Alice and Amos who also died aged one in June 1836. William senior died a month later aged fifty-six. In 1841 William's widow Mary lived along the West End in Oundle with her family William, Anne, Isaac, John, Michael and Alice.

At the Oundle Petty Sessions on December 21st Wm. Billing and Michael Roughton, both of Oundle, labourers, were charged with trespassing in search of conies on the estate of Jesse Watts Russell, Esq., at Biggen: reprimanded and discharged. *Stamford Mercury 1 January 1847*

At Oundle on Monday last, Widow Roughton. *Stamford Mercury 10 November 1848*

In 1851 Michael aged eighteen was lodging with John and Mary Wilson just off West Street at 10 Oddfellows Place. No further trace of Michael could be found.

William and Mary's son Samuel married Elizabeth Cunnington during 1840. By 1841 they were living along West Street, Samuel was an agricultural labourer. Elizabeth died in 1845 aged twenty-eight. Samuel, a widower, married Dinah Negus during 1846. Samuel died in 1848 aged thirty-one. At the time of the 1851 census Dianna (Dinah), a widow aged twenty-nine and her daughter Mary aged three were living with Dianna's parents John and Dina Negus in the hamlet of Ashton.

Dinah Roughton married George Steers at the end of the year in 1851. George died in 1853. Dinah Steers married James Chapman in 1858. (See Chapman family details).

Samuel and Dinah's daughter Emma (Mary Emma) was a house servant for James Bucknall, a house and land owner who lived along the High Street in Cotterstock at the time of the 1861 census. By 1871 Mary Emma was a domestic servant for Robert Turner, a chemist, druggist and postmaster who lived along the Market Place with his wife and five children. He also employed four other people. Mary Emma married Alfred Smith from Ashton during 1872. They were living in Ashton at the time of the 1881 census.

William and Mary's son William married Mary Ruff during 1845. Mary died in 1848. By 1851 William, a widower and his four-year-old daughter Elizabeth lodged with Mary Ruff senior, a widow, and her two daughters Catherine and Elizabeth who lived along Church Lane. In 1861 William, a stone mason and his daughter Elizabeth continued to lodge with Mary Ruff and her family along New Street. William lived along the Angel Inn Yard near St Osyth's Lane during 1871. Catherine Ruffe was his housekeeper. William died in 1874 aged fifty-seven.

William and Mary's daughter Hannah married James Laxton in 1847. By 1851 they lived along Stoke Road with their one-year-old daughter Louisa. Hannah's brothers' Isaac and John also lived with them. At the time of the 1861 census they had three daughters' Louisa, Matilda and Anne they lived at 51 West Street.

William and Mary's daughter Charlotte married John Wilson in 1850. (See Wilson family details).

William and Mary's daughter Alice was a parlour maid in 1861 living and working for Samuel and Emma Woods at Ford Lodge in Croydon. Samuel Woods was a member of the stock exchange. It has not been possible to find Alice through 1861 to 1891. By 1901 Alice was a boarder with Alice Maynard, a widow, she had eight sons. They lived at 20 Scott's Road in Bromley Kent. At the time of the 1911 census Alice had moved back to Oundle, she lived at 7 Havelock cottages along North Street. Alice, who never married, died during 1918 aged ninety.

William and Mary's son John married Mary Ann Giddings, daughter of Benjamin during 1851. By 1861 John, was an agricultural labourer, he and Mary Ann, a dressmaker. lived along North Street with Alfred thirteen and William six. In 1871 John and Mary Ann lived along North Street with son William a footman. John died in 1877 aged forty-seven.

John and Mary Anne's son Alfred married Ellen Gumm in the district of Middlesex during 1869. By 1871 Alfred, a cellarman and Ellen, a dressmaker from Wiltshire with son Charles one-year-old lived along North Street. Included in the Death's column of the Northampton Mercury dated 27 May 1871 was – May 22, at Oundle, Charles Henry infant son of Alfred Roughton. By 1881 they had moved to Fulham where Alfred was a grocer. Alfred and Ellen had three sons, William, Alfred and John all born in Oundle.

John and Mary Anne's son William, a post office messenger, and his wife Sarah lived along North Street in 1881 with John William two and Ada six months. William's mother Mary A, a widow, also lived with them. By 1891 William, a general labourer and Sarah a charwoman lived along Drumming Well Yard with family John Wm thirteen worked in spruce factory, Ada eleven, Elizabeth nine, Harry six, Eliza four and James one-year-old all shown as attending school.

William's mother Mary Ann was recorded on census as living on parish relief in North Street during 1891, her granddaughter Ada aged ten lived with her and attended school. (Query as to whether Ada was with her parents William and Sarah or her grandmother Mary Ann on the night of the census. She was recorded in both places.) Mary Ann died in 1896 aged seventy-four.

William and Sarah's son John William Roughton signed up for the Norfolk Artillery Regiment in 1895 when he was seventeen years old.

William and Sarah had moved by 1901 to North Street with John William a brickyard labourer, Harry an Ag lab, Eliza fourteen, James eleven, Alfred nine, Annie six and Albert three. William, a road labourer for the urban council and Sarah were living at 2 Havelock cottages in 1911 with their sons Alfred and Albert farm labourers. William and Sarah had been married for 32 years had nine children one of whom had died.

William and Sarah's son John William married Susan Rebecca Smith during 1906. By 1911 they were living at Finedon with their three children.

William and Sarah's son Albert Edward signed up to the army in 1917 and served his country for two years.

Birthday Honour's – The King's birthday on Tuesday was marked by the issue of a very long list of honours, chiefly for war service – EGYPT – D.C.M. – Pte. A. Roughton, ¼ Northants R. (Oundle) *Northampton Mercury 6 June 1919*

William and Mary's son Isaac married Sarah Ann Slater daughter of Thomas and Mary during 1853. At the time of marriage Sarah had a daughter Harriett born in 1849. By 1861 Isaac a sawyer and Ann lived along Danford's Square along West Street with their children Harriett Slater thirteen, Samuel George five, Alice two and Amos one month.

Harriett died in a fatal accident during 1869 aged twenty-one. - Shocking Death. – Between ten and eleven o'clock on Christmas Eve, a domestic servant named Harriet Roughton, arrived at the Oundle Station from London, intending to spend Christmas with her relatives at Oundle. The unfortunate young woman after getting out of the train reached forward for the basket or parcel she had brought with her, when the wheel of the carriage caught her dress, and she was instantly dragged underneath the train and killed, her head and one arm being severed from her body. The deceased was in service in London with Miss Lloyd, a sister of Mr D. Lloyd, of Castle Street. *Stamford Mercury 31 December 1869 also reported in the* Cambridge. *Cambridge Chronicle and Journal 1 January 1870.*

In 1871 Isaac, a general labourer and Sarah Ann had moved to 12 Inkerman Square, this was to be the family home. Their children at home were Samuel fifteen an errand boy, Alice twelve, Amos ten and Earnest aged three were scholars, the youngest child was Alfred John aged seven months. At the time of the 1881 census Isaac was a wheelwright labourer, his wife (Sarah) Ann and their family at home were Amos a slater, Earnest Harry a tailor's apprentice and Alfred was a scholar. Isaac and Sarah's daughter Alice was a cook for Charles York and his brother Frederick who were wine and spirit merchants', living along West Street in 1881.

Isaac died in 1886 aged fifty-eight.

By 1891 Sarah lived alone in Inkerman Yard, she was a laundress.

Isaac and Sarah's daughter Alice married Henry Sivers during 1884.

Isaac and Sarah's son Samuel married Virtue Wheatley during 1878. In 1881 they were living near Rotherham where Samuel was a railway signalman. By 1891 Samuel and Virtue had moved to Oundle and lived along Benefield Road with their nine-year-old son Percy. Samuel was an ironmonger's warehouseman. Samuel and Virtue had moved again in 1901 and made their home at 12 Inkerman's yard, their son Percy was a draper's assistant. In 1911 Samuel was an ironmonger's warehouseman, he and Virtue continued to live at 12 Inkerman Yard. They had been married for thirty-two years and had one child. Virtue died during 1917 aged sixty-six. Samuel died during 1940 aged eighty-three.

Samuel and Virtue's son Percy married Agnes Plowman during 1909. By 1911 they were living at Nottingham where Percy was a shop assistant in a drapery shop.

Isaac and Ann's son Amos married Emma Smith during 1884. By 1891 Amos and Emma lived along Binders Row where they made it the family home with Montague Wilfred six, Jessie Paulina three and Herbert E one-year-old. Jessie Paulina died in 1893 aged six. Montague Wilfred died in 1898 aged thirteen. In 1901 Amos and Emma's family had increased with Herbert E twelve, Alice M nine and Emma K four at. At the time of the 1911 census Amos, a slaters journeyman, and his wife Emma only had their

Isaac Roughton and his family's grave in the town cemetery.

daughter Emma Kathleen a nursemaid and Ellen Jessie Smith niece (orphan) aged eight living at home. Amos and Emma had been married twenty-six years had seven children four of whom had died.

A RESPECTED INHABITANT – passed away suddenly on Thursday morning in Mr Amos Roughton, of Binder-row. He was a slater on the Lilford Estate for many years. *Northampton Mercury 6 January 1933*

Amos and Emma's son Herbert married Priscilla Rycroft during 1914.

The RYCRAFT families

In 1841 Sarah Rycroft aged twelve and Martha aged ten were pupils living along West Street. The schoolmistress was Maria Brood (spelling unsure) her sister Anne helped her with the school. They were twenty-five and twenty-four respectively. There were ten pupils in the school.

Also in 1841 living along Town Street in Nassington were William Rycraft, a carpenter, his wife Mary and their family. Robert thirty, Winifred twenty, James and Susanna twins aged fifteen, Thomas eight, Winifred Abbott Rycraft aged two. James and Susanna were baptized during 1820 and 1823 respectively as recorded in the Oundle baptisms. By 1851 William senior a wheelwright, widowed, had his son James a carpenter and his granddaughter Jane fourteen and Winifred thirteen living with him.

William and Mary's son William married Rebecca Lightfoot during 1839. At the time of the 1841 census they were living not far from William's parents. By 1851 both families were shown as living along Church Street in Nassington. William and Rebecca lived a bit further along Church Street from William and Mary, with their children Ann aged eight, Martin aged six, Sarah aged three and William seven months. In 1861 William, a sawyer, and Rebecca were living along the High Street in Nassington with Martin, Sarah, William, John eight, Robert four and Henry two. At the time of the 1871 census William and Rebecca only had three of their sons living at home, John a farm servant, Robert and Henry. They had no children at home in 1881 and by 1891 they were shown as living on own means. William died in 1895 aged eighty and Rebecca in 1896 aged seventy-nine.

William and Rebecca's son Martin married Susan Newton from Tallington during 1870 and made their home at Brown Lane in Thurlby by the time of the 1871 census. William Newton thirteen and Christopher Newton nine also lived with Martin and Susan. In 1881 Martin and Sarah Ann (Susan) had moved to Oundle and were living along Drumming Well Lane with their son Christopher aged eighteen a bricklayer born in Morton.

Martin Rycroft, in the employ of Messrs. Siddons, Oundle, was summoned for locking the wheel of a wagon without using a skid pad, while going down Stoke-hill, on July 13th. Dismissed on payment of costs 6s. *Northampton Mercury 5 August 1882.*

OUNDLE – A young man named Rycraft, in the employ of Mr Storey, was engaged casting moulds the other day, when the chain of his watch was accidentally caught, and dropped into some molten iron, never to be seen any more. *Northampton Mercury 21 April 1883.*

Martin and Susan (name change again) continued to live along Drumming Well Lane in 1891. At the time of the 1901 census they had moved from Oundle and were living at 32 St Margaret's Road in Old Fletton. Martin worked as a labourer in the brickyards. By 1911 they had moved back to Oundle and were living along East Road although Charles Alfred Wright filled out the census for them as Martin seemed to make a mark of a cross. Charles lived along North Street and was a baker. Martin and Sarah had been married for thirty years, had eight children seven of whom had died. Susan died in 1913 aged seventy-five, Martin died in 1914 aged seventy.

William and Rebecca's son Henry married Mary Powell during 1881. Mary was only eighteen at the time of the marriage and was the daughter of Stephen and Ellen from Fotheringhay. By the time of the 1881 census they were living in Nassington. Lily Powell, Mary's sister aged ten was visiting them. In 1891 they had four children Ernest nine, Annie seven, Margaret five and William one. At the time of the 1901 census they had moved to Main Street in Fotheringhay where Henry worked as a yardman on a farm. Ernest was an agricultural labourer the other children living at home were William, Edith aged nine, Stephen five and Albert two. Henry and Mary's daughter Margaret was a domestic servant living at the Vicarage in Fotheringhay where she worked for Richard Croyden-Burton, the Vicar, and his wife Annie. By 1911 Henry and Mary had been married thirty years, had twelve children, nine were still alive and three had died. Henry was a shepherd on a farm. Still living at home were William and Stephen both labourers on a farm, Albert, Nelly nine and Alfred six.

The majority of William and Rebecca's family had moved to Fotheringhay or Lutton at the time of the 1911 census.

The SHARP/SHARPE families

James and Sarah Sharpe's family

James Sharpe from Gt Addington married Sarah Howes during 1836. By 1841 James, a fellmonger, and Sarah lived along Chapel End in Oundle with John aged one. John Howes, a butcher, his wife Anne and their son Joseph aged fifteen also lived with James and Sarah. In 1851 James and Sarah were living along West Street with their family John eleven, Joseph nine, Jane five and two-year-old Thomas. John and Ann Howes lived next door.

At the time of the 1861 census James and Sarah's son Joseph was living at the Rectory in Clapton near to Thrapston where he worked as a footman.

By 1871 Sarah Sharp, a widow, was housekeeper for Joseph Langham a farm bailiff who lived along Mill Lane. In 1881 Sarah was an inmate at the Latham's Almhouse along North Street. Sarah died in 1883 aged seventy-seven.

Adam and Elizabeth Sharpe's family

Adam and Ann Sharpe from Stamford had a son Adam born at Stamford around 1806. At the time of the 1841 census Adam junior, and his wife Elizabeth born at Wigsthorpe, were living at Thorpe Achurch near Oundle with their two sons, Thomas nine and John five. From the 1851 census and through to 1861 they lived at Aldwinkle. In 1861 their children at home were Elizabeth nineteen, William sixteen a farm labourer, Charlotte Jane twelve (Sarah Jane), Frederick ten, Ann six, Susannah one, Stephen Arthur three and grandson Walter was six months old.

At the Petty Sessions held at Aldwinkle All Saints – An application was made by Mr Allen, the overseer of the poor of this parish, for an order to remove Adam Sharp, his wife, and six children, to Thorpe Achurch, as the place of their settlement. It appeared from the evidence of the pauper that his father was a settled and an acknowledged inhabitant of Thorpe Achurch, and that in the year 1847 the pauper worked for Mr Freeman, a respectable farmer, and then a guardian of the parish, and that, being unable to get a house there, he got one at Aldwinkle; that in the year 1826 he had been removed by order of justices from All Saints, Stamford, to Thorpe

Achurch, and had always been recognised as a settled inhabitant; that in 1848 he had an accident, and had never since been able to work, and that he applied to the relieving officer of the Thrapston Union, in which Aldwinkle is situated, for relief, and he and his family were taken into the workhouse, but by an arrangement of Mr Freeman, they returned to the house at Aldwinkle, and continued to receive relief through the Thrapston relieving officer, which was repaid by the Oundle Union until 1861, when it was stopped. (Further on in the report it reads) 'Elizabeth Sharp, the pauper's wife, deposed to some additional facts, and said: We have been regularly paid by Mr Sanders Leete, the guardian of Thorpe Achurch, from June 1861 to about two months ago. Mr Leete allowed us 8s. a-week, but he made us take it out in flour. Mr Leete charged us 2s 8d. a stone for the flour, which would come to 10s 8d. a-week, so that we had two shillings and eight pence a-week to pay back to Mr Leete for the flour, and if we did not pay it, Mr Leete would not let us have any more flour, or any money until it was paid. For the last nine weeks that Mr Leete gave us anything, the allowance was 9s. a-week, but he stopped 7s. of it for flour. I used to go to Mr Leete's house for it, and he paid me himself. – The magistrates, in granting the order, said they were surprised that a neighbouring parish should put the parish of Aldwinkle to such unnecessary trouble and expense in obtaining an order in such a case, and animadverted strongly on the system of paying the paupers in the manner stated to have been done by the guardians of Thorpe Achurch. *Northampton Mercury 28 June 1862*

Oundle – Adam Sharp, of Oundle, was ordered to pay an Improvement rate of 2s.3d and expenses in a month. *Northampton Mercury 28 May 1870*

By 1871 Adam, shown as an Invalid (formerly an Ag lab), and Elizabeth lived along St Osyth's lane with Jane a lace-maker aged twenty-three, Arthur twelve an errand boy and Eliza aged seven.

Adam and Elizabeth's daughter Charlotte Jane married Michael Parker during 1873. Michael was the son of Thomas Parker a shoemaker from Oundle. In 1881 they were living along St Osythes Lane with their children Susannah aged six and John five months old.

Adam died during 1877 aged seventy-two. Elizabeth was a nurse at the time of the 1881 census, her daughter Annie, a dressmaker, lived with her along St Osythes Lane. At the time of the 1891 census

Elizabeth lived by herself. Elizabeth had moved to East Road by 1901 and was a general shopkeeper, working from home. Elizabeth died during 1906 aged eighty-three.

Adam and Elizabeth's daughter Eliza aged nineteen was a general servant for John and Ann Bunning at the Red Lion along New Street in 1881. During the summer of 1881 Eliza married Charles Loakes, a labourer, also from Oundle. Charles was the son of Thomas and Ann who lived at Setchells yard. By 1891 they were living along North Street with their children, Alice nine, Alfred six, Winnie three and one-year-old Tom. Charles was a brewery labourer in 1901 he and Eliza lived along North Street in number 3 Havelock cottage. Their children at home were Alfred a labourer in a mineral water factory, Winnie, Ethel eight, Kerman seven, Berty five, Harry four and William was two years old.

Charles and Eliza Loakes daughter Alice Annie was a domestic servant for Horatio William Horton, a bank manager, who lived along the Market Place with his wife May and their three children. Alice married Frederick Sharpe, the son of Arthur and Charlotte, in 1908.

Charles and Eliza's daughter Winifred Mary married Albert Edward Sharpe during 1908. Albert, known in previous census as Edward was the son of Stephen and Charlotte Sharpe. By 1911 Albert and Winifred Mary lived at Baker's Yard in Oundle with their daughter Nance Alice aged one, they were all born in Oundle.

Charles and Eliza had moved by 1911 to Station Road with three sons still at home. Bertie was a carpenter, Harry a farm labourer and William was a school boy. Charles and Eliza were shown as having had twelve children but only seven were still living. Eliza shown as Elizabeth died during 1920 aged fifty-six.

Adam and Elizabeth's son Stephen Arthur married Charlotte Coulson from Polebrook, during 1878. In 1881 Stephen, a merchant's labourer, and Charlotte lived along North Street with son Adam A aged two. By 1891 Stephen had dropped his first name and was shown as Arthur, a bricklayer's labourer. He and Charlotte were living along Drumming Well Yard with Arthur (Adam A), Edward Albert, William, Harry and Fred all attended school. In 1901 Arthur, a Navvy, and Charlotte lived at No 10 Havelock Cottages with Adam A, a groom, William, Harry and Fred all general labourers Tom was seven. Arthur continued to live at 10 Havelock Cottages along South

View Oundle with Charlotte in 1911. They had been married for 32 years had fifteen children nine of whom had died. They had three sons at home Harry, William and Tom all worked as farm labourers as did their father.

The death has occurred of Mr Stephen Arthur Sharpe, of Havelock cottages, Oundle, at the age of 78 years. Mr Sharpe leaves a widow and six sons. *Northampton Mercury 1 November 1935*

Arthur and Charlotte's son Frederick married Alice Annie E Loakes in the spring of 1908. Alice was the daughter of Charles and Eliza Loakes. At the time of the 1911 census Frederick and Alice lived in Lower Glapthorne with their son Alfred Arthur aged ten months.

Arthur and Charlotte's son Albert Edward enlisted with the Northamptonshire Regiment in 1903. Albert Edward married Winifred Mary Loakes, daughter of Charles and Eliza Loakes, in the winter of 1908. By 1911 Albert Edward Sharpe lived at Baker's Yard in Oundle with Winifred Mary and their daughter Nance Alice aged one all born in Oundle.

A GALLANT RESCUE – On Tuesday afternoon some little children were on Ashton high bridge, when one named James Palmer, the three-year old son of Mr John Palmer, St. Osythe's-lane fell into the stream. The call "Jimmy's in the water" was heard by several fishermen, including ex-Sergeant Edward Sharpe who, without divesting any clothing, and with a useless arm through a wound, dived in the river and rescued the boy who was restored by artificial respiration. *Northampton Mercury 13 August 1920.*

Adam and Elizabeth's daughter Annie married Samuel Loomes, son of Joseph and Jane from Wilbarston, not long after the 1881 census was recorded. At the time of the census Samuel was lodging with George and Susan Woods who lived further along St Osythe's lane. Samuel died a few months later aged twenty-two. Annie Loomes, nee Sharpe married Isaac Cullop in 1883. By 1891 they were living along St Osythes Lane with their young family. Percy Edward was six, Frederick Hensan Cullop five, John William was four and Sydney was one-year-old. Isaac was an agricultural labourer (army reserve). John William died not long after the census was recorded in 1891.

A section of a report from the Barrowden Parish council – The Chairman stated the committee delegated to see if water could be obtained for a public supply at the east end and decided to set a man to work in making a hole, but they had to get the permission of Mr Northern, the surveyor. He advised them to employ a "water diviner," and they acted on his advice. Mr Isaac Cullop, of Oundle, was engaged for a fee of 25s, his visit with the "magic twig" showed that four springs ran under the village, all these being traceable from a single spring. Mr Cullop guaranteed they would find water on the east green at a depth of perhaps 40ft or even less. He had clearly shown where water could be got, and they now had to decide what steps to take. *Stamford Mercury 19 November 1897*

Isaac and Annie had moved by 1901 and were living along Carters Row on Benefield Road Isaac was a mason's labourer. Percy was a bricklayer's labourer and Frederick an agricultural labourer, Sydney was eleven and Annie Elizabeth eight. Sydney died during 1903 aged fourteen. Isaac and Annie were still living along Benefield Road in 1911 Isaac had changed his job and was a roadman for the rural district council. They had three children at home Percy was shown as a coal hosker, Frederick a bricklayer's labourer and a new daughter Maggie aged nine. Isaac and Annie had been married for twenty-seven years, had ten children six of whom had died. Annie died during 1914 aged fifty-nine.

Adam and Elizabeth's son Frederick Sharp married Mary Ann Clipson, daughter of Joseph, in 1875. By 1881 Frederick and Mary Ann lived along Redheads Yard, West Street with Ellen Annie, Amy and Maggie. In 1891 Frederick, a general labourer and Mary Ann were living along North Street with Ellen Annie fourteen, Amy Clipson twelve, Maggie Jane ten, Herbert eight, Walter Edwin six, and Kate five, Bessie three, Charlie one year and seven months and Emily Mary five months. They had moved again by 1901, Fred, a Mason, and Mary Ann were living along East Road with Maggie a housemaid domestic, Herbert apprentice to saddler and harness maker, Edwin was an ag lab and Charles was eleven.

So many deaths from drowning have occurred during the last few days, several of which might have been averted with a little presence of mind and courage, that the brave conduct of an Oundle boy, Charles Sharp, stands out in pleasing contrast. He was standing on Oundle Bridge when he saw a little child fall into the river. He immediately dived in and brought the child safely to shore. It is a strange commentary on the facts of human life that so many of these rescues are accomplished by mere boys, whilst grown-up people have been known frequently to stand by and see the person drown before their eyes. *Northampton Mercury 29 August 1902*

In 1911 Frederick was a general labourer in the building trade he and Mary Ann continued to live along East Road. They had been married for 35 years, had fourteen children eight of whom had died. Their grandson Ronald aged nine lived with them.

Frederick and Mary Ann's son Herbert Loomes Sharp married Alice Miriam Smith, from Elton, in 1909. By 1911 Herbert, a carpenter's labourer, and Alice Miriam lived along Drumming Well Yard, West Street with their son Eric Herbert aged one.

DRAMA OF MIDNIGHT DISCOVERY ON NORTHANTS ROAD – Driving along a Northamptonshire road late at night, a motorist came upon the body of a man lying in the road. Apparently, he had been knocked down by a vehicle. The identity of the vehicle is not known. This was revealed at the inquest. The man was Herbert Loomes Sharpe, aged 56, of Cotterstock, whose body was found near the Tansor cross-roads on the Peterborough-Oundle road, towards midnight last Saturday. Recording a verdict of accidental death at the inquest, which was at the Public Assistance Institution, Oundle, the East Northamptonshire Coroner, Mr J. Cairns Parker, said that death was caused by multiple injuries received by coming into collision with a heavy motor vehicle, such as a heavy motor lorry. *Further details relating to earlier events in the day can be found in the Northampton Mercury 29 September 1939.*

There were families with the surname Sharp/Sharpe also living at Kings Cliffe, Barnwell, Thorpe Achurch, Wadenhoe, Apethorpe and Pilton.

The SIDDONS families

In 1851 George Siddons, born in Kings Cliffe c.1820, was a surveyor of public works and coal merchant employing thirty-five men. George and his wife Ann c.1817 also from Kings Cliffe were living along West Street in Oundle with their family, Ann six, Mary five, Sarah three and Henry Arthur eleven months old. They employed Martha Burrows aged sixteen from Essex as their cook/governess. Arthur Adams aged sixteen from Buckinghamshire was a pupil to the surveyor. By 1861 George, shown as a timber and coal merchant, and Ann had a large family to support Ann, Henry, George aged eight, Grace seven, James Carvill five, Lucy four and twins John and Harriet aged two all were born in Oundle. Sarah Arnold and Mary Billing were their house servants. George was shown as a merchant surveyor in 1871 he and Ann only had four of their children at home, Annie, George a mechanical engineer and the twins John and Harriet. Their son Henry Arthur was a clerk cashier visiting John and Elizabeth Taylor who lived at Ashby de la Zouch in Leicestershire.

OUNDLE – In our obituary of the 3rd instant, we announced the decease of Mr Henry Arthur Siddons, the eldest son of our respected townsman, Mr George Siddons. He was a young man greatly esteemed and deeply lamented. *Northampton Mercury 10 April 1875*

OUNDLE – A fire broke out in the stackyard of Mr William Smith, farmer of Ashton, near this town, and resulted in the destruction of a hay-stack. On the following afternoon Mr George Siddons, West-end, Oundle, lost part of a splendid stack of hay, the fire being attributed to incendiary. The Oundle Fire Brigade was in each case of great service. *Northampton Mercury 15 September 1877*

In 1881 George and Lucy ('Ann' often people would change their names on the census) had moved from West Street to the Market Place, George was described as a merchant surveyor and farmer. Their son James was an assistant to his father, his sisters' Lucy and Harriet also lived at home. George died during 1889 aged sixty-nine. Ann (Lucy on last census), a widow, was living on her own means back along West Street by 1891 with her son James a coal merchant and her daughter Harriet. Eliza Lovell aged twenty-six was visiting the family, she was born in India.

OUNDLE – Accident – On Saturday evening Mr James Siddons was riding home from Polebrook on a bicycle, and when descending the hill near Ashton hollow his lamp went out and, the night being very dark, he dashed into a drove of beasts coming in an opposite direction. Mr Siddons was thrown heavily from his machine on to the road and terribly bruised and injured. He was removed home, and is now progressing favourably. *Stamford Mercury 29 October 1897.*

By 1901 Ann was continuing to live by own means and had Edith Swann aged sixteen living with her as a general domestic servant. Edith was born in Warmington.

George and Ann's daughter Mary Elizabeth married William Francis Scott (son of the Rev. C. Scott Broomfield Belfast), on the 12 June 1872. This announcement was recorded in the Stamford Mercury on 14 June 1872. Another announcement in the same newspaper dated 18 July 1873 read – At Oundle, on the 25th June, (by the Rev. C. Hopkins) the Rev. C. Eacott, to Annie Maria eldest daughter of Mr Siddons; - and on the 30th June, Wm. Parker, to Mary Ann Billing, 15 years' servant to Mr. Geo. Siddons.

On July 25 at St. Sepulchre's Northampton, John Miller Siddons of Oundle, to Eleanor Mary, eldest daughter of Edmund Muscott of Northampton. *Northampton Mercury 28 July 1883*

OUNDLE – IN MEMORIAM – This town and neighbourhood have sustained a severe loss by the death of Mr G. Siddons, after a protracted and painful illness, borne with great patience. No name in the county was more familiar – no person more respected than he who bore it. In every department of social life in connection with the people, among whom he dwelt, his presence and influence for good were constantly felt. As a man of business, his upright and honourable conduct and strict integrity ever commended themselves to all who had dealings with him. In all his public associations, and they were numerous, he deservedly won and enjoyed the confidence of all his colleagues, assured as they were that his ripe judgment and great experience were always brought to bear on the consideration of all matters submitted to him. In all the philanthropic and religious movements in operation in the locality, and altogether irrespective of name or denomination, he took a deep interest, and his uniform and substantial assistance was always to be depended on; while in the more private acts of benevolence he often made the widow's heart sing for joy, dried the tears of the orphan, and relieved the really necessitous poor with no niggard hand. "The righteous shall be held in everlasting remembrance." The funeral took place on Wednesday, when all the shops in the town were closed, and a large number of tradesmen, &c., followed the funeral in procession from St Peter's Church to the Cemetery. The Vicar (the Rev. James C. Hopkins), the Rev. F. L. Denman, and the Rev. James Skinner, took part in the service. The deceased gentleman has held many public offices in the town, amongst them being Surveyor to the Nene Commissioners (Second District), the Oundle Improvement Commissioners, and Kings-Cliffe Highway Board. He was also a member of the Board of Guardians, and Manager of the British and National School. He also, up to the time of his death, served on many committees in connection with the Board of Guardians. Much sympathy is felt throughout the town with the bereaved family. *Northampton Mercury 15 June 1889*

SKEFFINGTON – SIDDONS – June 14, at Oundle, Thomas Skeffington, of Medbourne Leicestershire, to Harriet Ellen (Nellie), daughter of the late George Siddons. *Northampton Mercury 17 June 1892*

At the time of the 1911 census Ann, at the amazing age of ninety-four, was still living along West Street. It showed she had been married for forty-five years, had ten children, seven were still alive but three of them had died. Living with Ann was her granddaughter Edith Mary Scott aged thirty-five born in Belfast, Charlotte Maria Green aged fifty-six her niece from Lincolnshire, Eliza Randall aged fifty-seven was the housekeeper, she was born in Clipston and Edith Ellen Fisher a servant aged fourteen born in Australia. All Ann's house guests were single.

Many were the congratulations extended to Mrs Siddons on reaching her 94th birthday on Wednesday. This was recorded in the Northampton Mercury 13 January 1911. Also in the newspaper was a small article which read – "OLD LADIES AT TEA – Mrs Ross, of Laxton School, very kindly invited the old ladies of Latham's Hospital to a New Year's tea last week, according to her usual custom; and on Wednesday this week Mrs. Siddons, who reached her 94th birthday, sent to the hospital a tea for each of the inmates to commemorate the event."

OUNDLE'S OLDEST INHABITANT – Mrs Ann Siddons, widow of the late Mr George Siddons, passed away on November 19 at the advanced old age of 96. She was a charming old lady, the senior of all the inhabitants of Oundle. She was the mother of 10 children, seven of whom survive, and had 30 grandchildren and 11 great-grandchildren.' A full report of the obituary can be seen in the Northampton Mercury dated 28 November 1913 – page 7 – column 7.

George and Ann's son James family details

INTERESTING WEDDING – The interest of a large proportion of the population of Oundle was aroused over the marriage, on Wednesday, of Miss Ethel Barnes to Mr James C. Siddons. Both parties are natives of the town, the bride being the youngest daughter of Mr Thomas Barnes, of West-street, and the bridegroom a son of the late Mr George Siddons (founder of the present firm of George Siddons and son of Oundle). The event took place in the Parish Church. The Rev. Caleb Eacott (Gaulby), brother-in-law of the bridegroom, officiated, assisted by the Rev. Newbury, of Oundle. During the service, appropriate wedding music was rendered on the organ by Mr C. M. Spinling (should have read Spurling). The bride was dressed in a grey cloth travelling dress and the bridesmaids, who were Miss Evelin Siddons, of Oundle and Miss Gray, of Stamford were dressed in white muslin. Mr Siddons was attended by Mr H. Tilling, of London, as his best man. The bells rang merrily throughout the day. Mr and Mrs Siddons left by the four o'clock train to spend their honeymoon in North Wales. The wedding gifts were of a costly and beautiful character. *Northampton Mercury 23 June 1899*

OUNDLE – TEA – The employees of Messrs. Siddon and Sons were entertained to a meat tea on Saturday on the occasion of the wedding of Mr James Siddons, which took place a few weeks back. About 180 were present. After tea, an entertainment was held, which was greatly enjoyed. *Northampton Mercury 21 July 1899*

In the 'Places Wanted' section of the Stamford Mercury on 11 August 1899 was the following – 'General (experienced) wanted. Two in family – apply Mrs James Siddons, Yorke House, Oundle.'

BIRTHS - SIDDONS – On the 18th inst., at Thornecliffe, Oundle Northamptonshire, the wife of James Carvill Siddons, of a daughter. *London Evening Standard 27 March 1900*

By 1901 James and Lucy lived along West Street with their one-year-old daughter Constance. Margaret Hill, born in Elton, was a servant living with them. James was a land agent and corn merchant. In 1911 James, a corn and coal merchant, and Lucy still only had one daughter Constance. Annie Bannard aged twenty-three was their cook and Maggie Hinman, aged eighteen born in Oundle, was their housemaid.

SERIOUS ACCIDENT AT OUNDLE – Mr J.C. Siddons injured – About midday on Wednesday a serious accident befell Mr J. C. Siddons, the well-known merchant. It appears that, accompanied by Mr C. Wilmott, hay trusser, he was driving a pony and trap along Peterborough-road, and when nearing the village of Warmington, the animal shied at a car coming in the direction of Oundle, and in which was seated Lady Proby and two other ladies. The animal was so severely injured that it had to be shot. Mr Siddons and his companion were thrown out of the trap, with the result that the former sustained a fractured jaw and other injuries, and Mr Wilmott had one of his shoulders injured, while the driver of the trap was so badly hurt that he had to be taken to Peterborough Infirmary. Both the shafts of the trap were smashed, as was also the splash-board. Fortunately, Lady Proby and her companions escaped unhurt, and the car was not damaged. Mr Siddons is going on as well as can be expected. *Northampton Mercury 7 November 1913*

OUNDLE – We are pleased to state that Mr J. C. Siddons has so far recovered from the serious motor accident of more than three months ago as to be able to get out, and on Thursday he journeyed by motor to Hunstanton to recuperate. His many friends hope he will return thoroughly restored to health. *Northampton Mercury 6 February 1914*

George and Ann's son John Miller Siddons married Eleanor Mary Muscott in the Northampton district in 1883. By 1891 they lived along West Street and had three children Ethel M aged six, Bruce five and Evelyn was two years. In 1901 they were living in Jericho Lane, John was a surveyor and building contractor, Eleanor was busy looking after their four children. Bruce was fourteen, Evelyn eleven, Victor eight and Violet was seven. Edith Loveday from Islip was the family cook and Annie M Smith from Stoke Doyle was their housemaid. Ten years later John and Eleanor had moved to Milton Road and had only one son at home, Victor Donald was shown as being an articled pupil for the above, (possibly for his father). Annie Maria Smith continued working for them and was described as a sewing maid, Carry Lizzie Templeman aged twenty-three was a general domestic servant from Thorney.

The THURLBY families

William Thurlby married Millicent French during 1828 at St Peter's church in Oundle. Millicent was the daughter of William French from Oundle. William and Millicent made their home along West Street. In 1841 William, a sweep, and Millicent had five children, Ann eleven, Eliza eight, Robert seven, William four and Jane one-year-old. Thos' Brown aged sixteen was an apprentice sweep and lived with the Thurlby family. By 1861 they lived at 4 Poplar Row, just off West Street, where William was a chimney sweeper employing one man. Their son Mark, aged fifteen, a shoemaker lived with his parents. John Hicks from Oundle was employed by William as a chimney sweeper. Millicent died in 1868 aged sixty-one.

OUNDLE – Rival Smuts – William Thurlby of Oundle, chimney sweeper, was charged by Thos. Emmerton, another member of the black business, with using a boy under 21 to sweep a chimney. Complainant adhered to the fact of hearing the boy in the chimney at work and seeing him come down, which was denied by the mistress of the house and the boy, they stating the machine had been used, and the boy was clearing the soot out of the grate. - Dismissed, complainant to pay costs. *Northampton Mercury 30 May 1868.*

William and Millicent's son William married Catherine Redhead during 1859. By 1861 they were living along Benefield Road with their fourteen-month old daughter Anne. William, a wheelwright, and Kate had moved to West Street in 1871 with their children, Anne eleven, William eight born at Great Gidding and five-year-old Kate born in Oundle. William and Kate had moved again in 1881 to Odys Yard with their son William a wheelwright and daughter Kate a pupil teacher. They were back along West Street by 1891 with their son William a wheelwright and Kate a certified elementary teacher. In 1901 they only had William at home.

WEDDING – A very pretty wedding was solemnised in Oundle parish church on Monday when Mr Charles T. Maddison, the well-known violinist, and Miss Kate Thurlby for many years' head infant mistress at the National school, were united in holy matrimony. The Rev. A.E. Oldroyd officiated. The bride, who was prettily attired in white, was given away by her father Mr W. Thurlby. The bridesmaids Misses J Thurlby and H Maddison wore spotted muslin dresses. Mr

Chas. Dugdale was best man. The happy couple left for Kettering in the evening, now the residence of the bridegroom. *Peterborough Advertiser 5 May 1900*

William senior died during 1906 aged sixty-nine.

OBITUARY – The death took place on Tuesday of Mrs Kate Thurlby, who was in her 90th year, and was the widow of Mr William Thurlby, who died some years ago. She was much esteemed and leaves one son and two daughters. *Northampton Mercury 5 June 1925.*

William and Millicent's son Mark married Clara Goodman King in 1869. Clara was the daughter of William and Mary Ann King; William was a Sexton. In 1871 Mark, his wife Clara and their one-year-old daughter Clara lived with William and Mary Ann King in St Osyth's lane. Mark died in 1875 aged thirty-one. By 1881 Clara was shown as 'Jack of all trades' she lived along West Street with her family Clara King Thurlby eleven, Ada Marian eight, Edith Mary six and Pearl Maggie was one-year-old. Clara was house keeper for Francis and Mary Ann King in 1901, they lived along West Street, Mary Ann was shown as sister to Clara.

William and Millicent's son Robert married Mary Ann Pratt, the daughter of James Pratt a labourer from Oundle during 1858. In 1861 they lived at 5 Poplar Row with their son Mark William aged one. Mary Ann died in 1865 aged twenty-five. Robert re-married in 1869 to Charlotte Louth, daughter of Thomas Louth from Oundle. By 1871 Robert and Charlotte were living along West Street with their children Mark William eleven, Robert nine and Mary Jane was ten months old. They lived with Robert's father William. William died during 1874 aged seventy-one. In 1881 Robert and Charlotte still lived along West Street with their children Robert, Mary Jane and Maurice aged five, also James South aged eighteen son of Charlotte. At the time of the 1891 census they were living at Calcott's yard along West Street Robert was a master sweep, their daughter Jane was a dressmaker, Maurice was a shoe finisher. They had moved to New Street in 1901 their daughter Mary Jane was a dressmaker and son Maurice was a carpenter. Robert died in 1905 aged seventy-two. Charlotte died in 1908 aged seventy-five.

*Graves of Robert and Mary Ann Thurlby also William
and Millicent Thurlby in the town cemetery.*

Robert and Mary's son Maurice married Edith Ellen Fox, daughter of Thomas a gardener, in 1903. Maurice was a carpenter.

FUNERAL – The remains of Edith, the youngest daughter of Mr Thomas Fox, of Rock-road, were interred in the Cemetery on Saturday afternoon. The deceased passed away at the early age of 28 years, and her death is a particularly sad one, for she was only just recently married, being the wife of Mr Morris Thurlby, of Oundle. For the past few months she has been a great sufferer from a complication of diseases, and the end was caused by a severe attack of bronchitis. Great sympathy is felt for the husband, who is left with a motherless babe. The funeral took place from deceased father's house. The wreaths were extremely beautiful. *Northampton Mercury 25 May 1906*

In 1911 Maurice was living with his married sister Mary Jane Wright at 71 Channel View Road in Eastbourne. Mary married Tom Wright in Oundle towards the end months in 1903.

Robert and Mary's son Robert married Sarah Ann Walton during 1888. By 1891 they were living along West Street with their six-month old son Benjamin. In 1901 they had a brother for Benjamin who they called Charles Morris he was four months old.

At the Divisional Petty Sessions on Thursday 20 August 1908 – Before Colonel Costobadie (in the chair) and Mr L Brassey – The charge against Benjamin Thurlby, chimney sweep, Oundle, of allowing a dog to be large at night was dismissed on payment of costs, 6s. *Northampton Mercury 21 August 1908.*

In 1911, still along West Street, was Robert a chimney sweep, shown as being totally blind for three years, and his wife Sarah who assisted in the family business had filled out the census return. They were shown as having had five children two of whom had died. Benjamin aged twenty was a chimney sweep, Charles aged ten and Ned aged eight attended school. Robert Abbott aged thirty-one, an assistant in the family business, was shown as being deaf and dumb from birth.

Robert and Sarah's son Benjamin married Florence Willis in 1913. They had three sons Maurice B, Robert Charles and Richard Mark, and a daughter Ellen.

MOTOR ACCIDENT – On Wednesday morning about 10.30 Mr. B. Thurlby, a chimney sweep, was driving his pony and cart along the Milton-road, and when crossing for Blackpot-lane, a motor car, containing Colonel Milne Redhead and his chauffer, came into collision with him. Thurlby was thrown out and was badly shaken and bruised. His cart was broken, and the pony was scratched. The car was damaged, but was able to convey Thurlby to his home in West-street. *Northampton Mercury 28 November 1913*

Benjamin Thurlby joined the Army in 1915 as a Gunner with the Royal Horse and Field Artillery.

OUNDLE – Mr B Thurlby, fishing in the Nene, caught a Tench weighing 4lbs 2 ½ ozs. *Northampton Mercury and Herald 27 July 1934*

WAR SERVICE AT 14 – Following a claim put forward for Mr C. M. Thurlby, of Oundle, that he was the youngest soldier in the war, the "Mercury and Herald" has received a letter from Mr E.L. Willett, of Peterson, Buckingham-road, Bletchley, who states that he was 14 on January 7, 1915, and joined the South Wales Borderers on May 3, 1916. Mr Thurlby served with the Northamptonshire Territorials. He joined up with the 4th Battalion on April 25, 1915, when 14, and on Armistice Day he was still 18 days off his 18th birthday. *Northampton Mercury 5 April 1935.*

Robert and Charlotte's son Mark William married Lucy Elizabeth Clarke, daughter of Thomas and Mary Clarke during 1880. Thomas was a hawker. They lived at Victoria Yard along West Street in 1881 with Lucy's son Henry Clarke aged eleven. Mark was a mason's labourer. Lucy Thurlby, married woman, was a domestic servant living at the Red Lion along New Street where John Bunning was the licensed victualler in 1891. Her husband, shown as William Mark was lodging with James and Mary Bailey along Knight Street in Wellingborough, he was a farm labourer, he was recorded on the census as being the son of James and Mary Bailey (not sure why that was recorded). Their daughter Nellie born in 1881 was living with her Grandmother Mary Clarke at the Victoria Yard along West Street. Mary Clarke's sons Richard and Herbert also lived with her. Lucy died in 1895 aged forty-four. Mark, a widower, was living at 5 Montague Street in Rushden in 1901, he was a stone mason. Mary Parrish was his house keeper, also living there was Sarah Parrish aged twenty-one as well as Ada nine, May six, Millicent three and one-year-old Winifred. They were shown as children of Mark. In 1908 Mark and Mary Parrish married. By 1911 Mark and Mary were living at 5 Windmill Road in Rushden, Mark was a club steward and Mary a club stewardess. Their daughter's Ada, May and Millicent were shoe hands in the Closing Dept., Winifred attended school. Mark and Mary had five children one of whom had died.

Mark and Lucy's daughter Nelly was a domestic servant for Walter and Helen Harris at the time of the 1901 census. Walter was a china and glass stall keeper for Henry Thurston the circus proprietor. They were staying in the Gipsy caravans along the Stansted Road in the Red Lion field at Bishop Stortford. Nellie Thurlby married John Thomas Steels during 1910. John was the son of Robert and Harriett who lived in Fletton Peterborough. By 1911 John Steels, a tea warehouseman, and Nellie lived at 16 Milton Street in Peterborough with their son John Thomas shown as being under one month old. He died not long after the census was recorded.

The TODD family

Thomas and Mary/Martha's children included Thos' c.1737, William c.1739, Richard c.1741 and Mary c.1747.

Thomas and Hannah's children included Thomas c.1764, William c.1766, Benjamin Leet Todd c.1770, Richard c.1772, Mary Millicent c.1775 and John c.1776.

Thomas and Hannah's son William married Elizabeth Edis during 1795. Their children were Rebecca Coates Todd c.1796, Hannah Leete Todd c.1798, Thomas and William were baptised together in 1800, Robert Edis Todd c.1801, Richard c.1803 and Mary Millicent who died 1827 aged eighteen. William senior died during 1824 aged fifty-seven.

Thomas and Hannah's son Benjamin Leet Todd married Elizabeth Kisbee on 2 January 1816, Mary Kisbee and Rebeckah Todd were witnesses. Benjamin, a schoolmaster, and Elizabeth had the following family, Thomas c.1816, Mary Millicent c.1818, William c.1820, Benjamin Leete c.1822, Hannah Leete c.1825 and Rebecca Leete born c.1826 and died in 1838.

In 1841 Benjamin and Elizabeth's son Benjamin Leete Todd was a junior hairdresser living and working for John Askham, hairdresser, and his family in the Market Place in Oundle. Living nearby was his brother William, a baker.

Benjamin and Elizabeth's son Benjamin Leete Todd, a hairdresser, married Elizabeth Belton from Spaldwick during 1845. They lived along New Street in 1851 with their family, Robert William aged four, Benjamin two and William was ten months old. Benjamin employed one apprentice John Belton aged sixteen from Spaldwick. Helena Auspital aged sixteen from Elton was their house servant. By 1861 Benjamin was shown as a hairdresser/tobacconist, he was also shown as being deaf. Their family had increased with two daughters Elizabeth eight and Emma seven. Emma Bishop from Nassington was their servant. Benjamin and Elizabeth only had William at home by 1871, he was an assistant hairdresser. Sarah Ann Caster from Brington was their house servant. Benjamin had retired from the hairdressing business in 1881 also he and Elizabeth had moved to North Street and employed Emma Barratt from Southwick as their domestic servant.

Four of Benjamin and Elizabeth's family were living along the Market Place in 1871. Robert was the head of household and was a draper, as was his brother Benjamin. Elizabeth and Emma also lived there. Benjamin died during 1872 aged twenty-four. By 1881 Robert was living along West Street, Elizabeth and Emma, milliners continued to live with their brother. Sarah Ann Sharman from Woodnewton was their general servant.

MARRIAGE – On Wednesday last the nuptials of Mr. Joseph William Willcocks, of Stamford, and Miss Emma, second daughter of Mr. Benjamin Todd, were celebrated in the parish church of Oundle. The bride was the daughter of an old and highly esteemed inhabitant. The sacred edifice was crowded. The bride was attired in cream satin with a bridal wreath and veil, and carrying a rich bouquet. She was led to the altar by her father. Mr. Bowmar acted as best man. The bridesmaids, who were costumed in blue satteen, cream lace, and velvet, with hats to match, were Miss Todd, sister to the bride; Misses Alice, Lizzie, and Katie Willcocks, sisters to the bridegroom; and Miss Ferriman, cousin to the bride. The marriage ceremony was performed by the Rev. C. Hopkins, vicar, and at the conclusion "The Wedding March" was effectively played by Dr. F. King on the organ, the bells shortly afterwards ringing out their merry peal. After the usual wedding breakfast, the bridal pair left for the south amid hearty good wishes. *Northampton Mercury 17 September 1881*

Benjamin Leete Todd died in 1891 aged sixty-nine. Elizabeth, a widow, was living with her son Robert along the Market Place. Robert's cousin Eva Brown from Spaldwick and Sarah Thompson from Peterborough, a domestic servant for the family also lived in the Todd household. Elizabeth died during 1900 aged eighty.

Robert Todd had moved on from his drapery business as in 1901 he was a town surveyor. His sister Elizabeth was still living with Robert, as was their nephew Robert William Willcocks born in Stamford. Hannah Pinder from Warmington was their domestic servant. By 1911 Robert and Elizabeth were living along New Street, neither of them had an occupation and both stayed single. Nellie Bird from Lutton was their general servant. Robert William Todd died in 1918 aged seventy.

OUNDLE – MISS ELIZABETH TODD passed away on Tuesday at the age of 80. She was the last of a very old Oundle family and was much esteemed. *Northampton Mercury 20 January 1933. (*Elizabeth was the daughter of the late Benjamin Snr., and Elizabeth Todd).

The Will of the late Elizabeth Todd was published in the *Northampton Mercury on* 2 June 1933, some of her wishes included the following – '£10 to Mary Todd- "to give her a little holiday; she has wealthy relatives on her own side, who, I hope will remember her"; £5 to Kate Cattermole, dressmaker; She desired Margaret E. Cook "to care for my dear dog."

Benjamin (jnr) and Elizabeth's son William married Louisa Dodwell during 1877 in Buckinghamshire where Louisa was born. At the time of the 1881 census William and Louisa lived along the Market Place with their son Benjamin aged two. William was shown as being deaf. Jonathan Lee was an apprentice hairdresser living with the family. Mary Ann Laxton aged fifteen from Oundle was their general servant. William, Louisa and Benjamin had moved to West Street in 1891, Agnes Pitts from Tansor was their domestic servant. By 1901 William and Louisa had moved to New Street, their son Benjamin lived at home, he was an ironmonger's assistant. Annie Shrive from Elton was their general servant.

ACCIDENT – An unfortunate accident happened on Monday morning to Mr. W. Todd, tobacconist, of West-street. Whilst cycling he collided with another cyclist at the bottom of the Black Pot-lane, causing him to be thrown to the ground. A broken ankle was the result. Mr Todd was quickly conveyed to his home by members of the St. John Ambulance Brigade on the wheeled litter. Mr Todd had a severe shaking, as well as a broken limb, and it will be month or two before he will be able to walk again. *Northampton Mercury 1 July 1904*

ACCIDENT – Mr William Todd, retired tobacconist, had a fall while skating on Saturday, causing a badly sprained ankle. *Northampton Mercury 10 January 1908*

In 1911 William and Louisa had moved and were living at 'Fairholm' along Glapthorne Road. Rosa Johnson from Great Gidding was their domestic servant. Their son Benjamin was living along Ebury Street in St George Hanover Square, London where he was a Clerk in Holy Orders.

DEATH OF MRS TODD – After a long illness, Mrs Todd, wife of Mr William Todd, passed away at her residence, Glapthorne-road, on Wednesday evening, at the age of 72. *Northampton Mercury 28 May 1926*

Mr William Todd, a retired hairdresser and tobacconist, of Oundle, dies on Wednesday aged 77. His health gave way on the death of his wife in May last year. His son, the Rev. B. Todd, is vicar of Hadlow Down, Uckfield, Sussex. *Northampton Mercury 22 July 1927*

TESTIMONIAL TO VICAR – A cheque for £22 has been sent to the Rev. Benjamin Todd, the retiring Vicar, as the result of a collection among the parishioners. Mr Todd, who was Vicar of Hadlow Down for twelve years, is now residing at Uckfield. *Sussex Agricultural Express 13 July 1928.*

FORMER VICAR OF HADLOW DOWN – There was a large congregation present at St. Mary's Church, Buxted on Monday morning, when the funeral took place of the Rev. Benjamin Todd, A.K.C.L., of "Northenden," London-road, Uckfield, who passed away last week. He became Vicar of Hadlow Down in 1916, and on his retirement on account of ill-health went to reside at Uckfield. The body was conveyed to the church overnight. The service was of a very impressive nature and there were numerous floral tributes. Mr Todd was 50 years of age. The interment was preceded by Requiem Mass in the Church, the Rev. H.H. Williams (Rural Dean of Uckfield, and Rector of Little Horsted) officiating. The mourners included the widow and son and daughter, while among the congregation were a number of clergy from the district, and parishioners from Hadlow Down. *Sussex Agricultural Express 7 December 1928.*

William and Elizabeth's son Richard's family

An entry in the Leicester chronicle dated 14 February 1829 under the heading of - From the London Gazette Friday, Jan.30. – Partnerships Dissolved – 'Richard Todd and William Williams, of Oundle Northamptonshire, booksellers.'

The following advertisements were submitted to the Stamford Mercury; -

15 January 1841 - To PRINTERS and BOOKBINDERS Wanted, a steady Man as Journeyman. - Apply (by letter) to RICHARD TODD, bookseller, Oundle ☞ None but good Workmen need apply.

On 27 August 1841 – To PRINTERS. Wanted, a respectable Man as above-none but good workmen need apply: one who can assist occasionally at the Binding would be preferred. Apply to RICHARD TODD, bookseller, Oundle.

Richard and Eliza Todd lived along New Street in Oundle where Richard ran the family business. Their children were Richard William, Eliza Martha, Mary Emily, Caroline Hannah, Isabella, Emma Rebecca, Frances Elizabeth and Flora Octavia. In 1851 Richard's address was shown as Stamford & Spalding Bank & Coup, New Street. He employed three people, Augustus Chilton from London was a governess for their children, George Horden from Stamford was a book seller's assistant and George Overbury from Wiltshire was a book seller's apprentice. Their three house servants were Jane Reed from Ashton, Mary Palmer from Glapthorn and Thomas Shrive from Oundle. Ten years later Richard was shown as a bank manager and bookseller employing 2 men. Richard and Eliza only had their daughter Frances and granddaughter Emmeline aged five at home.

On the 7th May RICHARD TODD aged 63, for 35 years' manager of the Stamford, Spalding and Boston Banking Company at Oundle. *Northampton Mercury 11 May 1867.* Richard's death was also reported in the Stamford Mercury, Lincolnshire Chronicle, Yorkshire Post and Nottinghamshire Guardian.

NEW-STREET OUNDLE, Northamptonshire All the valuable HOUSEHOLD FURNITURE, 2 Cottage Pianofortes, Oil Paintings, Engravings, books, Glass, China, Home-made Wine, Washing and Wringing Machine, Flower-stands, Pots and Plants &c., to be SOLD by AUCTION, by Samuel Deacon on Friday the 21st day of June 1867, on the premises of the late Mr RICHARD TODD, New-street Oundle. Descriptive catalogues may be had six days previous to sale on application at the principal Inns in the neighbourhood; King's Printing-office, Oundle; and at the Offices of the3 Auctioneer, Oundle. Sale to commence at 10 o'clock. *Stamford Mercury 7 June 1867*

Richard and Eliza's son Richard William married Fanny Prudence Cockle during 1854. They had a daughter Emmeline Dora. (In 1851 Prudence F. Cockle was a governess for a magistrate who lived at Easingwold in Yorkshire.) Richard, an agent for Burton ales, and Prudence lived at Basford, Nottinghamshire in 1861, they had two sons Henry two and Paul one. Ten years later Fanny had moved and was living along Star-lane in Peterborough with her children. Harry (Henry) twelve and Paul eleven born in Nottingham then Kate aged eight and Arthur six both born in Oundle. In 1881 Fanny, a widow, was living with her married daughter Emmeline Larratt, her husband Clement and their family in Bracebridge Lincoln. Ten years later they had all moved to Nottingham. Fanny Prudence Todd died during 1896 at Hailsham in Sussex aged sixty-four.

Richard and Eliza's daughter Caroline married William Eve in 1861. William was a surveyor from London. They were living at 113 Albion Road, Stoke Newington in 1871 where William was a surveyor and architect.

Richard and Eliza's daughter Isabella married George Horace David Chilton during 1864. George was a solicitor from Stoke Newington in Middlesex. They also lived in Stoke Newington at 115 Albion Road in 1871.

At St Mary's, Stoke Newington, on the 20th inst., Charles Edward second son of the late Rev. W.H. Marriott, M.A., minister of St Paul's Episcopal chapel, Edinburgh, to Mary Emily second daughter of the late Mr. Richard Todd of Oundle. *Stamford Mercury 26 July 1867.*

By 1871 Charles, a schoolmaster, and Mary were living at Seaford with their young family. Mary's sister' Eliza Martha also lived with them and was a governess.

At Seaford on the 15th inst, Eliza relict of Richard Todd, of Oundle, in her 60th year. *Stamford Mercury 24 June 1870.* Eliza was buried in the churchyard at St Leonards in Seaford, East Sussex.

At St Mary's Stoke Newington on the 30th ult., Wm. Eve Langford, of Hitchin Herts, to Frances Elizabeth youngest daughter of the late Richard Todd, of Oundle. *Stamford Mercury 2 May 1873*

The death took place on Sunday at Stoke Newington of Miss Eliza Martha Todd (late of Oundle), in her 82nd year. *Northampton Mercury 7 April 1916*

Family graves of the Todd family including
many children in St Peters churchyard.

'Dedication of a window - In 1845, and probably a few years earlier, there was a well-known bookseller and stationer in Oundle. Richard Todd, whose shop was in New Street, where Barclays Bank now is. He was also secretary to the Oundle Savings bank and was a leading tradesman of his day. Now one of his descendants, Miss Margaret Chilton, of Edinburgh, herself a Church window designer, has presented a stained-glass window to the parish Church and very appropriately it is being fixed near the spot in the churchyard where many of the TODD family are at rest and the inscription reads – designed by Miss Margaret Chilton, Edinburgh. In gratitude for the happy memories of the daughters of Richard and Eliza TODD, whose early years were spent in Oundle and whose gracious presence survives in many places in the younger generation.' (As an interesting note the business of the late Mr TODD was purchased by the later Mr Alfred King in 1862 and carried on until 1934 and now Mr V. E. Leayton. Such is the whirligig of times). *Peterborough Advertiser Friday 28th September 1934.*

The TOOKEY families

Samuel Tookey married Mary Drake in 1759 their children included Richard, Mary, William Watson, Catharina, Richard, Samuel, John and Catherine. Some of their children died whilst very young.

An announcement in the deaths column of the Northampton Mercury 23 July 1814 states –Wednesday last, at Oundle, Miss Tookey, aged 52, eldest daughter of the late Mr. Samuel Tookey, druggist of that place.

(In the early years the letter 's' were sometimes written as an 'f').

OUNDLE – WILLIAM WATSON TOOKEY, having Taken and Entered upon the Premifes, and Stock in Trade of MR JOHN BAKER, BOOKSELLER and STATIONER, oppofite the Talbot Inn, in the New-street, OUNDLE, humbly takes this Method of informing his Friends in Oundle and its Vicinity, as alfo the Public in general, that he intends laying in an intire new STOCK, together with a Variety of other Articles in the above Branches, and earneftly folicits their kind Patronage ; affuring them, every Endeavour fhall be exerted for their Intereft and Satisfaction, and the Favour of their Orders moft gratefully acknowledged, by their moft Obedient and very humble Servant. – N.B. STAMPS of all Sorts. Alfo, a great Variety of the neweft and moft fafhionable PAPER HANGINGS, BORDERS, &c. on the Fhorteft Notice, and loweft Prices. *Northampton Mercury 3 September 1791*

On Sunday laft, at Oundle, Mr John Tookey to Mifs Johnfon, of the fame place. *Northampton Mercury 28 September 1799*

John and Rebecca's children were Johnson c.1800 died 1802, William Watson c.1802, Letitia c.1803, Lewis born and died 1810.

On Sunday last, at Oundle, aged 69, Mary Ashby; who had lived in Mr Tookey's family, of that place, a good and faithful servant upwards of fifty years. *Northampton Mercury 1 September 1804.*

The following was reported in the Stamford Mercury 26 October 1810 – On Monday, aged 88, Mr Tookey, grocer, of Oundle. He was in his shop as well as usual, when he dropt down suddenly, and expired immediately. Another death was announced on 1 February

1811 that on Sunday last, Mr J. Tookey, farmer of Oundle. In the 30 August 1811 edition – On Tuesday, aged 76, Mrs Tookey, of Oundle.

At Oundle, on Sunday last, Mr Saml. George Leigh, grocer and tea-dealer, of Oundle, to Miss Tookey, daughter of Mrs Tookey of the same place. *Stamford Mercury 6 September 1822*

At Oundle, on Friday last, Mr W.W. Tookey, draper, to Miss Hannah Todd, milliner, both of that place. *Stamford Mercury 9 December 1825*

Wanted immediately, a respectable YOUTH, as an APPRENTICE to the LINEN & WOOLEN DRAPERY BUSINESS. Apply, if by letter, Postpaid, to MR W.W. TOOKEY, Oundle. *Northampton Mercury 10 December 1825*

On Wednesday, at Oundle, aged 26, Mrs Tookey, wife of Mr. W. W. Tookey, draper, and daughter of Mrs Todd, milliner of that place. The amiable disposition of this truly excellent woman will long be cherished in the recollection of her relatives and friends. *Stamford Mercury on 8 December 1826* Hannah was the daughter of Benjamin Todd, a school master, and Elizabeth Todd.

On Monday last, Mr Tookey, draper of Oundle, to Miss Margaret Cheeseman, of the same place, third daughter of the late Mr. Cheeseman of Apethorpe. *Stamford Mercury 2 November 1827.*

William and Margaret had two children Margaret Hannah c.1831 and William Watson c.1833.

On Monday last, aged 3 months, William Watson the infant son of Mr Tookey, draper of Oundle *Stamford Mercury 22 February 1833.*

A most impudent fraud was attempted to be practised at Oundle on Saturday last. A young woman went into the shop of Mr Tookey, draper, and presented to the shopman a note purporting to be written by Mrs Deacon, of Benefield, containing an order for goods to the amount of about 4/- : the shopman suspecting, from the girl's demeanour, and from other circumstances, that all was not right, desired her to call again, and in the interim sent for Mr Deacon, who happened to be in the town, and who upon seeing the note said it was not his wife's hand-writing. Upon the re-appearance of the delinquent, she was taken into custody, and conveyed before the magistrates, who were then sitting at the Swan Inn, where she gave a very vague account of herself, but at length acknowledged that the note had been written by a Mrs Chapman, of Oundle. Mrs Chapman was then sent for, and upon being asked how she came to be implicated in such a fraudulent transaction, stated that the girl called upon her with tears in her eyes told a most piteous tale of having lost a note with which Mrs Deacon had entrusted her ; that note contained an order for goods from Mr Tookey's ; that she was sure Mr Tookey would not let her have them without a written order ; that she dare not see Mrs Deacon again without executing her errand, &c, &c,; and she concluded by entreating Mrs C. to write another note in Mrs Deacon's name, as she could inform Mrs C. of every word contained in the order, having been present when Mrs Deacon wrote it. Mrs C. was thus induced to comply with the girl's request, and wrote the note, which was presented at Mr Tookey's shop as above stated. – The girl, not having completed her crime by obtaining possession of the goods, was discharged, after receiving a severe admonition from the magistrate. *Stamford Mercury 30 January 1829*

On Monday morning last some expert conveyancer succeeded in abstracting 18 yards of muslin, of the value of 30s., from the shop of Mr Tookey, draper, of Oundle. – The delinquent has not been discovered. *Stamford Mercury 10 April 1829.*

In 1841 W.W. Tookey, a draper, and his wife Margaret lived in the Market Place with their daughter Margaret and Lukey (Lucy?) Tookey aged seventy. There were twelve other people living with the Tookey family, they were drapers, dressmakers, apprentices in said occupations, or servants to the family.

Wanted immediately, two respectable young Ladies as Apprentices to the Millinery and Dress-making business. - Applications (if by letter, pre-paid) to Mrs Tookey, Oundle *Stamford Mercury 6 October 1843.*

On the 2nd inst., at the residence of her nephew Mr W.W. Tookey, draper, Oundle, Miss S. Tookey, in her 78th year, much respected by a numerous circle of friends. *Stamford Mercury 16 May 1845.*

By 1851 William and Margaret had moved to West Street, W.W. Tookey (as recorded on census), a draper, who employed 1 apprentice and 5 milliners. He also employed a house maid, a cook and a footman.

At Apethorpe, on Wednesday last, (by the Rev. M. J. Bexley) Mr Durrnas of Lascelles Hall, Yorkshire, to Margaret Hannah only daughter of Mr W.W. Tookey, of Oundle *Stamford Mercury 3 October*

1851. The wedding was also reported in the London Evening Standard on the same day.

At Oundle on the 8th inst., aged 75, Mrs Tookey, mother of Mr W.W. Tookey, of that place – *Stamford Mercury 10 February 1854*

At Oundle July 22 Margaret Hannah widow of W.W. Tookey, aged 74. Friends will kindly accept this intimation. *Stamford Mercury 30 July 1880.*

Graves of the Tookey family in St Peters churchyard.

The VESSEY families

In 1841 Charles Vessey was an agricultural labourer living with his wife Eliza and their daughter Charlotte aged one at Green Lane in Horncastle. They continued to live at Horncastle right through to the 1871 census Charles was a maltster's labourer. Their children were John a plumber aged nineteen, Charles a whitesmith aged seventeen, Eliza fifteen, William thirteen, George twelve, Mary ten, Rachel seven, Sarah five and Alice aged two, they all attended school. Charles died at Horncastle during 1878 aged sixty-six. Eliza worked as a laundress by the time of the 1881 census, her daughter Sarah was shown as a mother's help. Eliza's seven-year-old granddaughter Alice Harbour also lived with them, Alfred Cook a commercial clerk from Camberwell boarded with the family. Eliza's daughter Alice was a servant for William France, an accountant, and his family who lived along Alexander Terrace in Nether Hallam in Yorkshire during 1881. Eliza died during 1887 aged seventy-one.

Charles and Eliza's daughter Sarah was living along Stanhope Road in Horncastle during 1891. Her sister Alice and niece's Alice Harbour aged seventeen and Nellie Vessey aged five lived with Sarah. Sarah and both the Alice's were laundresses. Arthur Prestwood, a confectioner, lodged with them. In 1901 Sarah, a laundress was still living at 15 Stanhope Road, where she lived until her death. Sarah's niece Nellie was a chemist' packer and was still living with her aunt. Arthur Prestwood continued boarding with them. Sarah and Arthur were at 15 Stanhope Road in 1911, Sarah died during 1913 aged fifty-eight.

Charles and Eliza's daughter Alice married William Saltman during 1895 in Horncastle. At the time of the 1901 census they were living at North Gate in Market Weighton in Yorkshire where William was a master shoemaker. By 1911 William and Alice had Nellie Vessey living with them, she was a wool winder in a hose factory, and was shown as Williams' step daughter. Nellie married Stanley Warner during 1911.

Charles and Eliza's daughter Rachel was a house servant at the Dryden House Boarding house in North Street in 1871. Rachel worked with Sarah Plowright from Benefield and Mary Burrows from Tansor who was a cook. Rachel married William Lancaster during 1877 they made their home in Manningham near Bradford. William was a tailor. Rachel died in 1883 aged twenty-nine.

Charles and Eliza's son Charles married Patience Taylor during 1864 in Oundle. By 1871 they were living along New Street where Charles was a whitesmith. They had two children, Samuel Charles aged five and Elizabeth Patience aged two. Arthur Howitt, a saddler from Spalding lodged with Charles and Patience. At the time of the 1881 census Charles was a whitesmith journeyman, he was living along West Street with Patience and their family. Elizabeth Patience aged twelve, Arthur George nine, Ellen Mary six, Hannah Jane four and Charles Samuel aged two all born in Oundle.

Sad case of burning at Oundle – On Saturday at 7am a sad case of burning occurred to a woman named Pridmore. She had been sitting up all night nursing her children, who were ill, and, it appears, worn out, fell asleep before the fire. Her clothes caught fire, and she rushed out of the house in flames. A man named Charles Vessey, a member of the Fire Brigade, quickly extinguished the flames, not however, before the poor woman was very seriously burnt all over her body. She was speedily attended to by Dr L.B. Calcott, but lies in a very precarious condition, and is hardly expected to recover. *Northampton Mercury 1 March 1890.*

In 1901 Charles and Patience were living along Benefield Road. Patience died in 1902 aged sixty-two.

ACCIDENT – On Tuesday Mr Charles Vessey, a highly respected employee of Mr Ramshey of Oundle, was at work in Aldwinckle, when the ladder on which he was working slipped, throwing him some distance to the ground, fracturing two ribs and cutting him about the face. Mr Vessey was brought home to Oundle, and is making favourable progress under the circumstances. *Peterborough Advertiser 17 June 1905*

By 1911 Charles Vessey continued to live along Benefield Road where he lived alone. Charles had recorded on the census that he had been married for thirty-eight years had eight children two of whom had died. One of their children was Evelyn Patience who died from serious burns aged three months. Due to the sad nature of Evelyn's experience a full report of the inquest can be found in the *Northampton Mercury dated 23 February 1906.*

Charles died on 20 July 1915 at Benefield Road in Oundle aged seventy-one.

Charles and Patience's daughter Ellen Mary was a nurse living at The Hall in Southwick working for George Capron in 1891. Although Ellen was so named throughout the census years she was baptised as Helen Mary. Ellen/Helen seems to have evaded the 1901 census. Helen married George Chadburn during 1902 in the Dartford district. By 1911 they were living at 88 Aslett Street in Wandsworth with their sons Cyril and Alexander. George was a warden in the prison service.

Charles and Patience's daughter Elizabeth Patience married Frank Palmer, from Benefield, in 1892. They made their home at Southwick where they were in 1901 to 1911, Frank was a gardener. In 1911 their children were Ada Helen seventeen, Francis William fifteen, Evelyn Patience fourteen, Bertram Charles twelve, Enid Lilian ten and Bernard Vivian was seven.

Charles and Patience's son Arthur George married Sarah Ann Hill during 1896. In 1901 they lived a short distance away from Arthur's parents with their two sons, Arthur four and Charles W two years old.

Arthur took part in the Band of Hope entertainment held in the Queen Victoria Hall on Wednesday 3 February 1904. A section of the report in the Northampton Mercury reads as follows; 'An attractive and amusing entertainment was given by the members of the Congregational Band of Hope. Notwithstanding the wretched weather the new hall was packed to its utmost capacity by the biggest audience of any concert yet held there. Miss Emily Knight is to be congratulated on the success of the concert. She has been at great pains drilling the children and the result of her work does her great credit. A very amusing item of the programme was a recitation by Master Arthur Vessey, entitled "I Dunno." His acting and the history of his childhood days fairly captivated the company, and the little fellow had to present himself three times before the applause subsided.'

In 1911 Arthur was a gardener, he lived along West Street with his wife Sarah Ann; they had been married for fifteen years and had eight children two of whom had died. Their children at home were Arthur George aged fourteen a butcher's apprentice, Charlie William aged twelve, Gertrude Annie nine, Eric Lionel six and Mary Georgina aged four all attended school, then Alice May was two years old. William Afford aged seventy-three, shown as an Old Age Pensioner from Oundle George Wilson a farm labourer from Morton and Thomas Rivett a drover from Norfolk lodged with Charles and Sarah Ann.

A big branch of a poplar tree on Sunday crashed on to the roof of a cottage occupied by Mr Eric Vessey demolishing the tiles and rafters and considerably damaging the bedroom furniture. Fortunately, nobody was in the room. Sympathy is felt for Mr and Mrs Vessey as their house at Peterborough was demolished in an air raid some months ago and they came to Oundle to live. *Peterborough Advertiser 5 February 1943*

The WILLMOTT/WILLIMOTT families

An entry in the Stamford Mercury dated 3 June 1825 read –On Sunday last, at Oundle, Mr John Willmott, landlord of the White Lion public house, aged 56. – His death is supposed to have been occasioned by the injury he received from falling over a wheelbarrow in his yard the preceding Friday.

Most Willmott/Willimott families were living at Cotterstock then Oundle and some in Luddington. By 1911 they were also living at Elton, Warmington and Wadenhoe.

John Willimott c.1799 from Cotterstock married Elizabeth Stevens c.1793 from Barnwell during 1822. Their children were Elizabeth, Samuel, John, Leonard, William, Catherine and Frank. By the 1841 census John and Elizabeth were living along Chapel End in Oundle with their children, Elizabeth seventeen, Samuel fifteen, Leonard thirteen, William nine, Katherine six and Francis was two years old. In 1851 John, an agricultural labourer and Elizabeth had moved and were living along West Street with their family. Elizabeth, Edward (Leonard), William and Frank (Francis) all were born in Oundle. At the time of the 1861 census they were still living along West Street at the Boys Yard with their son Leonard an agricultural labourer. Their son Frank was a general servant for Joseph Ody, a baker, who lived along West Street in the Bakers house. By 1871 John and Elizabeth had no children at home. John died in 1880 aged eighty.

John and Elizabeth's daughter Catherine was a house-maid working for Thomas and Maria Spencer in their home at Keystone near Thrapston in 1851. Thomas was a farmer of 400 acres.

The following announcement was reported in the Stamford Mercury dated 25 November 1853 – As of Monday last (by Rev. J. Nussey) Thos Parker of Tansor to Catherine Willmott. It has not been possible to find anything further on Thomas and Catherine.

John and Elizabeth's son Samuel married Elizabeth Bourn in Horncastle during 1858. Elizabeth was born in Spalding. By 1861 they were living along Far Street in Horncastle where Samuel was a railway porter. In 1871 they lived along Lincoln Road in Horncastle their children were Elizabeth, John Thomas, George Henry and William. Ten years later their address was shown as 6 Moore's Yard Horncastle. Living at home with Samuel and Elizabeth were George and William who attended school they also had a sister Edith aged two.

Samuel and Elizabeth's daughter Elizabeth was married to James Gray and had a two-month old son John Robert, they all lived with Elizabeth's parents.

John and Elizabeth's son William married Rebecca Brawn during 1854. By the time of the 1861 census they were living along Benefield Road with their children, Sarah Ann aged five born in Daventry, William three and Samuel seven months both born in Oundle. Ten years later still along Benefield Road was William and Rebecca with William thirteen, Samuel ten, Mary seven, Kate five and Alice two. Their daughter Sarah Ann was visiting William and Caroline Brawn in Hamerton. By 1881 William, a general labourer, and Rebecca only had Samuel, Alice and Leonard aged six at home.

John and Elizabeth's son John was living along North Street in 1851 he was an agricultural labourer, and lodged with Charles Sismey a brewer's labourer from Oundle. John married Mary Palmer during 1851. Mary was the daughter of Thomas, a farmer from Oundle. Samuel and Catherine Willimott were witnesses to the marriage. Mary died in 1853. John, widower, married Ann Butler, son of Daniel, during 1854, John's brothers Leonard and William were witnesses to the marriage. By 1861 John and Ann lived at 33 West Street with Ann four, John two and Charles six months old. At the time of the 1871 census John and Ann still had all three of their children at home. John died during 1879 aged 54. In 1881 Ann had two of her sons living at home John and Charles. Her daughter Ann was a kitchen-maid living at the Rectory in Oundle.

John and Ann's daughter Ann married John Parker, from Oundle, during 1895. By 1891 they were living along West Street with their five-year-old son John. Ann's mother also lived with them. Ann senior died in 1892.

John and Ann's son Charles married Sarah Webb during 1883. By the time of the 1891 census they were living just off West Street in Inkermans Yard with Edith Annie six, John William four and Charles Webb Willmott two. In 1901 still in Inkermans Yard Charles, a hay-trusser, and Sarah had five children at home, William J fourteen a draper's errand boy, Charles twelve, Mabel nine, Percival seven and Kathleen four years old. Ten years later they were living at No 5 Inkermans Yard. Percival Ernest was a hay presser like his father, Kathleen was a general domestic help, Ethel nine and Mollie six were at school.

Charles and Sarah's son John William married Ethel Rose Cullop during 1910. Ethel was the daughter of William and Martha from Warmington. By 1911 John and Ethel were living with Ethel's widowed mother Martha in Warmington. John William was a houseman at the Grammar school.

Charles and Sarah's daughter Edith Annie married Charles William Pamplin at Oundle during 1912.

Mr and Mrs C Willmott received many congratulations on Christmas Day when they celebrated their golden wedding. They have lived in Oundle all their lives and were married at the Parish church. Of their nine children, the eldest son lost his life in the war, and the youngest died two years ago from the effects of wounds. *Northampton Mercury 29 December 1933*

The WILLS family

In 1841 William Wills, c.1781, and his wife Ann c.1786, lived along St Osythes Lane. William was an agricultural labourer.

William Wills, a shoemaker, married Sarah Steers during 1843. Sarah was the daughter of Charles and Ann Steers. William was born in Islip c.1821, and Sarah c.1824 was from Oundle. They lived along Mill Lane in Oundle in 1851 with their four children Charles was eight, Ann six, Mary four and William aged one. By 1861 they had moved to Danfords Square along West Street where William continued working as a shoemaker, their family had increased. Charles eighteen, Selina sixteen, shown as Ann in the previous census, William eleven, John nine, Jane seven, Alfred five, Eliza one and two-month-old Jacob. Jacob died not long after he was born.

AGRICULTURAL SOCIETY'S MEETING AT OUNDLE – The Flower Show – Cottagers' Section – Two fuchsias, 1st William Wills, Oundle. 1lb of gooseberries, flavour, 1st Daniel Harris, 2nd Henry Winston, 3rd William Wills.' A section of the full awards taken from the Northampton Mercury 11 July 1868. Also at the flower show in 1877 as reported in the Northampton Mercury, William Wills was awarded the following a 1st in the Cottagers' class for Two plants, various. Two fuchsias in pots 2nd. Two geraniums, 1st. Twelve round potatoes 1st. Six lettuces 1st. Six spring-sown onions 2nd. Six autumn-sown onions 2nd'.

William and his family had moved to Inkerman Square by 1871 (they stayed there right through to the 1891 census) their four children at home were Alfred aged fifteen, Eliza eleven, Sarah eight and Thomas Chr'is aged seven. In 1881 William and Sarah were shown as living at 4 Inkerman Place, and had two grandchildren living with them Christopher aged seventeen and Rose Annie aged four. (Parents unknown) At the time of the 1891 census William and Sarah had their grandchild Rose Annie and their great grandson Harold aged two living with them. During 1901 their grandson Harold aged twelve continued living with them. Sarah died in 1910 aged eighty-six. In 1911 William, aged ninety, a widow and blind, lived along Benefield Road with his grandson Harold Rufus who was a house painter. William died at the end of the year in 1911 aged ninety-one.

William and Sarah's grandson Harold Rufus Wills married Gertrude A. Toyne during 1912.

William and Sarah's daughter Selina married Alfred Cunnington during 1867. (See Cunnington family details).

William and Sarah's son Alfred George married Louisa Mary Bailey during 1878. By 1881 they were living along Benefield Road Industrious Terrace with their sons Alfred George aged two and Percy William aged eight months. Samuel Barnard Barbey, brother in law to Alfred also lived with them; he was twenty-one and worked as a tailor. Ten years later still along Benefield Road lived Alfred, a plumber, and Louisa with their children Alfred twelve, Percy ten, Louisa eight, Elizabeth six, Victor three, Elsie one and Nellie was two months old.

Alfred George Wills, Oundle, plumber, was summoned by Louisa Mary Wills, under the summary Jurisdiction Act, for a separation order, owing to her husband's cruelty. Mr Maudesly appeared for complainant and Mr Norris for defendant. The Bench made an order for a deed of separation, and an order of 10s a week, with custody of the children under 16 years of age. *Northampton Mercury 2 April 1897*

In 1901 Alfred George was boarding with Mary Hale, a greengrocer, and her family who lived along West Street.

By the time of the 1901 census Louisa worked at home as a laundress with her family of seven. Alfred aged twenty-two was a fireman (general), Percy aged twenty was a blacksmith, Louisa M aged eighteen a laundress, Elizabeth S aged fifteen a domestic servant, Victor O aged thirteen an errand Boy, Elsie A was seven and Nellie M was ten years old.

OUNDLE – Petty Sessions – Order Varied, Alfred George Wills applied for a reduction of an order made against him on April 1st 1897, for the maintenance of his wife and children. He informed the Bench that from then up to the present time he had regularly paid 10s, weekly. He now offered 5s. saying that only two of the children were now under 16 years of age. His earnings were 24s. weekly but he had to contend with short time. Mr Maudesly appeared on behalf of the respondent, Louisa Wills, and maintained that the order should not be reduced. One boy, a plumber, was an apprentice, and only earning 6s. weekly. Two little girls were more or less unwell. All three required more to keep them now than when the order was made. Louisa Wills, the wife, said that the other children were Elizabeth Sarah (17), a domestic servant, earning £12 a year; Louisa Mary (22) who was at home; and two grown up sons earning £1 and £ 1s. a week respectively. – In reply to the Bench respondent stated that the last named were lodgers and paid her as such. The Bench varied the order to 7s. 6d. per week. If an application was made at some future date the case would then be reconsidered. *Northampton Mercury 6 May 1904*

In 1911 census Louisa was living along South Road in the Bassett Villa with Louisa twenty-eight a laundress, Victor twenty-three an insurance agent for Pearl Assurance, Elsie twenty-one a domestic and Nellie aged twenty a school mistress for the County Council.

Alfred and Louisa's son Alfred George married Edith Ellen Abbott during 1908. Edith was born in Wollaston Northants. By the 1911 census they were living along West Street, Alfred was a tinsmith, he worked for an ironmonger, they had a son Ronal aged one.

William and Sarah's grandson Thomas Christopher Wills married Alice Barnes from Hemington during 1887. Alice died in 1889 aged twenty-four. Thomas then married Mary Ann Allaby during 1890. An announcement in the Stamford Mercury dated 17 October – Oct. 15, Christopher Wills to Mary daughter of Mr W Allaby.

Thomas and Mary had a daughter Alice Allaby Wills who was born and died in 1891. At the time of the 1891 census they lived along Inkermans Yard in Oundle where Thomas worked as a painter. Ten years later they had moved to Benefield Road with their children Bernard George eight, Jennie six, Alec four and Jack was 10 days old. Ellen Bentley aged forty-seven was employed by the family as a monthly nurse, she was born in the Peterborough district.

Listed in the children's section of Northampton Mercury dated 22 July 1910 under the section 'For the Boys and Girls in the Uncle Dick Society new members sent by Captain V. E. Leayton was the following – 4565 Fred Wills Benefield-rd; 11 – 4566 Jack Wills Benefield-rd; 9 – 4567 Horace Wills Benefield-rd; 7'

Thomas and Mary Ann continued to live along Benefield Road in 1911. They had seven sons at home, Bernard was a builder's clerk, Alec a news boy, Fred, Jack, Horace and Christopher attended school and Frank aged two was at home with his mother. Thomas and Mary

Ann had been married for twenty years, had nine children and eight of them were still living.

OUNDLE – Mr Thomas Christopher Wills (76), who died at Oundle on Tuesday, was for 40 years a member of Oundle Fire Brigade. He leaves seven sons and a daughter. *Northampton Mercury 24 November 1939.*

Alfred and Louisa's son Percy married Florence Fowler from Fotheringhay during 1906. By 1911 they were living at 8 Battenburg Street in Kempston Bedfordshire. Alfred was a shoeing smith and carman-contractor. They had two children Percy William aged two born in Thurlby Lincolnshire and Florence Louisa Mary aged one born in Kempston.

The WILSON families

John and Mary Ann Wilson

In 1837 John Wilson, a coachman, son of Jonah Wilson, married Mary Ann Robertson, daughter of Thos' Robertson at St Peter's church Oundle. At the time of the 1841 census they were living along West Street with their one-year-old son William, he died the same year.

In 1851 John, a miller's waggoner, and his wife Mary Ann lived at 10 Oddfellows Place in Oundle with their family, Emma aged six, Harriett four and John William was three years old. Michael Roughton from Oundle lodged with them he was the son of William and Mary Roughton. John Wilson was shown as being born at Brigstock around 1811.

By 1861 John, an agricultural labourer, and Mary Ann lived at 22 Danford's Square with their family Robert aged twenty an agricultural labourer, Emma aged sixteen a dressmaker, Harriet fourteen, John William a farm servant aged thirteen, Caroline Eva six and Herbert under one month old. Mary Ann died during 1870 aged fifty-three. John was living at 20 Inkerman Square in 1871 he was recorded as an 'Ag lab unwell'; and was born in Corby. His daughter Emma aged twenty-six was shown as a 'cripple lost one arm' his other daughter Harriet aged twenty-four was a servant 'out of place'. Also at home were John William an agricultural labourer and Herbert aged ten attended school. John Wilson died in 1875 aged sixty-three.

John and Mary Ann's daughter Caroline married Walter Borlase

John and Mary Ann's daughter Caroline married Walter Borlase towards the end of the year in 1881 in the Kensington district. Walter was a solicitor from Cornwall. By 1891 Walter and Caroline made their home at Alverton House in Madron near to Penzance they employed two servants from Cornwall. Charlotte Clay from Great Addington was visiting.

John and Charlotte Wilson

John Wilson married Charlotte Roughton, daughter of William and Mary Roughton during 1850 in Oundle. John was shown as being born at Wigsthorpe near Lilford in 1811. By 1851 they lived along West Street John was a brewer's waggoner. In 1861 John and Charlotte lived at 43 West Street with their family. George was nine, John seven, Thomas six, William four, Mark one and Samuel was one month old. John was recorded on the census as being born at Pilton. Charlotte died during 1862. John a brewer's labourer was living at Tookey's Row in West Street in 1871 with his sons Thomas and Samuel. Mary Hewitt from Oundle lodged with them and was their housekeeper. John shown as being born during 1807 had moved by 1881 to Binder's Row his son Samuel lived at home and was a groom.

John and Charlotte's son Samuel was lodging with Elizabeth Squires along Mill Lane in 1891. Samuel, a hotel ostler, also shown as 'totally blind at 45 years' was an inmate at the Workhouse along Glapthorn Road in 1911.

When leaving a concert at Oundle Workhouse on Monday, Samuel Wilson aged 67, who had been an inmate for many years, dropped dead from heart disease. *Northampton Mercury October 26 1928.*

John and Charlotte's son Mark was living at 3 Golden Square in Hampstead in 1871 with William and Mary Hayter, his uncle and aunt, where he attended school. Mark married Mary Ann Foreman in Hampstead during 1883. By 1891 Mark, a gardener, and Mary lived at 13 Golden Square with their young family Kenneth six, Harry three and Florence was one-year-old, all born in Hampstead. Mark and Mary were still living at the same address in 1901 with Kenneth a printer compositor, Henry an errand wine store then Florence twelve, Allan nine and Frank four attended school. By 1911 at Golden Square Mark and Mary only had three sons at home Allan a plumber's mate, Frank fourteen and nine-year-old Leonard. Mark and Mary had been married for twenty-seven years had eight children two of whom had died.

The WYLES families

William Wyles married Eliza Duncomb in Oundle during 1840. In 1841 they were living along Benefield Road where they stayed throughout their lives. William was a shoemaker born in Oundle Eliza was born in Uppingham and worked occasionally as a laundress. Their children included George, William, Eliza (Louisa), Margaret, Mary Ann, Emma (Emily) and Marian. The daughters either worked as dressmakers or laundresses. Most of the sons became shoemakers. William died during 1895 aged eighty-two. Eliza died in 1900 aged seventy-nine. In 1911 William and Eliza's daughter Margaret lived along North Street where she ran her dressmaker's business from home. Margaret's sister Mary Ann also lived with her.

William and Eliza's son George married Rebecca Leigh during 1870. Rebecca was the daughter of Robert and Harriet Leigh who lived along Benefield Road. In 1871 and through to 1901 George and Rebecca lived at the shoe makers shop along West Street, William his brother also lived with them. George and Rebecca's children were Eliza Eleanor, Louie Margaret, Ada Leigh Wyles, Charles William, George Percy, Arthur Edward, Alfred Reginald, Willie and Robert Duncombe Wyles.

Oundle Petty Sessions, May 20 – Before G.H. Capron (chairman), and M. Biggs Esq. – Eliza Ann Braines (17), Clapton Lodge, domestic servant, was charged with obtaining, by false pretences, two pairs of shoes, valued at 11s., from George Wyles, shoemaker, West Street Oundle. – The wife of the prosecutor stated that between the 30th of April and the 3rd of May prisoner went to the shop and asked for a pair of shoes for one of the young ladies in Mr Beal's shop, saying she was a servant there. She tried a pair on; saying what fitted her would do for the young lady. Those produced were the same shoes. – Emma Johnson, housekeeper to Mr Fortescue, of Ashton, said prisoner was in his service from Michaelmas last. About three weeks since the prisoner went to Oundle. When she returned, she had a pair of tennis shoes, which she wore next morning. Witness asked where she bought them. She replied at Adkins'. Those produced were the same. – P.C. Evans said he went to prisoner's parents' house, and received a pair of cloth top shoes, and also from Miss Johnson a pair of tennis shoes. On the 15th instant he apprehended the prisoner, and charged her with obtaining the shoes from Mr Wyles. The full report can be seen in the *Northampton Mercury 24 May 1884*

By 1891 Margaret (she seemed to drop the name Louie and used it as her second name) was a school teacher and Ada was a draper's apprentice. In 1901 George Percy was a post office telegraphist, Alfred Reginald was a grocer's assistant and Willie was a boot and shoemaker.

George and Rebecca had moved by 1911 to 35 Mount Road in Hendon Midddlesex with four of their sons. Charles William was a 1st assistant clerk for Hendon Council, George Percy was a civil servant for the post office, Willie had no occupation and Robert Duncombe was a clerk to a dramatist manager. George died in 1913 aged seventy-one and Rebecca died in 1926 at the age of eighty both in Hendon where their son Charles lived.

William and Eliza's son William married Catherine Louisa Skillett during 1877. Louisa was the daughter of Thomas and Esther from Pilton. William and Louisa lived along Binder's Row in 1881 with Louisa's eight-year-old son John Skillet. William died in 1882 aged thirty-five. Louisa died in 1888 also aged thirty-five.

Joseph Wyles from Catworth

Joseph Wyles married Caroline Eliza Brudenell during 1867. Caroline was the daughter of William and Jane from North Street in Oundle. They originally came from Warmington. In 1871 Joseph, a railway labourer and Caroline a dressmaker lived along North Street with their three-year-old daughter Flora Agnes Jane. Caroline died in 1878 aged thirty-four. By 1881 Joseph lived along North Street with his children. Agnes was thirteen, Herbert eight and Jessie was six years old. Jessie was a domestic servant for Nelson Cobbald in 1891; he was a mathematics and science master at Oundle School, who lived at Sydney Villa along Glapthorn Road. Jessie died during 1896 aged twenty. Jessie's father Joseph, a labourer, and her sister Laura the house keeper still lived along North Street. Laura was born Flora Agnes Jane but had changed her name on the census. Ten years later Joseph was a maltster in a brewery, he and Laura lived in Gray's Yard on the west side of North Street.

A very extensive report can be found in the Northampton Mercury dated 11 September 1903 with regards to Joseph and Caroline's daughter's death. "Laura Agnes Jane aged 34 at the time of death. Laura sadly took her own life. An inquest was held which Dr C.N.

Elliott from Oundle performed. He found the stomach inflamed, and he said the death was due to poisoning from oxalic acid. The deceased could not have taken a large dose of oxalic acid. It must have been diluted, and would take longer to kill her. One of the witnesses was Amy Ashton, wife of George Ashton, schoolmaster, Oundle. Amy knew the deceased who often worked for her at housework. About three weeks ago deceased told witness she was likely to become a mother. She was afraid her sweetheart would not marry her, and she said that if he did not do so she would do away with herself. The jury returned a verdict of "Suicide whilst temporarily insane".

The report of the inquest included the following – The deceased was found on the hearth-rug by a female friend, in great pain, and died soon afterwards. A young man who kept company with the deceased denied that he was the cause of her trouble. She was jealous, and said that if he went out with anyone else she would throw herself in the river. *Stamford Mercury 11 September 1903*

In 1911 Joseph was a boarder at the home of Louis Hodson, an engineer - motor maker, at the Motor Works in Oundle. Joseph died during 1913 aged sixty-nine.

School children place and date unknown.
Photograph courtesy of Peterborough Images

Children c.1907 place unknown.
Photograph courtesy of Peterborough Images

241

Oundle Cricket Team date unknown.
Photograph courtesy of Peterborough Images

Oundle Football Team date unknown.
Photograph courtesy of Peterborough Images

OUNDLE SNIPPETS
(All spellings as recorded in newspapers).

(Peterborough Advertiser – PA) (Northampton Mercury – NM) (Stamford Mercury – SM)

1700's

<u>24 October 1717</u> (SM) The Apothecary's Shop in Oundle in Northamptonshire, which was Mr Selby's, lately deceas'd; is now possess'd by Henry Smith from Stamford, where any Person may be furnished with Coffee, Tea, Chocolate, and snuff, at reasonable Rates.

<u>18 October 1722</u> (SM) At Oundle in the County of Northampton, on Thursday the 25th of this Instant October, a Purse of 10 Guineas will be run for (either in the Meadow, or on the New Course, which shall be thought best in order at the time of running, by the clerk of the race) by any Horse, Mare, or Gelding carrying 10 stone weight, with briddle and saddle. The winning horse &c. to be thrown for by the Contributors at 30/-. The horses to be entred in the right owners names, to have been bona fide, in the owners possession, one month before entry, no less than 3 horses &C. to start of 3 several persons, to be shewn and entered on Monday the 22d. of October before the Clerk of the Race at the Turk's Head in Oundle aforesaid, between the hours of two and 6 in the afternoon, and be kept till the time of running, at such Public Houses only who subscribed 1/- or more to the Town Purses lately run for, or to have no share in the same. A contributor to pay Half a Guinea, a Non contributor a Guinea entrance. If any dispute arises in Entring, or any other Matter, Reference is to be had to the Articles for Determination: And the following Day will be run for on the same course, a Saddle of 30s. value, for the Horse that wins the best of three Heats, two Miles a Heat; a Whip for the second a Briddle for the third, a Pair of Spurs for the 4th, and a Wooden Spoon for the last. The Horses to be entered between 10 and 12 the Morning before Running. Note, The Meadow (barring floods) which is now set out, is one of the best Courses in England.

23 October 1735 (Derby Mercury) We hear from Oundle in Northamptonshire, that on Michaelmas-Day last, Mr Benjamin Foley of Binnifield near that Town, a Gentleman of 53 years of Age, was

married to a seventh Wife. 'Tis said he lived with his first Wife above twenty years.

1800

2 May (SM) A few days ago, whilst in the act of yawning, a young woman of Oundle, dislocated her jaw, which is likely to be attended with bad consequence. Ten days later it was reported in the Reading Mercury on 12 May 1800 – Some days since a young woman of Oundle, whilst in the act of yawning, dislocated her jaw, and it is apprehended will die in consequence.

2 August (NM) TALBOT INN to be LETT, and entered upon immediately, or at Michaelmas next, that commodious and good-accustomed INN, eligibly situated in OUNDLE, with Stabling for upwards of one Hundred Horses, and very excellent Gardens. Also, THIRTY ACRES of very rich MEADOW, and, if required, TWENTY ACRES of ARABLE LAND. For particulars, and to treat for the fame, apply to Mr John Smith, of Oundle, Northamptonshire. N.B. The furniture, and stock in trade, may be taken at an Appraisement, if required.

21 November (SM) VACCINE INOCULATION Mr Campion, of Oundle, is prepared to conduct the new INOCULATION, now found to be certainly preventive of the Small Pox, and much milder than even the inoculated Small Pox. Those who apply about the 25th, 26th, or 27th of this Month, will have great Advantages.

1856

5 July (PA) Some dissatisfaction has been caused amongst the rural postmen by an order from the General Post Office compelling them to walk and deliver their letters at the rate of three miles an hour, and to perform the return journey at the rate of three and a half miles an hour. When it is understood that their pay, which seldom exceeds 11s per week, is not to be increased, and that to make an average income they have hitherto been allowed to take parcels, which of course to a certain extent cause a little loss of time in their delivery, but no complaints on that score have been made by the public, it must be allowed to be a hard case, and one which we hope will be taken into consideration, by those who put some value on the services of a hard-working and responsible class of public servants.

1857

6 August (PA) An Unwelcome Visitor – The residence of E. Webster Esq., suffered considerable damage on Thursday last by the sudden intrusion of an over-driven cow, which poked its head through the parlour window breaking the glass casement &c.

16 October (SM) Gas – The streets of Oundle have again assumed something like brilliancy, the lamps having been put in "lighting order." There can now be no excuse for parties coming into collision with each other as previously.

1863

16 October - Lincoln Rutland and Stamford Mercury – Miscellaneous. Matrimony, Two Independent Gentlemen, residing in the neighbourhood of Oundle, are desirous of Corresponding with two suitable young Ladies, thoroughly domesticated, with a view to Matrimony. The strictest confidence may be relied on. Address enclosing carte de visite, to A.B.C., Post-office Oundle and a return carte de visite will be sent to the Lady selected.

1874

21 February (NM) OUNDLE – Police, Feb. 17th – Before J. W. Smith, Esq, Mary Reed, a vagrant of the old school, was committed for seven days, for following her professional duties with too great pertinacity. Being given a half loaf by a baker, she, seeing some sausage on the counter, requested some to go with the bread.

1899

5 May 1899 (NM) A Freak of Nature – No doubt some of our poultry fanciers will be interested to read the following: - A well-known poultry breeder, named Mr Hewitt, residing at Rock-road, Oundle, has had out of a batch of thirteen eggs a chicken with two perfectly-formed bodies and four legs and only one head, and out of another batch of eggs he had another chicken formed in every particular excepting its head, which was minus. As they did not hatch out at the proper time Mr Hewitt broke both the shells and in doing so bled them to death. They were both living when the eggs were smashed. Both eggs were from a per of pure white Leghorns, two-year-old birds. They are now preserved in spirits. *(Words and spellings are as appears in newspaper)*

Rock Road Oundle c.1905.
Photograph courtesy of Peterborough Images.

1900

24 March (PA) Late on Wednesday evening a young man named John Smith, an assistant to Mr Claridge, grocer, Oundle, was practising with a toy revolver and under the impression that it was not loaded he pulled the trigger and the contents lodged in the head of a girl named Fox in the employ of Mr Claridge. On Thursday afternoon, the girl was still unconscious, and in a critical condition. The girl Fox regained consciousness on Thursday evening and hopes are expressed for her recovery.

31 March (PA) The girl Fox, who was accidently shot last week, is now making favourable progress towards recovery.

17 July (PA) The shed at the bathing place has been removed, as owing to mischievous destruction by youths it had become useless and a positive eyesore. At the council meeting on Monday evening, the chairman said he would have been pleased to erect a new shed for the use of all alike, but owing to the wanton conduct of boys, he couldn't see his way clear to do so. At present the ladder attached to the live-saving apparatus is missing. It is a thousand pities a lot of reckless boys cannot be taught a salutary lesson as it prevents those who would enjoy the privileges from doing so.

Photograph c.1910 courtesy of Peterborough Images

<u>21 July</u> (PA) On Wednesday morning a man named William Giddings while engaged cleaning windows in the Market Place fell from a ladder about ten feet, seriously injuring his face and head, although no bones were broken.

<u>8 September</u> (PA) Urban District Council Meeting - On Thursday evening Mr H. Bletsoe sold by auction the fully licensed house known as 'The George' Tilley Hill Oundle. After spirited competition it was knocked down to Messrs Smith & Co Oundle for £1200/£1290 (not clear in newspaper). It was decided to plant Lime trees on the Glapthorne Road from Wood Lane cottages to near Tilley Hill.

<u>15 December</u> (PA) We have pleasure in acknowledging the receipt of the 1901 issue 'Markham's Oundle Almanac and compendium' because it surpasses its predecessors in its literary excellence and in its encyclopaedic information – and all for Twopence. We have often been at a loss for the moment for some local item of information and have invariably found it here, and thus been able to preserve the Editorial peace of mind, which is worth a good deal. Next year we would suggest the title being printed on the book for ready reference when in a bookcase.

1901

5 July (NM) SERIOUS FIRE AT OUNDLE – Early on Monday morning an outbreak of fire occurred in the New-street on the premises of Miss Negus, who has a needlework and fancy business. That lady at once gave the alarm to Mr R. Marlow, her neighbour, who quickly dressed, sent for the Fire Brigade, and helped Miss Negus to escape by a back staircase, which at that time had escaped the fire. Within ten minutes the Fire Brigade were on the spot, and they found on arrival that already the ground premises were well alight. Two hoses were at once fixed on the hydrants close by, and with an excellent supply of water the fire was soon under control, not before, however, serious damage had been done, for the rooms on the ground floor were gutted. Fortunately, the fire did not have time to spread to the upstairs rooms. Had it done so the result would have been alarming, for near is a gunpowder storage owned by Mr W. Todd. The premises are said to be over 200 years old. The origin of the fire remains a mystery. The loss is fully covered by insurance.

1904

13 May (PA) LOST AND FOUND – The Town Crier cried a lost watch some fortnight since, and on Saturday the lady who lost same went for a walk and on opening her umbrella the watch dropped out.

1905

25 February (PA) The Oundle School Cadets Corps had a field day at Lamport near Northampton. During the mimic warfare, the Oundle boys were made prisoners, but they arrived back by special train none the worse from it, having had an excellent day.

4 March (PA) Telephone – It will not be long now before the telephone system in the town will be an accomplished fact, as engineers have been in the town this week arranging for the fixing of the instruments and connections, and thus Avondolians who have arranged to go on the system can begin practising calling "Are you there".

4 March (PA) Our readers will learn with interest tinged with regret that Mr Woodward, the esteemed stationmaster at Oundle, is shortly retiring from his post. Mr Woodward has been in the services of the L. & N.W. Railway Co., forty-five years, the last eight as stationmaster at Oundle, where he has, by his unfailing courtesy and obliging

disposition, earned the esteem and respect of the towns people, and all those whose business is concerned in railway matters, and he will carry with him in his retirement the best wishes and respect of all. Mr Woodward will not leave the town, where he has taken a residence. His successor has not yet been appointed.

18 March (PA) So great is the interest taken in the newly formed Athletic and Cycling club that the Old Town Hall has been taken, and it makes an excellent Gymnasium. The number of members is increasing.

28 April (SM) OUNDLE BAND CONCERT – In place of the athletic sports usually held on Easter Monday, a brass band contest, promoted by the Oundle Town Band, was held in the cricket field, and proved a great success, nearly 2000 people being present. The weather was fine, although cold. There were 16 entries, comprising twelve bands, divided into two sections. – further down the report continues – The Oundle Town Band are to be congratulated upon the success of their first venture in this direction. The arrangements for the gathering, which were excellent, were made by a business-like committee, headed by the President, Vice-Presidents, Mr J. Pullan, Mr A. Laxton. Mr J. R. Webb. Mr T. Taylor. Mr J. Chapman and Mr F. Fox, with Mr T. A. Harris (assistant bandmaster and secretary of the Oundle Band) and Mr H. Richards (formerly secretary of Oundle Sports Committee), hon, secretaries.

Oundle Town Band. Photograph courtesy of Peterborough Images.

<u>14 October</u> (PA) The telephone system is now being installed, and the work of erecting some of the massive poles 65 feet high has been watched with great interest. To erect one in the back premises of the Post Office it was necessary to hoist the 60-foot pole over the roof from the Talbot Hotel yard, entailing a large number of men and a considerable amount of time. On the top of the pole near the old Town Hall an ornamental weather vane has been placed. This will be useful for the weather prophets. It is expected the installation will be completed in about a month, and it should prove of great service for business purposes.

1910

<u>15 January</u> (PA) A well-known resident in the town who had suffered considerably from thefts in his garden has put the following notice on his garden entrance. 'If I can catch the thief who visits my premises after dark, I will do the best I can for him. A thick stick will be the best remedy if caught.'

<u>12 February</u> (PA) Re Pancake Day – Tradition says that pancakes are thrown from the church tower and many juveniles are deluded with it.

<u>28 May</u> (PA) Mr Arthur Wright, the Oundle photographer, sent a photo of the Proclamation at Oundle to H.M. the King and has received the following letter. "Buckingham Palace May 28th – The Private Secretary has been commanded by the King to thank Mr Arthur Wright for his photograph of the Oundle Proclamation."

1913

<u>30 May</u> (NM) HOME HINTS – A prize of 2s. 6d. is offered every week for the best cookery recipe or any suggestion that will help housewives in the care of the home and family. Postcards or letters should be addressed to Home hints, "Mercury" office, Northampton. The prize this week is awarded to Mrs Coleman Binder, West-street, Oundle. BIRDS' NESTS OR SCOTCH EGGS – A TASTY SUPPER DISH – Three hard boiled eggs, 1/2 lb sausage meat. Wrap each egg around with the meat, brush over with egg, and roll in fine breadcrumbs. Fry in boiling lard or fat a few minutes (or until they are a nice brown), when the meat will be found to be sufficiently cooked. Cut them in halves with a sharp knives, and serve with a nice brown sauce or gravy. If these are eaten cold, garnish with parsley,

and the dish will be very effective and appetising. - Mrs Coleman Binder, West-street, Oundle.

1915

6 March (PA) In the window of Markham's library are two German shells and a German pewter drinking mug, all picked up by Pte. John Fox of Oundle, near La Bassco (query spelling). The objects have excited great interest.

1918

25 January (NM) OUNDLE. An absurd rumour of murder was conveyed through the town from the fact of a man discovering a bundle of clothes on the roadside leading from Oundle to Glapthorne. The bundle in question was subsequently identified by a servant living in the town who had forwarded it to her parents for washing and which had dropped from the carrier's cart.

1920

21 February (PA) In a village near Oundle there is a very estimable young man in a very perturbed state of mind just now, for on Valentine's Day (Saturday), he received by post a leap year proposal of marriage. From enquiries made it apparently came from a young lady in Oundle. Efforts are being made to trace the source, and if successful we hope to hear the wedding bells.

21 February (PA) The pancake bell was duly rung on Shrove Tuesday warming the good ladies of the town to prepare the pancakes. It would be rather interesting to know how many years the pancake bell has been rung in Oundle.

15 May (PA) The white railings on the Station road are this week being removed, thus removing another landmark. They belong to the Feoffees of the town estates, and efforts were recently made to obtain tenders for repairing and painting them but not one tender was received and the Feoffees decided to remove them. It is said that when Oundle had its big fairs these railings were used for tethering horses. For sentimental reasons, many will be sorry to see them disappear, but this is not a sentimental age so the railings must go.

19 June (PA) On Monday afternoon a runaway horse created a good deal of excitement in the town. It ran into Mr. W. Michael's office

which is the labour exchange but not being eligible for unemployment pay, it was ejected after considerable trouble.

24 July (PA) There is every possibility of Oundle having Housing bonds, and we hope they will be well taken up. Anyone with five pounds can invest and receive six per cent interest. Look what a feeling of pride investors will have when they walk up the Benefield Road and see the houses being erected, and can say a few (not many bricks today for five pounds) of those bricks belong to me. Watch our advertisement columns.

31 July (PA) HOUSING BONDS – As will be seen by our advertising column, Oundle has embarked on the Housing Bond campaign and it is up to every inhabitant to do his and her bit in investing in these bonds which pay six per cent interest, and are absolutely safe, and will considerably help the housing scheme. Don't be afraid to apply even for five pounds worth, although bigger sums will be welcomed. During the war Oundle nobly did its' bit in investing in War Bonds and now the time has come again in the Housing Scheme. We used to ask our readers to turn out their old tin box, and we feel sure there are a few pounds still reposing there that could be used. During the war one of our friends told us he could take us straight to a house where four hundred pounds was in a box under the bed. It earns nothing there whereas it would bring twenty-four pounds per year interest in housing bonds, and the four hundred pounds would still be intact. We believe there are many Oundle people who have left their native town and perhaps become rich who would like to invest in the town of their birth. Their money will be welcomed. We hope there will be a big rush, and if any of our readers require any further information they can obtain it from Mr R. Knight or Markham's information bureau, but don't forget to turn out the old tin box or bureau where the moths will eat your Treasury notes, but will not touch the housing bonds. Probably there are some friendly societies or clubs with fifty pounds to spare. They can invest it in housing bonds.

9 October (PA) In a London paper last week was an advertisement of a house in a village near Oundle for sale. One of the allurements of the advertisement was 'within a stone's throw of the church'. An applicant came to view the house, and after carefully noting the distance to the church, suddenly said to the agent, "I should like to see the man that threw that stone."

<u>16 October</u> (PA) In a village near Oundle a young man decided to take his sweetheart to the Peterborough fair. They went by train, and when about to enter Wansford tunnel, the young man thought it was a good opportunity to squeeze the young ladies hand to show his affectation, but on emerging from the tunnel he was horrified to find he was squeezing another ladies hand, the carriage being rather full. Fortunately, his sweetheart did not notice it, and the other lady was a good sport and took it quite good humouredly.

<u>6 November</u> (PA) In a village near Oundle a young man was very much perturbed at his hair getting rather thin. Being a great reader of the Periodicals containing small advertisements, such as 'How to cure blushing, Fits cured in five minutes, etc., he read of a new growth of hair for a shilling postal order. Having sent this, the young man was disgusted to receive the following recipe. 'Before retiring for the night rub salt well into the roots of the hair, and put a basin of water at the bedside. When the rats are thirsty and come out to drink, grab them tight so that they cannot get back again, and you will then have a new growth of hair. The young man has asked the local hairdresser their opinion, but it was not favourable.

1926

<u>10 September</u> (NM) ICE HOUSE AND SEWER – Unpleasant Experiences at Oundle – A six-year-old Oundle girl and an Oundle youth have each had an unpleasant experience this week. On Tuesday afternoon, Mrs Bonser, of Southwick Grange, who was in the town, heard cries coming from the pavement near Laxton School House, and on investigating, found that they came from a little girl who had fallen down a sewer manhole ten feet deep. The girl whose name is Pridmore, and who lives in East-road, Oundle, was lifted out, and taken to Dr Elliott, who was able to say she was only bruised. The cover of the hole had been removed whilst work was in progress, but the approach was guarded, and it is difficult to know how the child got near to it. - A few days ago, a youth named Phillipson, who is employed by Mr Brudenell, Market-place, Oundle, had occasion to go into the ice chamber. When inside, the door closed behind him and he was forced to stay in the chamber for ten minutes before being released.

1930

Cable laying along West Street c.1930

1934

27 July (PA) OUNDLE SUCCESS – Our congratulations to Miss Margaret Gale (elder daughter of Mrs J.W. Gale, of Oundle) who has been at the Homerton Training College for teachers and has now passed her final examination with distinction in advanced drawing and credit in educational handwork.

28 December (PA) Tale of a lost Pudding – On Monday our Oundle correspondent was kindly presented with a Christmas pudding. This was left in a green paper shopping bag and was left in Mr Leayton's shop, but in the afternoon when our correspondent went to fetch the pudding it had disappeared. Probably some customer had taken the bag and pudding by mistake. If so our correspondent would be glad to receive his pudding back. (Later: Please take out the Lost Pudding Report: it has come back.)

2 November (PA) DIPS INTO THE PAST – The Great Plague in Oundle – Those of our readers who knew their history will need telling of the Great Plague in London in 1665. This appears to have struck Oundle very badly in 1666 and from an interesting document our Oundle Correspondent has had given him we find that from

April 29 to October 31 of that year people literally died off like flies from the plague, burials taking place almost every day, and it is impossible to think they were burned off in coffins so rapidly did they die. A most horrible name for some of the houses in Oundle at that time was "Pest Houses" and we learn from Canon Smalley Laws Oundle story that these were at the bottom of Mill Lane. Some of the names of these days seem strange now, such as John Bing, Mrs Wine Rose Clifton, Widow Yernist, George Mokes, John Tomblston, Zach Mews wife and Griffin Ladson's wife, Old George West, Peter Cranck, Elizabeth Boaz and Thomas Skotney. Butcherron Street – Some of the present generation know where that was at the back of the Rose and Crown, Bernware Street we do not know; possible the Canon may know. During the six months there were 223 burials (105 males 118 females) and the plague was responsible for 200 deaths. The record is a most interesting one of Oundle of 268 years ago.

1935

6 September (NM) JUVENILE ODDFELLOWS – 160 juveniles and friends, members of the Providence Juvenile Lodge of Oddfellows, Manchester Unity, took part in an outing to Wicksteed Park. After tea Bro. E. A. Mowbray paid tribute to the secretary, Bro. E. A. Howitt. Members of the committee who assisted at the gathering were Bros. E. A. Mowbray, S. B. Bailey, A. J. Marlow, J. D. Pridmore and V. E. Leayton

Trip to Wicksteed Park. Photograph courtesy of Peterborough Images

1941

<u>5 September</u> (NM) Four young Oundle girls, Anne and Ruth Leayton, Reah Kettle and Joan Vessey, have sent £1 to Mrs Markham's knitting party to purchase wool for comforts for the Merchant Navy. These industrious girls during their holidays have been painting d'oyleys and selling them.

1942

<u>8 May</u> (NM) Scholars of Oundle Church School sang traditional songs and danced round the maypole on the lawn fronting the Great Hall of Oundle School on May Day. Each carried a posy of flowers and Mrs K Fisher and Mrs Squire awarded prizes to Jean Evans, Violet Underwood, Michael Turland, John Fellows and Tony Wilson. The children afterwards paraded the town and collected £14. 1s. 9d for the Aid-to-Russia fund.

1943

<u>15 January</u> (PA) There is probably only one man today throughout all England who is still riding a 'penny farthing' bicycle, and that is Mr Arthur Dicks of Wealdstone who a short time ago celebrated his 74th birthday and his diamond jubilee and riding this old time-cycle. A native of Pilton Mr Dicks is one of the few surviving members of the old Oundle Cycling Club which had a strong membership in the 1890's. Mr Dicks won many trophies on his penny farthing.

<u>22 October</u> (PA) A horse named 'Oundle' on Saturday won a big race at Windsor. It would be interesting to know how it derived its name. Its sire was 'Early School'. We understand that many local sportsmen backed 'Oundle' on account of its name. Perhaps its owner was an old Oundelian.

1954

<u>13 August</u> (NM) Oundle Party off to Austrian Tyrol – A party has left Oundle on a journey of over 900 miles by train and steamer. Mr K. D. Evans, the Headmaster of Oundle County Secondary Modern School is conducting a party – 33 in all – of scholars, accompanied by some of the staff to Sistrans, just outside Innsbrook in the Austrian Tyrol. The party hopes to visit Italy and Germany during their 10 days stay.

Oundle Station c,1900.
Photograph courtesy of Peterborough Images.

West street c.1904.
Photograph courtesy of Peterborough Images.

OUNDLE SOLDIERS

The following details were reported in the Peterborough Advertiser newspapers.

13 January 1900 – OUNDLE MANS DESCRIPTION OF A WONDERFUL GUN – The following letter, dated 11 December has been received by Mrs Peacock, wife of Private Peacock of Oundle 2nd Northants Regiment and now with Lord Methuen's force: - We had been over a week in camp when I wrote your last letter on Sunday last. We had a grand capture of Boers ambulance wagons the day after. We had a good fight at Enslin and got through with a few wounded but it was a severe go for a time. Two days after we had another, the worst of the three we have had. The Boers were on one side of the river and we were the other side. Some of us had to swim across in places. We could plainly see the Boers firing, their bullets flying through the bushes. Several of the Grenadier Guards were shot. When we reached the other side of the river what was left of the Boers rushed off. They take most of their wounded away if they can and have time. After the battle, which lasted thirteen and a half hours our stretcher bearers were bringing a wounded man in when the Boers started firing again and hit this poor chap on the stretcher, killing him on the spot. They dropped him off and picked another up. We have a gun here which carries twelve miles when the bell explodes it covers about 300 yards, killing and suffocating within that distance. We are using this on account of their firing at our wounded. I must tell you more when I get home and it won't be long I think if God spares me. Paper is very scarce here, cigars are 6d, clay pipes 6d, box of matches 3d.

20 January 1900 – NORTHAMPTON WELL IN FRONT – A letter dated December 14 has been received by Mr Lillaker of Oundle, from Private J. Hill, 2nd Northants and now with Lord Methuen's force at Modder River. In it he says. We have had plenty to do with the Boers and are at them now nearly every day. We have got a hard job to tackle they have a position, if you like. We have had four days trying to shift them, but cannot work it yet. The first day we had a large number of men in the 42nd Black watch cut up. We are waiting now for reinforcements and then we shall manage them. I think there are eighteen or twenty thousand Boers. We are only about twenty-one miles from Kimberley, but we have to shift the Boers first. I don't

think it will take long when we get more troops. It was said our regiment was only for the line of communication, but we have been well in the front line at present and I hope we shall remain so.

17 February 1900 – The Oundle men attached to S.B. Imperial Yeomanry sailed from Southampton on Saturday by the S.S. Norman for South Africa. A safe and speedy return is the wish of all.

24 February 1900 – AN OUNDLE WARRIOR THANKS THE BOERS – Private E. Hinman of Oundle, with Methuen's force at Modder River writing to his brother and sister at Oundle. On January 26 states that at Graspan he lay for six hours under the fire of the Boer big guns, and with his mates dare not show himself. The Boers do not like cold steel and as soon as bayonets are fixed they jump on their horses and ride for their lives. The Boers may say what they like, but there was no doubt that they have lost 10,000 wounded and killed. He was at Belmont with the rest of the Northamptons. They had a hot time at Belmont before the guns and reinforcements arrived which soon made the Boers shift. Amongst the enemy it was very evident there are "all sorts" – Irish, Scotch, Germans, Blacks and English, for now and again the writer adds "we catch some of them" but they are veritable demons for pulling up the line and blowing down the posts, turning people out of their houses and homes and making them fight by standing over them with 'pistols'. Eggs 1s apiece, matches 6d packet but he was glad to say tobacco was cheap.

3 March 1900 – On Tuesday morning shortly after 11 o'clock, the welcome news was posted outside Mrs Markham's establishment that Cronje had surrendered and big crowds gathered during the day to read and re-read the gratifying intelligence. The utmost enthusiasm was shown, the bells were rung, flags were flying from houses, the children at the schools were granted a holiday and Oundle was not one whit behind in testifying to the national joy at this great British victory

24 March 1900 – SEND OFF – Mr E.A. Caborn, the Oundle Volunteer for the Ambulance Corps., for South Africa had an enthusiastic send off on Thursday night by the 6.54 train. The ambulance brigade assembled at the Fire Station in full force and with a few members of the fire brigade and the Town Crier (Mr O Leayton in his official uniform). The whole being under the command of Captain R. Knight, marched to the station with the out-

going volunteer followed by a huge crowd. On reaching the station the National Anthem and Rule Brittania were lustily rendered and as the train steamed out Auld Lang Syne was sung. A safe, speedy return is the wish of all Avondalians.

<u>16 June 1900</u> – DEATH OF TROOPER GUNN – Trooper P. Gunn, who left Oundle to join the Bucks Imperial Yeomanry for service in the Transvaal, who was invalided home, after suffering from enteric fever, succumbed to a relapse on Saturday as the transport was nearing Gravesend. The body was removed, and interred in that place on Monday. Great sympathy is felt in Oundle for the friends of the deceased, as he was a fine, manly fellow, and when he left Oundle looked the picture of health and his premature end is deeply deplored.

<u>The following details were reported in the Northampton Mercury newspapers.</u>

<u>30 October 1914</u> - OUNDLE – Louis Afford, son of Mr W. Afford, a private in the Northampton's, is now home for a rest, having just left hospital. He was wounded in the left shoulder at the battle of Mons.

<u>18 December 1914</u> – OUNDLE MILITARY NEWS – Quite a batch of Oundle soldiers have been home this week for a seven days' leave. Private John Fox, 2nd Northants, has been wounded in the leg, and is now in Bristol Military Hospital. The parents of Private Robert Butt, 1st Battalion, West Yorkshires, and of Private George Jacobs, 1st Northants, both of whom are prisoners, have heard from them saying they are well. They complain of not hearing from their friends.

<u>29 January 1915</u> – WOUNDED – BURROWS PTE. MARK, 2nd Northamptonshire Regiment. Private Burrows, of Oundle, who was wounded by shrapnel in the wrist, is home on leave for a few days. He referred in a conversation with our Oundle representative to the nearness with which the forces get to each other at times. On one occasion he says he heard a German who spoke in good English shout, "What are King George and you people doing killing our wives and children?" Burrows speaks in the highest terms of the treatment he received in hospital at Ampthill.

<u>29 January 1915</u> – WILLIAMS, PTE. ARTHUR, A.S.C. Private Williams, whose home is at Oundle, is in hospital suffering from an injury to his back which he sustained in making his escape from a cellar in which he had been imprisoned by the Germans.

19 March 1915 – FOX, PTE. C. 4th Northamptonshire Regiment. COTTINGHAM, PTE. G., 1st Northamptonshire Regiment. PHILLIPSON, PTE., Northamptonshire Regiment. LOAKES, PTE. B. All the above belong to Oundle. Private Loakes, writing home, says he had a lucky escape from serious injury, for the missile that struck him cut through his pocket, in which there were some letters, and his face was grazed.

19 March 1915 – LEES, BERNARD, Oundle. It is reported that Mr Bernard Lees, who is the son of Colonel P. Lees, of Oundle, has been killed in action.

15 October 1915 - CULLOP, PTE. P. 1st/4th Northamptonshire Regiment. Private Cullop was the son of Mr another son through the war.

22 October 1915 – SHARPE, PTE. E., 1st Northamptonshire Regiment. Private Sharpe, of Oundle, who has been wounded and gassed, is now spending a few days at his home.

26 November 1915 – Interesting letters home – Private M. Fox, of 1st/4th Battalion Lincolnshire Regiment, son of Mr J. Fox, of West-street, Oundle, has written a letter to relatives describing the attack on the Hohenzollern redoubt on Oct. 13. He was wounded in the left arm on the evening of the same day. Company Quartermaster Sergeant R. Bell, 5th Bedfordshire Regiment, son of Mr J. Bell, of Oundle, writes of the capture of "Kidney Hill" (Gallipoli) at the point of the bayonet. He says an officer and he went out from the trenches 300 yards to bring in a wounded Londoner. The officer was hit in the leg, and Quartermaster Sergt. Bell had to take him back. Then he returned for the wounded Londoner, and, he says, "I seemed to bear a charmed life that day. They could not hit me, though they riddled my water-bottle, helmet and through his boot, skinning a couple of toes. The Colonel recommended me for a D.C.M.

Also printed in the same edition was – 'Private Fox is the son of Mr J. Fox, of West-street, Oundle. He is now in hospital at Rouen with a wound in the left arm.'

26 November 1915 - WOUNDED – BELL. QUARTERMASTER SERGEANT REGINALD, 1st/5th Battalion Bedfordshire Regiment. Information has been received by his father, Mr J. Bell, a member of the Oundle Postal Staff that his son, Q.M.S. Bell has been wounded and is in hospital at Malta.

<u>26 May 1916</u> CONSTABLE D.C.M. – A BOUGHTON MAN'S DECORATION – News has been received at Boughton that Lance-Sergeant Harry Roughton, of the Northamptonshire Regiment, has been awarded the D.C.M. Details of the act of gallantry which have been thus recognised are not to hand, but it is believed to be good work done in the taking of German trenches. Lance-Sergeant Roughton is a member of the Northamptonshire Constabulary. He is a native of Oundle, and rather more at Boughton on transference from Kettering where he had been a constable for about six years. His wife is still at Boughton. He comes of a fighting family, for he was a reservist when called up on the declaration of war, and he landed in France on August 10, 1914. He fought at Loos in September of last year, and was wounded. He was sent to England, and had only been back at the front about a week when he accomplished the deed that has brought him an honour that is coveted by every non-commissioned officer and private. Lance-Sergeant Roughton has two brothers on active service, and another brother was killed at the Dardanelles.

<u>29 September 1916</u> – AFFORD, PTE. GEORGE, Northamptonshire Regiment, the son of Mr. and Mrs. C. Afford, East-road, Oundle, has been killed. He was 28 years old.

<u>13 October 1916</u> – Killed - COOPER, PTE. THOS., also CRAYTHORNE, PTE. W., both soldiers of the Northamptonshire Regiment, of Oundle.

<u>5 January 1917</u> – PALMER, PTE. R.P., Northamptonshire Regiment, (machine-gun section), died in hospital on Christmas Day from nephritis. He belonged to Oundle.

<u>27 April 1917</u> – Died of Wounds – BENNETT PTE. A. F., Queen's Royal West Surrey Regiment, the son of Mr and Mrs Bennett, West-street, Oundle, has died of wounds. He was one of six soldier sons, and formerly worked for Mr. R. Goosey.

<u>25 May 1917</u> – Killed – Garrett, Pte. F. (39), Suffolks, Oundle. Cooper, Pte., R.A.M.C., Oundle, reported to have been lost on a torpedoed vessel.

<u>3 August 1917</u> – Included in the list of soldiers who were missing since the Battle of the Dunes on July 10: Phillipson, Corpl. C., son of Mr S. Phillipson, of Oundle; two brothers have been killed and another reported missing.

17 August 1917 – Wilson, Corpl. Wallis (19), a son of Mr Wilson, caretaker at the Brereton rooms, Oundle, has died of wounds.

26 October 1917 – Lilleker, Gunner Ralph, son of Mr R. Lilleker, Victoria Inn, West-street, Oundle, killed in action.

26 October 1917 – Willmott. Pte. J., whose parents reside in Inkerman-place, Oundle, killed; was in the transport service.

23 November 1917 – Stafford, Pte. Wm. (27), Northants, son of Mr and Mrs Stafford, of Oundle, killed on November 20; had seen eight years' service; was invalided home, but was recalled when time had expired; was on the Transylvania, but saved himself by means of a rope after being several hours in the water; had been gassed and wounded; leaves a widow and one child; three brothers are serving.

28 December 1917 – Sad intelligence comes to hand that more Oundle soldiers have fallen. One is James Pridmore, aged 34, private in the Tank Gun section who was home three months ago looking fit and well, although he had been several timers wounded. He was in the battle of Mons and other heavy engagements. His widowed mother has four other sons serving. Pte. Reg. Barrett, son of Mr. E. Barrett, Rock-road, Oundle, is also among the killed. He was formerly employed by Mr Horton, grocer.

10 May 1918 – Bell. R. (22), son of Mr John Bell, postman, of Oundle, has died of wounds.

31 May 1918 – WOUNDED – Sawford, Corpl. Tom, Scottish Rifles, son of Mrs. and the late Sergt. Instructor Sawford, of Rock-road, Oundle; was in the county Police Force, stationed at Rushden. MISSING – Sawford, Sergt. Victor Harry (27), Royal Fusiliers, son of Mrs. and the late Sergt'. Instructor Sawford of Rock-road. Oundle; worked at Baker and Co.'s provision stores, Oundle.

6 June 1919 - Birthday Honour's – The King's birthday on Tuesday was marked by the issue of a very long list of honours, chiefly for war service. – Included in the list was – France and Flanders - D.C.M. Sergt. J. Baker, M.M., 2/4th Yorkshire L.I. (Oundle); Corpl. F. Barber, 49th Battery, R.F.A. (Oundle); Gunner W. Lane, R.F.A. (Oundle). - Italy – D.C.M. Sgt S. W. Moore, ¼ Royal Berks (Oundle); Egypt – D.C.M. Pte. A. Roughton, ¼ Northants R. (Oundle)

22 June 1945 – To celebrate the return of Pte George Abbott, Northamptonshire Regt., youngest son of Mrs Abbott, of Church-street, Oundle, who had been a prisoner of war for nearly three years, a Welcome Home Party was given in the Brereton Rooms when over 60 relatives and friends were present, including the vicar of Oundle. A collection was taken for the Red Cross.

9 November 1945 – Home with his wife, Mrs R. Leigh, of 9 East-road, Oundle, is Lance-Bomb Leigh, who was taken prisoner by the Germans at Tobruk in May 1942. After spending some months in Camp 85 Italy, where he became a member of the Northamptonshire Club for prisoners-of-war he was moved to Stalag 4A in Germany. He was released by Russians in May this year. He is an old boy of Oundle School.

Oundle School Cadet Corps. And Band.
Photograph courtesy of Peterborough Images.

Oundle School OTC c.1930
Photograph courtesy of Peterborough Images.

Forming a Company of Rifle Volunteers 1894.